Coinage and Administration in the Athenian and Persian Empires

The Ninth Oxford Symposium on Coinage and Monetary History

edited by

Ian Carradice

BAR International Series 343
1987

B.A.R.

5, Centremead, Osney Mead, Oxford OX2 0DQ, England.

BAR-S343, 1987 : 'Coinage and Administration in the Athenian and Persian Empires'

ISBN 9780860544425 paperback
ISBN 9781407346168 e-book
DOI https://doi.org/10.30861/9780860544425
A catalogue record for this book is available from the British Library
This book is available at www.barpublishing.com

CONTENTS

Preface

THE subject of the Ninth Oxford Symposium on Coinage and Monetary History, which took place at St Hilda's College in April 1986 under the auspices of the Heberden Coin Room, was *The Impact of Empire on Fifth Century Coinage*. Subtitled *Persia, the Athenian Coinage Decree and other matters*, the main intention was to provide an occasion for discussion of coinage and finances in both the major empires in the Aegean area and, importantly, to bring into the discussion the exciting new evidence provided by the 'Decadrachm' hoard. The meeting, organized by Dr Daphne Nash and the Editor, was designed to bring together historians and archaeologists as well as numismatists, to help broaden the basis for discussion and for evaluation of the new evidence being presented.

For the publication the new title, *Coinage and Administration in the Athenian and Persian Empires*, has been adopted. The papers are published in the order they were presented at the Symposium. Athens and her allies dominate most of the proceedings, as they did the Symposium, with a total of six papers, as against two on Persian subjects. No excuses are made for this imbalance (which is, in any case, redressed by the greater length of the two Persian papers).

A sample of coins from the Decadrachm hoard was on display in the Heberden Coin Room at the time of the Symposium. The coins were provided by a foundation in Boston, whose generosity and cooperation is gratefully acknowledged.

British Archaeological Reports again kindly agreed to accept camera-ready copy produced by the Lasercomp facility of the University Computing Service, the Heberden Coin Room providing the necessary financial support. Mrs Jennifer Baines was responsible for typesetting the volume.

IAN CARRADICE

The Decadrachm hoard: an introduction

SALLIE FRIED

[PLATES I–V]

THE recorded portion of the 'Decadrachm hoard' consists at present of more than 1,700 silver coins. Most are uncirculated and the quality of the silver is exceptionally good: almost all the pieces required no cleaning. Coins from the hoard first came on the market in 1984 in two large lots, with several smaller groups appearing subsequently. Almost 1,000 of the coins are Lycian issues and the remainder are from Athens, north Greece, the Aegean, and Asia Minor. The find spot is probably somewhere in southern Anatolia. The geographical distribution of the coins by mint is shown in Table 1. This paper will consider the coins from a dozen or so of the north and central Greek, Island, and Asia Minor mints in the find.[1]

North Greece is well represented with about 8 per cent. of the total number of coins, accounting for some 15 per cent. of the total silver content of the hoard (see Table 2; all percentages given here are approximate). The 68 octadrachms of the Bisaltai were struck from 26 obverse and as many as 45 reverse dies, most of which were previously unknown. The reverse is always a simple four-part incuse square.

I would like to thank the participants in the Ninth Oxford Symposium on Coinage and Monetary History for their helpful comments when this paper was given in April 1986. I am especially grateful to Dr Daphne Nash for providing the opportunity to present the material. I also wish to thank the dealers and collectors who made the study of the hoard possible.

Abbreviations. Asyut: M. J. Price and N. Waggoner, *Archaic Greek Silver Coinage: the Asyut Hoard*, London, 1975 (*IGCH* 1644). Balcer: J. M. Balcer, 'Peparethos: the early coinage reconsidered', *SNR* 56 (1967), 25–33. Barron: J. P. Barron, *The Silver Coinage of Samos*, London, 1966. Cahn: H. A. Cahn, 'Die archaischen Silberstatere von Lindos', in K. Schauenberg, ed., *Charites. Studien zur Altertumswissenschaft*, Bonn, 1957, pp. 18–26. Desneux: J. Desneux, 'Les tetradrachmes d'Akanthos', *RBN* 90 (1949), 1–122. Jordan hoard: C. M. Kraay and P. R. S. Moorey, 'Two fifth century hoards from the Near East', *RN* 1968, 181–235 (*IGCH* 1482). Kraay: C. M. Kraay, 'Greek coins recently acquired by the Ashmolean Museum, Oxford', *NC* 1954, 10–15. May: J. M. F. May, *The Coinage of Abdera*, London, 1966. Seltman: C. T. Seltman, *Athens—Its History and Coinage before the Persian Invasion*, Cambridge, 1924. South Anatolian hoard: E. S. G. Robinson, 'A hoard of archaic Greek silver coins from Anatolia', *NC* 1954, 107–17. Starr: C. G. Starr, *Athenian Coinage 480–449 B.C.*, Oxford, 1970 and 'New specimens of Athenian coinage, 480–449 B.C.', *NC* 1982, 129–34. Svoronos: J. Svoronos, *L'hellénisme primitif de la Macédoine*, Paris–Athens, 1919. *Traité*: E. Babelon, *Traité des monnaies Grecques et Romaines*, I–IV, Paris, 1901–1933. Zagazig hoard: H. Dressel and K. Regling, 'Zwei ägyptische Funde altgriechischer Silbermünzen', *ZfN* 37 (1927), 1–138, especially 104–38 (*IGCH* 1645).

[1] For a discussion of the Lycian issues and for further comments on the date and context of the hoard, see the accompanying articles by J. Spier and J. H. Kagan. These three papers represent a preliminary study of the hoard: a separate complete publication is also planned.

The obverse is a youth, sometimes identified as Ares or Rhesus, holding two spears and standing behind a horse with the ethnic spelled out around the inside of the border. The earliest inscription is retrograde with the initial letter resembling the Greek beta. **Pl. I, 1** was struck with the dies of *Traité* 1489. Subsequent variations on the obverse include the inscription not retrograde but still with the initial letter written as a beta, and both retrograde and non-retrograde inscriptions with the initial letter written just as the sigma (**Pl. I, 2**). This letter-form remains in use on the latest coins from this mint in the hoard. The type remains very much the same on all the dies; only the position of the spears changes, from horizontal to vertical. The type with the upright spears seems to have been used on only a few dies in the middle of the series (**Pl. I, 3**).

The latest coins of the Bisaltai, seven from one obverse die, have a helmet in the right field (**Pl. I, 4**). The type with a bearded head in the right field does not appear in the Decadrachm hoard but there was a coin of this type in the Jordan hoard (no. 6). Although the right field is not preserved on that specimen, it is said to be a die duplicate of *Traité* 1494, where the head is clearly visible. The variety with the head seems to be the latest before the coins with the ethnic on the reverse are struck by the Bisaltai. The only known octadrachm with the reverse inscription was found in the late-fifth century Black Sea hoard, no. 2.[2]

The three octadrachms of Getas, King of the Edoni, were struck from three different obverse and reverse dies. The obverse type is a herdsman, perhaps Hermes, standing behind two oxen. The inscription around the four-part incuse square on the reverse takes two forms: *ΓΕΤΑΣ ΒΑΣΙΛΕΩΣ ΗΔΩΝΕΥΝ* (**Pl. I, 5**) and *ΒΑΣΙΛΕΥΣ ΓΕΤΑΣ ΗΔΟΝΕΟΝ*. One specimen with the latter reading is from the same dies as Svoronos, pl. 4, 2. These octadrachms, which are the only north Greek coins with reverse inscription in the hoard, are very close in style to the early octadrachms of Alexander I of Macedon, with rather crude inscription, for example, Raymond Group I.[3] We have no certain dates for Getas' reign. His coins were not in the Asyut hoard. The very fresh condition of these specimens and the presence of the reverse inscription place them among the latest coins from this area in the find.

The obverse of the single octadrachm of the Derrones, Sternberg xv, 11/12 April 1985, 115[4], has an ox drawing a cart with a bearded man, perhaps Ares, holding a stick; above are a branch and an eagle. The retrograde inscription around the inside of the border is as on the Bisaltai issues. This is an early coin in the triskeles series, a type which is not in the Asyut hoard. The presence of this coin in the Decadrachm hoard helps to confirm Price's speculation[5] that the Derrones octadrachms with triskeles reverse are later in date than the coins in the Asyut hoard. It is worth noting again that the other provenanced specimens of the triskeles series have been found in hoards from Yugoslavia and Bulgaria rather than the Near East. The octadrachm of the Derrones is in the same excellent condition as almost all of the other north Greek coins in the hoard, and the similarity of its

[2] C. M. Kraay and P. R. S. Moorey, 'A Black Sea hoard of the late fifth century BC', *NC* 1981, 2–3.

[3] D. Raymond, *Macedonian Regal Coinages to 413 B.C.*, *NNM* 125, New York, 1953, pl. III, 1–3.

[4] This coin was also published by C. Sternberg, 'Ein umgeschnittener Vorderseitenstempel einer Grossmünze der Derronen', *SM*, 37 (1985), 2 ff.

[5] Asyut, p. 29.

obverse inscription to the ethnic on the Bisaltai pieces suggests that this coin should be contemporary with the others from this area.

There are nine staters of Thasos with the centaur abducting a nymph on the obverse and the characteristic four-part incuse square on the reverse (**Pl. I, 6**). These were struck from six obverse and eight reverse dies. The coins are similar to the pieces from the Asyut hoard but there are no shared dies. Given their proximity in style to the Asyut specimens, the Thasos pieces should pre-date the island's revolt from Athens in 465. It is perhaps important that the nine coins from the Decadrachm hoard are considerably fewer than the 29 found in the smaller Asyut hoard.

The 19 Abdera coins from this hoard fall into May Period II (dated in that volume to *c.* 520/15–492) and Period III (*c.* 492–473/2). All these pieces have a griffin left with symbols and/or letters to the left on the obverse and the four-part incuse on the reverse. The Period II coins are five octadrachms and one tetradrachm. The earliest octadrachm, dies of May 44, with *A B* to the left was probably struck with the same dies as South Anatolian hoard number 3, and the tetradrachm with *E P* on the obverse shares its dies with Asyut 143, the latest coin from Abdera in that hoard. The other octadrachms have to left, *A B Δ H* on one, *E K A T* (May 45) on another, a negro head on the third, and on the fourth, *A Π O Λ* and a negro head (**Pl. I, 7**); this last is not recorded in May. The tetradrachm of Period II is one of the most worn coins in this hoard but the octadrachms are in remarkably good condition.

The 13 tetradrachms of Period III represent four magistrates, one of whom is indicated by a scallop shell alone *above* the griffin. Magistrates known to use this symbol, ANTI-, HERO-, and HIKES- are among the first in this period. HEGE- (*HΓH* with pellet, May 72) and ZEN (*ΖHN*: **Pl. I, 8**), are each present in three examples; the latter is listed by May only as a drachm, number 81. TELE- (*TEΛE* with a palmette, May 83: **Pl. I, 9**; and *TEΛE*- alone, May 84) is represented by six coins with four obverse dies. These three magistrates are placed early in Period III by May.[6] While the presence of only these four magistrates tends to confirm May's arrangement of the coins, the dates he gives for this period must be too early. The Period III tetradrachms show no signs of circulation.

The Decadrachm hoard also includes 37 tetradrachms of Acanthus with the lion or lioness attacking a bull on the obverse and the usual four-part incuse on the reverse. There are virtually no shared dies among these coins and almost all were struck with previously unknown dies, providing more evidence that this tetradrachm issue was extremely large. The earliest are as Desneux 16, with the facing lioness and floral symbol in the exergue (**Pl. II, 10**). While there are nine early specimens with the lion/lioness and bull in varying positions, most of the tetradrachms are part of Desneux's extensive rosette or theta series which have this symbol in the upper left field (**Pl. II, 11**). One piece shares dies with Desneux 52, another with Desneux 71. The latter bears a tiny delta or triangle next to the rosette. On several of the dies the rosette is replaced by a pellet, and in one case there is a large boss in the exergue (**Pl. II, 12**). The latest four coins are as Desneux

[6] May, p. 84.

90 (one struck from these dies) with an alpha above the type on the obverse (**Pl. II, 13**). Neither the rosette nor alpha varieties were present in the Asyut hoard and these later issues should presumably be dated after 475, as suggested in the publication of that find.[7]

Terone is represented by only two tetradrachms but both are new varieties. The obverse has an amphora with inscription: *ΣΠΓ* to the left on one (**Pl. II, 14**) and *ΠΟ* (or *Θ*) flanking the vase on the other (**Pl. II, 15**). In fabric, style, and weight these coins are very close to Kraay number 17 (BMC Terone 3) and Asyut 228–9, which have the letters *H E* flanking the amphora. The two coins in this hoard should join those pieces in Kraay's Group C. His suggestion,[8] followed in Asyut, that the *H E* is an abbreviation for the ethnic Heracleia, parallel to *T E* standing for Terone, is unlikely now that these other two inscribed coins have come to light. The three different inscriptions are perhaps magistrate's names, as is the case at Abdera.

There are also two tetradrachms of Peparethus from this find. The earlier has dies of Balcer 3 and Asyut 232, and the other (Bank Leu 38, 13 May 1986, 78) was struck from the same dies as Balcer 4. This type, with the bunch of grapes on the obverse and helmet on the reverse, was not present in the Asyut hoard. Although the dies were quite worn when this specimen was struck, it is very fresh and could not have been issued much before its burial.

The 187 Athenian coins are among the most important in the hoard. They comprise approximately 11 per cent. of the total number of coins, and 16 per cent. of the silver. There are 12 pre-Persian tetradrachms, two each of Asyut Group IV (Seltman Group G) and Asyut Group V a (Seltman Group C). The others are Asyut Group VI (Seltman Group E). There are no shared dies and many of the coins are worn. The rendering of the ear as a thick single line, the crude style of the obverse, and the heavy pendant leaves with large, straight epsilon on the reverse are characteristic of this last group of 'wreathless' tetradrachms (**Pl. II, 16**).

Among the eight tetradrachms attributable to Starr Group I, there is one which should be among the earliest wreathed coins (**Pl. II, 17**). The obverse—possibly the same die as Starr number 1—has the 'rick-rack' crest attachment, four upright olive leaves, and hair rendered as a mass of dots, and the reverse has the almost vertical owl with olive leaves hanging straight down along its back. These are the normal features of this group. The positioning of what appears to be a crescent with a dot, however, to the right of the owl rather than to the left should belong to an early experimental period when the crescent was first added. The other coins have the moon where it always is hereafter, namely between the owl and the olive branch (**Pl. II, 18**).

There are ten tetradrachms of Group II (all but three from II C) and they have the following features which distinguish them from the earlier coins (**Pl. II, 19** and **III, 20**): on the obverse, the hair is drawn along the forehead in parallel wavy lines, the spiral on the helmet breaks into a palmette, the crest is attached to the helmet by a row of dots and there are only three graduated olive leaves. The olive twig on the reverse branches at an approximately 90-degree angle and the left leaf is attached to

[7] Asyut, p. 42.

[8] Kraay, p. 15.

the stem below the right. Also, the owl's legs are slightly parted and the letters curve along the body of the bird with the epsilon somewhat larger than the theta. Only two Group II tetradrachms share an obverse die.

The 14 decadrachms of Group IIC share ten obverse and 11 reverse dies. There are at least five new obverse and six new reverse dies, bringing the total number of obverse dies to 16. The obverses of ten specimens (**Pl. III, 21**) are close in style to the tetradrachms illustrated above, but the earring is pendant and the palmette is more elaborate. The full frontal owl with outstretched wings surrounded by the *Α Θ Ε* and olive branch, and no moon, is a completely new type and is used only for the decadrachms. The obverses of the other four coins (**Pl. III, 22**) have one noteworthy difference: the right olive leaf clearly breaks into the crest. This is one of the main criteria used to distinguish between Group II and III tetradrachms.[9] The 'ogival' eye is also more common in Group III. The 'later' features on some of the decadrachms suggest that these coins should have been minted very close in time to the Group III as well as the Group II tetradrachms. This stylistic development within the decadrachm series as well as the number of dies used indicates that the issue was substantial and unlikely to have been intended as a one-time commemorative minting.

There are almost three times as many Starr Group III as Group II tetradrachms. The 28 coins share 18 obverse and 25 reverse dies, many not in Starr (**Pl. III, 23** and **24**). As mentioned above, one of the salient features of this group is the interruption of the crest by the right olive leaf. Other changes from Group II on the obverse are the more frequent appearance of the 'ogival' eye and the markedly curving spiral with the palmette breaking out further down along the left leaf. On the reverse, the owl's wing now always touches the left edge of the incuse and the letters are aligned along the right edge; the epsilon is still slightly larger than the other two letters. The legs of the owl are further apart and the tail feathers bend close to the claw. The sole Athenian didrachm found in the hoard shares its dies with Starr 106. The large leaves, almost square frame, and large epsilon of the reverse are typical of Group III didrachms.

The largest number of tetradrachms, 82, fall into Starr Group IV. Again, many of the obverse and reverse dies are new (**Pl. III, 25, 26** and **27**). On the obverse, the palmette extends further down along the left leaf and sometimes touches the ear. The waves on the forehead are less pronounced and the lips are full. The olive leaves on the reverse branch almost at the same spot and both leaves touch the owl. The bird's left leg slants back slightly. There are many more shared dies within this group.

The last 32 tetradrachms, all in exceptionally good condition, belong with Starr Group V A, Series (1). There are 13 obverse dies and probably 25 reverse dies, none of which are recorded by Starr (**Pl. III, 28**). On the obverse, the hair on the forehead is rendered by parallel curves, all the wave having disappeared. The front of the helmet is almost straight and extends to the ear. The lips are long and drawn into a slight smile. On the reverse, the owl's legs are longer and the tail does not touch the claw even though it hangs almost vertically in most cases. The bird's legs

9 Starr, p. 44.

on most of these pieces have not yet become the 'parallel stilts' which are characteristic of many later Group V issues.[10] The similarity of the over-all reverse appearance to the Group IV tetradrachms places these Group V A, series (1) pieces very early in their period.

Three Group V coins from one obverse die (**Pl. III, 29**) are very close to a tetradrachm from the Jordan hoard, no. 44. It is not the latest Athenian coin in that hoard, but these are the latest in the Decadrachm hoard. Starr has placed the starting date of Group V around 455.[11]

The presence of the eight Seltman Group E, 'crude, barbarous' pre-Persian tetradrachms in the hoard with the many wreathed tetradrachms helps confirm Kraay's arrangement of the 'wreathless' Athenian tetradrachms, which placed the Seltman Group E coins as the last minted at Athens.[12] The distribution and condition of the wreathed tetradrachms found in the hoard support the arrangement put forward by Starr. The very large number of new dies, however, especially in Groups III, IV and V A, indicates that these issues were much more extensive than previously thought.

Three of the Aeginetan staters are early and worn. The other two are quite fresh and are among the latest coins in this hoard. The T-back turtle with trefoil collar on the obverse is paired with a 'large skew' reverse, a Brown Class 5 type. Coins from this class are dated from the early 470s to 457.[13] One of these latest Aeginetan staters is Sternberg xv, 11/12 April 1985, 124.

The islands of the Cyclades are represented by two staters (**Pl. IV, 30**) and Sternberg xv, 11/12 April 1985, 128) and one drachm of Melos, 39 drachms of Paros, and perhaps a group of uncertain coins with a boar's head on the obverse. All the Parian coins have the goat on the obverse and four-part incuse on the reverse. The earliest group in the Decadrachm hoard, the heavy goat kneeling on a groundline, consists of 14 coins from nine obverse dies. They are similar to the later coins from the Paros hoard (**Pl. IV, 31**). Two of these drachms share obverse dies with coins from the Paros hoard, *SNG Paris (Delepierre)* 2453–5. Two coins of the same type in the Decadrachm hoard also share an obverse die with Zagazig hoard 234.

There are three dies with goats of much different style. On the two earlier (**Pl. IV, 32**), the animal is still kneeling, but the body is more slender, the groundline is absent and there is a very faint *Δ* above the goat. On the third die (**Pl. IV, 33**), which must be the latest in the hoard, the goat is now standing and has a distinctly equine body. Above the animal is the *Δ*.[14] While this last die was worn when striking most of the specimens from this hoard, the coins themselves are not.

Most of the drachms of Ephesus, 34 struck from 12 obverse dies, are from Head Group I.[15] They have a bee with curved wings and volutes in the left and right fields on the obverse (**Pl. IV, 34**). These are not inscribed except for two coins which have a *Φ* on the right wing (**Pl. IV, 35**). The left wing is off the flan in both

[10] ibid., p. 54.

[11] ibid., p. 63.

[12] C. M. Kraay, 'The archaic owls of Athens: classification and chronology', *NC* 1956, 43–68.

[13] Asyut, pp. 73–76.

[14] Another drachm struck from these dies is *SNG Paris (Delepierre)* 2456, which is specifically labelled as not from the Paros hoard.

[15] B. V. Head, *History of the Coinage of Ephesus*, London, 1880.

cases but it would undoubtedly have had the *E*. This is a new variety which anticipates the better-known coins of Head Group II which have the *E* and *Φ* flanking the bee. There are four fractions with this inscription from the hoard, three sharing the same dies. The fourth is noteworthy in that the antennae break into the border of dots (**Pl. IV, 36**).

All but five of the 41 Samian staters belong to Barron Class III. Some of the early coins (**Pl. IV, 37**, dies of Barron 1) are worn and one, which is not worn, has a chisel cut. There are coins from Barron Class III(i) through (viii) except (vii), and groups (ii), (iii), and (iv) are die-linked. While the hoard includes several new Samian dies, there are no unknown types and the coins fall well within the arrangement proposed by Barron. **Pl. IV, 38** is from III(iii), dies of Barron 21 (A13–P21) and **Pl. IV, 39** is part of III(v), dies of Barron 29 (A15–P29).

The latest Samian stater (**Pl. IV, 40**), dies of Barron 36 (A20–P36), has the olive branch as the symbol on the reverse. This variety is placed in a subgroup with three other issues:[16] the anchor (vi), the prow (vii), and the amphora (ix). Because coins with the prow are not present among the known specimens from this hoard and the olive branch is, it is possible that the latter may in fact precede the former. Coins with the olive branch are dated by Barron to 468/67.[17]

The weights of these Samian coins are high compared to the sample available to Barron, despite the fact that some of them are worn. They average 13·18 g, with only four coins weighing less than 13·05 g. This is surprising since 13·05 g is the weight at which Barron placed his light Samian standard, theoretically in use from 513 to 439 BC.[18] At 13·05 g. the Samian stater is equal to three-quarters of the Euboeic tetradrachm (17·40 g) and would pass as an Attic tridrachm. Now, however, it must seem that Samos did not abandon its heavy Samian standard of 13·40 g when it began striking tetradrachms. The three heaviest staters in the hoard weigh 13·38 g and above. At the heavier weight the Samian coins did not easily exchange with the Attic and the shift to that standard later in the century can perhaps be given more of an economic explanation. It follows that the Ephesian drachms discussed above, weighing about 3·35 g, were struck on the same standard as the Samian coins.

Coins from Caria and the Carian Islands account for 18 per cent. of the coins and about 18 per cent. of the silver. The 289 coins from Camirus on Rhodes, the largest number of coins from a single mint outside Lycia, form the bulk of this group. The 286 staters were struck from 16 obverse and 15 reverse dies.[19] The type is always the fig leaf on the obverse and the two-part rectangular incuse on the reverse. The later reverse type with inscriptions was not represented. The earliest coins have 'fruit' flanking the stem of the obverse leaf (**Pl. V, 41**). There are six obverse dies with 'figs' used to strike 31 coins. One is the same as Asyut 694. Four coins without figs were struck with the dies of Asyut 701. Most of the coins were struck from seven dies. One die seems to have been recut along the veins after it had worn out. In the hoard, there are 17 coins struck before the recutting and four

[16] Barron, p. 53.
[17] ibid., p. 48.
[18] ibid., pp. 9–10.
[19] Four coins are not included in these numbers because either the dies or the pieces are too worn to attribute them with reasonable certainty.

after it (**Pl. V, 42** and **43**); these 21 coins all have the same reverse die. One obverse (**Pl. V, 44**) exists in 20 specimens which share the same reverse with 101 other coins, all having the same obverse die. They are probably the latest coins from this mint in the hoard. The three drachms are die-duplicates (**Pl. V, 45**). The types are identical to the stater except that the incuses of the reverse are stippled.

The large number of die-duplicates and die-links and the mint condition of these coins (other than the earliest ones with the 'fruit') indicates that the Camirus issues came to the hoard as a group which had not been disturbed prior to burial.

The six staters of Lindos all have the lion head on the obverse. Unlike Camirus, one of them does have an inscription on the bar between the reverse incuses, *IΔNIΛ* (**Pl. V, 46**). The coin is a die duplicate of Cahn 63, which is the latest example with incuses from this mint; the reverse type of Cahn H1 has an inscription around a dolphin swimming right. This last Lindos stater in the Decadrachm hoard must post-date Asyut 707–11, which have no reverse inscription.

After looking at the condition, distribution, and die-linkage within the different issues, it is clear that this is neither a 'commerce' nor savings hoard.[20] While there are certainly a few strays in the Decadrachm hoard, most mints from the areas considered above are represented by groups of coins which came together; one should note here again the large number of die-linked Group IV Athenian tetradrachms, followed by the linked Group VA series (1) coins; the mint condition of the latest seven Bisaltai octadrachms (all from one obverse die); the 12 drachms with the delta from Paros struck with the same obverse die; and the 121 staters of Camirus from the same reverse die. Moreover, the almost complete absence of mutilated or fragmentary pieces, only six coins with chisel cuts and one piece of a pre-Persian Athenian tetradrachm, sets this find apart from the other deposits recorded from the same period, the Asyut and Jordan hoards. Unlike these finds, the Decadrachm hoard apparently contained no bullion. These differences make the hoard unique for late archaic and early classical times.

[20] For a discussion of different types of hoards, see P. Grierson, *Numismatics*, Oxford, 1975, pp. 130–6.

TABLE 1: *Geographical Distribution of Coins*

Region/City	*Before 480/475*	*Between 480/475 and 460*
GREECE		
Bisaltai	–	68
Edoni (Getas)	–	3
Derrones	–	1
Ichnai? Lita(s)	–	1
Incert. Thraco–Macedon	1	–
'Orescii'	2	–
'Tunteni'	–	1
Thasos	–	9
Abdera octadrachms	5	–
tetradrachms	1	13
Acanthus	9	28
Mende	1	–
Potidaea	1	–
Terone	–	2
Peparethus	1	1
Eretria	–	1
Athens 'unwreathed'	12	–
'wreathed'	–	175
Aegina	–	5
ISLANDS		
Melos	1	2
Paros	13	26
Incert.	–	7
ASIA MINOR		
Parium	1	–
Ephesus	–	34
Miletus	2	–
Chios	4	–
Samos	4	37
Cos	4	1
Cnidus	1	–
Caria 'lion' (Mylasa)	10?	–
Carpathos	–	3
Camirus	38	251
Lindos	–	6
LYCIA		
Dynasts	some?	c.970
UNCERTAIN	–	2

TABLE 2: *Geographical Distribution of Coins by Percent*

	No. of coins	*Volume of silver*
North Greece	8	15
Athens	11	16
Ionia	7	5
Caria and Carian Islands	18	18
Lycia	56	46
	100	100

KEY TO PLATES I–V

1 Bisaltai, octadrachm, 28·92 g. Dies of *Traité* 1489.
2 Bisaltai, octadrachm, 28·39 g.
3 Bisaltai, octadrachm, 28·56 g.
4 Bisaltai, octadrachm, 28·68 g.
5 Edoni, King Getas, octadrachm, 28·57 g.
6 Thasos, stater, 9·58 g.
7 Abdera, octadrachm, 29·80 g.
8 Abdera, tetradrachm, 14·89 g.
9 Abdera, tetradrachm, 15·25 g. Dies of May 83.
10 Acanthus, tetradrachm, 17·22 g.
11 Acanthus, tetradrachm, 17·02 g.
12 Acanthus, tetradrachm, 17·18 g.
13 Acanthus, tetradrachm, 17·44 g.
14 Terone, stater, 17·20 g.
15 Terone, stater, 17·32 g.
16 Athens, tetradrachm, 17·90 g. 3:00.
17 Athens, tetradrachm (cast).
18 Athens, tetradrachm, 17·19 g. 7:00.
19 Athens, tetradrachm, 17·18 g. 5:00.
20 Athens, tetradrachm, 17·22 g. 8:00
21 Athens, decadrachm, 43·05 g. 11:00.
22 Athens, decadrachm, 43·05 g. 5:00
23 Athens, tetradrachm, 17·21 g. 5:00.
24 Athens, tetradrachm, 17·19 g. 5:00.
25 Athens, tetradrachm, 17·19 g. 10:00.
26 Athens, tetradrachm, 17·19 g. 4:00.
27 Athens, tetradrachm, 17·18 g. 3:00. Dies of Starr 136.
28 Athens, tetradrachm, 17·21 g. 3:00.
29 Athens, tetradrachm, 17·19 g. 7:00.
30 Melos, stater, 14·46 g.
31 Paros, drachm, 6·02 g.
32 Paros, drachm, 5·95 g.
33 Paros, drachm, 6·09 g.
34 Ephesus, drachm, 3·36 g.
35 Ephesus, drachm, 3·37 g.
36 Ephesus, drachm, 3·35 g.
37 Samos, stater, 13·27 g. 12:00. Dies of Barron 1.
38 Samos, stater, 13·04 g. 2:00. Dies of Barron 21.
39 Samos, stater, 13·26 g. 7:00. Dies of Barron 29.
40 Samos, stater, 13·15 g. 6:00. Dies of Barron 36.
41 Camirus, stater, 12·23 g.
42 Camirus, stater, 12·02 g. Dies of number 43 below.
43 Camirus, stater, 11·95 g. Obv. recut.
44 Camirus, stater, 12·10 g.
45 Camirus, drachm, 6·05 g.
46 Lindos, stater, 13·45 g.

PLATE I

10

11

12

13

14

15

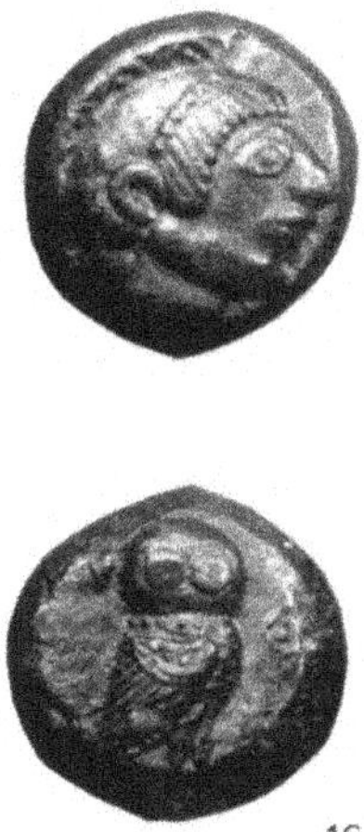

16

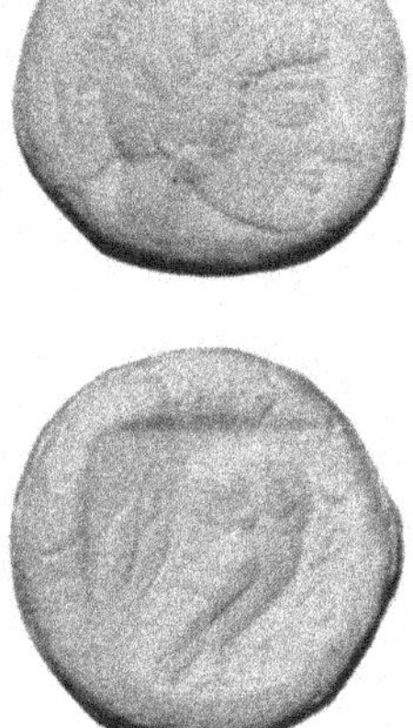

17

18

19

PLATE II

PLATE III

30 31 32 33

34 35 36

37 38 39 40

PLATE IV

41

42

43

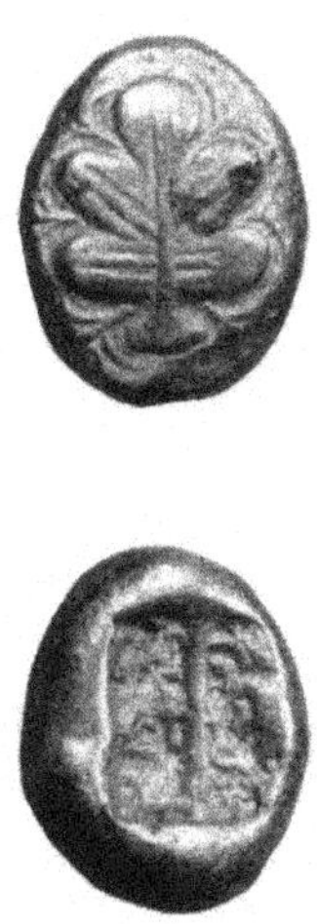

44

45

46

PLATE V

The Decadrachm Hoard: Chronology and Consequences

JONATHAN H. KAGAN

DATING archaic and early classical Greek hoards is rarely without some controversy and uncertainty. The decadrachm hoard will probably not be an exception. Before we can arrive at a date, one important assumption has to be made: that at least the large groups of Macedonian, Thracian, Athenian, and maybe Aegean island elements are contemporary.[1] It also seems likely that these coinages arrived at the place of burial as a single group, having been put together as individual blocks from each city. The case for this can be made as follows: 1) the coins from these regions show remarkably little wear; this is true not of just the latest strikings, but of almost all the coins; 2) the latest coin dies from the mints are the most frequent. It is therefore possible that the coins of these groups came out of treasuries or a single treasury rather than general circulation. If the coins had come directly from the mints themselves, we would not expect the variety of dies. More wear would be expected if the coins came out of commerce, especially on the earlier pieces. The Macedonian and Thracian elements are all at approximately the same point in the stylistic development of their reverse types. This further supports the notion that the coins are contemporary and probably came as a single lot.

If this hypothesis can be accepted, we can see quickly that problems with the conventional dating of certain coinages in the hoard are created. Starr would date the beginnings of his Athens Group V to approximately 454 BC.[2] May would date the Group III Abdera tetradrachms to no later than 473/470.[3] Kraay would place the Acanthus at about 470/465.[4] The latest Samian tetradrachm is placed by Barron in 468.[5] The Samos coins seem a little less fresh than the other large groups but they should not be appreciably earlier. All these dates are reasonably close, but they cannot all be right. It is important if the decadrachm hoard is going to prove a useful tool to historians of the Pentacontaetia that greater precision be achieved.

It may be worthwhile to consider what firm chronological anchors really exist for the mints under question for this period. The eight Seltman Group E archaic Athenian tetradrachms present in this hoard should put to an end any lingering

[1] For further comments on some of the coins from these areas, see the accompanying article by S. Fried; hereafter cited as Fried.

[2] C. G. Starr, *Athenian Coinage 480–449 B.C.*, Oxford 1970, p. 63; hereafter cited as Starr.

[3] J. M. F. May, *The Coinage of Abdera*, 1966, pp. 82 ff.

[4] C. M. Kraay, *Archaic and Classical Greek Coins*, 1976, p. 135; hereafter cited as *ACGC* and 'The Asyut hoard: some comments on chronology', *NC* 1977, 192; hereafter cited as Kraay.

[5] J. P. Barron, *The Silver Coinage of Samos*, 1966, p. 48.

controversy about the order of archaic Athenian owls; Kraay's sequence is confirmed.[6] The Group E coins are the latest unwreathed owls. This hoard also helps confirm the dating of the Acropolis hoard, which contains Group E coins, to the Persian destruction. The context that could best explain the large strikings of crude archaic owls, the burial of Group E coins on the Acropolis, the change to the wreathed style and the relative rarity of the early wreathed coins compared to the latest archaic issues is the Persian invasion and destruction of the Acropolis.[7] It is more than coincidence that the decadrachm hoard has as many Group E coins as wreathed coins of Starr's first period. Starr's Group I can safely be assigned to the early 470s.

The dates for Starr Groups II to V and the massive strikings of conventionalized coins are not as clear. Starr's arguments for his chronological arrangements depend largely on historical considerations: the date of Eurymedon, the transfer of the Delian treasury and the Coinage Decree. The major numismatic argument is based on the Jordan hoard, which contains some of the last Athenian issues before the regularized massive strikings.[8] Kraay's date of *c.* 445 for the Jordan hoard is largely derived from his view, without the benefit of Starr's die study, of the date of the Athenian specimens. There is circularity here.[9] In summary, we can be reasonably certain about the date of Starr's Group I, but not about the date of the latest Athenian specimens in the decadrachm hoard.

The confirmation provided here for Kraay's dating of the archaic owls should make us even more comfortable with a 475 BC closing date for the bulk of the Asyut hoard. The authors' arguments for this do not need to be repeated here.[10]

The dating of the Macedonian and Thracian issues after Asyut is fairly fluid. May's implicit acceptance of the workings of the Athenian coinage decree at Abdera in 449 is, to an important degree, a major assumption in his dating of the series with magistrate names. Asyut has already shown that his starting dates for that mint are too early.[11]

While Asyut presents a pretty clear picture of the north Greek mints at the end of the archaic period, it has led, because of one troublesome coin, to some disagreements concerning the dating of the coinage of Alexander I of Macedon.[12] Because he is one of the few historical personages with reasonably certain dates minting in this period, his coins are crucial. The key to dating as argued by Raymond[13] and more recently Kraay[14] is the development of the reverse type. The trend is from no reverse inscription, to a crudely inscribed reverse, to a neatly inscribed reverse.[15] While no coins of Alexander were present in the decadrachm hoard, comparisons can be made. Acanthus and the Bisaltai went through a similar

[6] C. M. Kraay, 'The archaic owls of Athens: classification and chronology', *NC* 1956, 43–63.

[7] Starr, pp. 3–6; for an alternative view, see M. Vickers, 'Early Greek coinage, a reassessment', *NC* 1985, 1–44.

[8] Starr, p. 63.

[9] C. M. Kraay and P. R. S. Moorey, 'Two fifth-century hoards from the Near East', *RN* 1968, 181–235 (p. 210); and R. T. Williams, review of Starr in *Phoenix* 26 (1972) 411–2.

[10] M. J. Price and N. Waggoner, *Archaic Greek Silver Coinage: the Asyut Hoard*, London, 1975, 117–25; hereafter cited as Asyut.

[11] Asyut, pp. 36–7.

[12] Asyut, pp. 38–9; Kraay, pp. 190–3; and H. A. Cahn, 'Asiut: kritische Bemerkungen zu einer Schatzfundpublikation', *SNR* 56 (1977), 284.

[13] D. Raymond, *Macedonian Regal Coinage to 413 B.C.*, NNM 125, (New York, 1953), pp. 100 ff.

[14] Kraay, pp. 190–3.

[15] Kraay, p. 192.

transition except that the trend is from an obverse inscription to a neatly inscribed reverse.[16] The three Getas octadrachms in the hoard have a fully inscribed reverse in a rather crude style similar to that of Raymond Group I Alexander of Macedon octadrachms.[17] We have the next-to-last variety of Acanthus and the Bisaltai before the adoption of reverse inscriptions.[18] A date between 470 and 460 for the Acanthus and Bisaltai seems assured for the latest of our coins. Asyut closed *c.* 475, before the introduction of the rosette symbol at Acanthus, and had no Bisaltai octadrachms. It is hard seeing all the Acanthian dies (there are 20 new obverse dies alone in the hoard) of that type being squeezed into less than 7–10 years. This point can be made despite the fact that this hoard clearly shows how dangerous it is to make chronological arguments based on die The same can be said about the Bisaltai. On the other hand, a date after 460 is unlikely. The transitional reverse-inscribed Acanthian tetradrachms,[19] which were struck just after the latest Acanthian coins in the decadrachm hoard, have a somewhat asymmetrical reverse. They must have been minted before the die-cutter became aware of the Group II octadrachms of Alexander of Macedon with symmetrical reverses.[20] It was such a Group II octadrachm that was found in Asyut. Should the Group II coins be much after 460, there would be no time for the development of Alexander's Group III coins, of a much finer style, before his reign came to an end in the late 450s.

The decadrachm hoard offers confirmation that the Asyut Alexander is indeed likely to be substantially later than the bulk of that hoard. Kraay's argument that the Acanthian stylistic development could not lag so far behind is even more convincing given the number of new dies found that are later than Asyut but still uninscribed on the reverse. Also, the absence of any reverse inscribed Bisaltai despite the long sequence is good evidence for arguing that Alexander's neatly inscribed reverse did not come in until 465/460, which is where Raymond originally dated it.[21] A late date within this range may be preferable.

The small Thasos group is close in style, but not linked, to Asyut. The coins are not circulated, but are perhaps less fresh than the Athenian and Acanthian coins. Their late archaic style and proximity to Asyut make a date before the 465/3 revolt probable.

Barron's 468 date for the latest Samos coins in the hoard may well be approximately correct. For Samos we have some reason to accept dates without relying on hoard evidence; the changing sequence of symbols and letters seem indeed to indicate annual periods. A plausible arrangement that would allow for a different date is that proposed by Kraay.[22] He would, in an effort to preserve Samos' compliance with the Coinage Decree, downdate the coins by about ten years, putting a break at the end of Class III. In that the Samian coins do not appear to be among the latest in the hoard on the basis of condition, it seems best to retain Barron's original dating. The Samian coins' appearance may partly be explained by the possibility that they were restruck on older coins. The flans are irregular. The later specimens in the series do not show even wear and are high in weight.

[16] Kraay, pp. 190–3.
[17] Fried, p. 2.
[18] Fried, pp. 2–4.
[19] J. Desneux, 'Les tetradrachms d'Akanthos', *RBN* 90 (1949), 83–4.
[20] Kraay, p. 192.
[21] Kraay, p. 192.
[22] *ACGC*, 'Appendix', pp. 332–3.

What other coins are helpful? The answer is not many. We know that we have many issues that are later than Asyut, but it is hard to judge how much later. Places such as Paros, Camirus, and Lindos may have been infrequent minters which used single dies for long periods. Note should be taken of the two latest Aeginetan coins in the hoard. They are not worn and are of a style not found in Asyut; they have been dated beween 470 and 457.[23]

In conclusion, then, a closing date of 465/462 seems reasonable for the non-Lycian elements. The Lycian issues may perhaps extend to a year or two later if we allow a natural time lag, but these coins unfortunately provide no firm anchors for dating.[24] The absence from the hoard of any coins from Phaselis is noteworthy; it may be explained by the fact that the city was geographically removed from the rest of Lycia and looked to the east (note the Persian standard) for its trade. Nevertheless, this is surprising if the hoard is to be dated after Eurymedon, given that the city was brought into the Delian League and paid a 10 talent indemnity.[25] If, on the other hand, one follows Plutarch and Meiggs[26] in accepting that Caria and Lycia were brought into the League prior to Eurymedon, and if one also accepts a later date for the battle, then a plausible historical context for a hoard of this magnitude may exist. But this should not be argued too strenuously.

Some of the ramifications of a 465/2 closing date for the non-Asia Minor elements are as follows. For Athens, we can no longer hold with Starr, that the city was a comparatively poor place in the 470s and 460s compared to the 480s or 450s and 440s.[27] Starr's division into groups still essentially holds, but by increasing so dramatically the numbers of known dies and shrinking the time frame, his historical conclusions are weakened. It should be noted that Kraay was uncomfortable with Starr's views, although not his dating and arrangements, well before this hoard.[28] The lack of die duplicates indicated that Starr was not dealing with a complete picture. The very success of the Athenian Empire has led to our inadequate hoard record; stability is not conducive to hoarding. It should be no surprise that our first significant recorded hoard from the Athenian Empire during the Pentacontaetia should come from its very fringes.[29]

The large Bisaltai element in the hoard, while not totally unexpected, requires some rethinking about the history of the Macedonian region. The presence of Bisaltai coins in the Jordan and Black Sea hoard and their absence from Asyut led Price and Kraay to the belief that the coinage was post-475, but one had no reason to think of it as massive.[30] The decadrachm hoard has 29 separate obverse dies; this compares to only 22 recorded octadrachm dies for Alexander I of Macedon.[31] The Bisaltai are known to have lived along the west banks of the Strymon and it has customarily been thought that their control over the Lake Prasias mines passed to

[23] Fried, p. 6.

[24] See the accompanying article by J. Spier for a discussion of the Lycian issues found with this hoard.

[25] Plutarch, *Cimon* 12.3–4.

[26] R. Meiggs, *The Athenian Empire*, Oxford, 1972, p. 74.

[27] Starr, pp. 27 ff.

[28] C. M. Kraay, review of *Athenian Coinage 480–449 B.C.*, in *NC* 1972, 313–17.

[29] One interesting note, an Athenian tetradrachm that, using Starr's chronology, would have been dated to the 430s has recently been found in a mid-century context at the Agora excavations. I am indebted to Professor Kroll for this observation.

[30] Asyut, p. 120; C. M. Kraay and P. R. S. Moorey, 'A Black Sea hoard of the late fifth century BC', *NC* 1981, 2–3.

[31] *ACGC*, p. 143.

Alexander immediately after the Persian retreat.[32] This needs to be rethought. We know from Herodotus that Alexander was mining a talent a day from the mine at some later date.[33] It seems probable that the Bisaltai were the initial beneficiary of the Persian withdrawal—we know again from Herodotus that their king resisted Xerxes and blinded his sons who sided with the Persians.[34] The Bisaltai must have controlled substantial silver sources until some time shortly after the burial of the hoard. The hoard lacks only the last two known octadrachm dies of the series.

Interestingly, the Bisaltai octadrachms seem to come to an end just at the time of Athens' involvement in the area. The colony at Ennea Hodoi and the campaign against the Thracians ending in the disaster at Drabescus in 465/4 may have had some effect on the fortunes of the Bisaltai. If, for a moment, we assume that the Bisaltai were on good economic terms with the Athenians then it becomes interesting that Cimon, according to Plutarch, was prosecuted after this period for his failure to attack Macedon.[35] One possible consequence of the Athenian disaster may have been that Alexander used the opportunity to dislodge the Bisaltai from their silver source. It is worth mentioning again that we have coins of King Getas of the Edoni but not of Alexander. Such a scenario has interesting historical implications for Alexander. Only in the last decade or so of his reign did he have access to truly great wealth.

Abdera and Acanthus, if the hoard date of 465/462 is correct, are not far displaced from currently accepted dates. But the downdating that we are proposing creates serious difficulties for a 449 BC coinage decree in northern Greece. There would be no room for a break at Abdera until the end of the 440s or early 430s, if one wishes to maintain annual magistracies; for Acanthus it is hard to see the Attic weight series ending in 449. Kraay could argue this because he accepted the beginning of the reverse inscription in 470.[36] Changing this to after 465 and accounting for the number of new dies make the case much harder to argue.

Moving the Abdera dates for Group III down by 10 to 20 years has a similar effect on Aenus, which is dated by an overstrike on an Abdera Group III coin.[37] The single Mende tetradrachm in the hoard, of the donkey-only type, leads to no new conclusions. The mid-century Gela overstrike on a Dionysus type makes it impossible to place a break in that mint for a 449 BC coinage decree between the two types.[38] Other mints not represented in the hoard may have their dates similarly affected on the basis of stylistic comparison.[39]

While the decadrachm hoard does not support the Coinage Decree's application in the north Aegean, it provides some interesting evidence for Rhodes. The mints of Camirus and Lindos are now clearly seen to be active after the archaic period.[40] There are later issues of staters with reverse inscriptions that are not in this hoard. These are closely related to the coins found in the decadrachm hoard and must be only a few years later. There exists, however, electrum coinage at Camirus[41] and

[32] N. G. L. Hammond and G. T. Griffith, *A History of Macedonia*, vol. 2, Oxford, 1979, p. 84.

[33] Herodotus 5.17.

[34] Herodotus 8.116.

[35] Plutarch, *Cimon* 12.3–4.

[36] *ACGC*, p. 136.

[37] May (op. cit., n. 3), pp. 90–1.

[38] *ACGC*, p. 137.

[39] See the accompanying paper by M. J. Price.

[40] For the conventional view, see *ACGC*, p. 245.

[41] N. Waggoner, *Early Greek Coins from the Collection of Jonathan P. Rosen*, ACNAC 5 (New York, 1983), no. 644.

Ialysus.[42] The Camirus electrum with KA inscriptions should be later than this hoard (there are also related silver fractions[43]). The appearance of isolated electrum issues such as these, a small series from Lampsacus and the one known issue from Chios[44] have as one possible explanation the existence of a restriction on silver coinage.

Regardless of the Decree, it is not surprising, looking at the hoard, that the weight standard confusion must have been serious. Athenian coinage and the Attic weight standard (note the Lycian changes shortly after this hoard[45]) were bound to force out existing coinages on local standards. It would have been far more convenient for Athens to have received, as does not always seem to have been the case,[46] the tribute in Attic-weight coin, if not actual owls.

It is interesting to observe that several of the mints represented in the decadrachm hoard are close to the end of their periods of operation. There are no other known dies for Paros drachms in this period. Several of the other Aegean island mints active after the archaic period, which are not represented in the hoard, also seem to close in this period.[47] Melos did not close, but is a special case in that the island did not join the League.[48]

The closing of several mints in the late 460s and early 450s does not need to be explained by the existence of an earlier decree. A useful parallel can be drawn between the members of the Athenian Empire in this period and the Thessalian cities under Macedonian influence in the late 4th century. Martin, in a recent study, has shown that the closing of the Thessalian mints was not due to any overt act on the part of Philip.[49] Independent coinage gradually came to an end. Hoard evidence demonstrates that Attic-weight tetradrachms, both Athenian and Macedonian, increasingly became the coinage of choice, in time making the local issues on the Aeginetan standard cumbersome.[50] One might speculate in both the case of Thessaly and the Athenian Empire in the late 460s and early 450s that once (for political or economic reasons) cities could not prevent the domestic circulation of Attic weight coins alongside local issues,then the profit in maintaining a mint disappeared. Local issues could not have commanded a sufficient premium to cover expenses. This problem would have been more acute for mints, like Paros, which did not have easy access to silver than for mints in the north Aegean. Such an explanation for the decline in minting during the period immediately following the decadrachm hoard would tie in well with an economic explanation for the Coinage Decree, whenever its date.[51]

In another direction, an exercise can be undertaken by looking not only at the coinages that are present in the decadrachm hoard, but also at those that are absent. When the pattern is compared to the Asyut, Zagazig, and Jordan hoards, an interesting phenomenon emerges.[52] Before going further, it is necessary to point

42 Babelon, *Traité* 105; H. A. Cahn, *Knidos* (Berlin 1970), 190, n. 584.

43 Waggoner (op. cit., n 41), no. 599; *BMCCaria*, p. 225, no. 14.

44 *ACGC*, pp. 243–5.

45 Spier (op. cit., n. 24), p. 37.

46 T. R. Martin, *Sovreignty and Coinage in Classical Greece*, Princeton, 1985, p. 201; hereafter cited as Martin.

47 E. Erxleben, 'Das Münzgesetz des delisch-attischen Seebundes', *Archiv für Papyrusforschung* 20 (1970), 72 ff.

48 C. M. Kraay, 'The Melos Hoard of 1907 re-examined', *NC* 1964, 1–25.

49 Martin, pp. 162 ff.

50 Martin, pp. 48 ff.

51 See Martin, pp. 196–207 for a convincing restatement of the economic argument.

52 Kraay, pp. 192–3.

out that there are a lot of pitfalls in this sort of analysis. With these four hoards we are dealing with a haphazard sample. Asyut, Zagazig, and Jordan are all eastern commerce hoards. Bullion was found with all three. Coins are likely to have entered the hoards at different times. Also, the Zagazig and Jordan hoards, with less than 90 identifiable coins in each, are perhaps too small to give an adequate cross section of what coinages were available. The decadrachm hoard on the other hand may have come together at one time for a special purpose. It, even more than they, may give a misleading picture of coin accumulations.

Having said all this, the pattern that emerges looks more than coincidental. It is remarkable how few coins there are in the decadrachm hoard from cities outside the sphere of Athenian influence. There is not a single coin from western Greece; nothing from Corinth; a few stray Aeginetan turtles, otherwise nothing from northwest or central Greece except Athens and one Eretrian piece. No coins of Alexander appear. There are only four coins from Melos. Despite the large Lycian run, there is nothing from Phaselis, no Persian sigloi whatsoever and nothing from Phoenicia, Cyprus, or Cyrene.

This pattern can only partly be explained by weight standards. There are few coins of Persian weight in the hoard (only Cos and certain Carian staters of Mylasan attribution that may be earlier). This may explain the absence of Phaselis, Persian sigloi, and Cyprus. But the weight argument is not in itself sufficient; the hoard already contains a number of different standards.

The distribution of mints in the hoard must, to a certain extent, represent the political realities of the situation. The creation of the Athenian Empire and the hostilities with Persia affected coin circulation. Non-league coinage from central Greece and the west did not find its way, unless restruck, into the coffers of the Delian League and did not flow freely between the League and the Persian Empire. The absence of even a stray siglos is remarkable. The somewhat official aspect of the decadrachm hoard and also the natural presumption that bullion travelled east, where the demand for it was greater, might mitigate against this theory of restricted circulation were it not for some surprising correlation provided by contemporary finds from within the Persian Empire.

Asyut contains, with the Alexander I octadrachm, at least one coin which is contemporary with, if not later than, the burial of our hoard. Aside from the two so-called Aegae tetradrachms with rosettes, what else might be later? Nothing for certain, but the best candidates are all from the East.[53] The Persian sigloi could be a few years later, although a crucial die link recorded in Asyut on which Kraay focused may be questionable,[54] and also some of the Cypriot and Cyrenean issues may be later. Some of the Lycian coins might not be before 470. If the Alexander is not a modern intrusion, then Asyut presents an interesting situation. The authors are clearly right in ending the bulk of the Aegean and western issues before 475, but the hoard itself remained open for some 10 to 15 years. It is tempting to explain the absence of any post-479 Athenian coins as well as coins of other Aegean mints by reference to the fact that the Athenian/Persian hostilities prevented the free flow of coinage that had existed in the archaic period.

53 Kraay, pp. 193–4.

54 Kraay, pp. 193–4; see also the accompanying article by I. Carradice.

Zagazig, which unfortunately is a difficult hoard to use because of the lack of some key illustrations, lends support to this view.[55] With the exception of the Athenian element, the Zagazig coins are all very close in date to the Asyut pieces. There are 16 archaic Athenian tetradrachms, one wreathed coin of the period of the decadrachm hoard and 17 coins which, based on the verbal descriptions, must be later. Kraay confirmed this after examining actual specimens in Berlin.[56] If the Athenian element indeed belongs to the hoard, we have another case of an Egyptian hoard basically closing to Greek coinage *c.* 475 but not being buried until later. Athenian coins alone re-enter the hoard at a date closer to mid-century, well after the decadrachm hoard.

Finally, the Jordan hoard presents a similar phenomenon. Excluding Cyprus, there are 46 coins out of 66 that are clearly archaic and minted before 475. Of the 29 Athenian coins, 24 are archaic. There are some 16 coins that could have been minted between 475 and 465/460, the date of burial of the decadrachm hoard. But then there are two Athenian coins, well preserved, of Starr's Group V, that are indeed later than the decadrachm hoard.[57]

Again, it is hard to draw conclusions from such a small hoard but it seems that the free flow of Athenian and other Greek coins, apart from areas controlled by Persia, declined to a mere trickle in the decades immediately after the failure of the Persian conquest. The decadrachm hoard was probably not a bullion hoard on its way to the east. The finely preserved Athens Group V coins from the Jordan hoard, when taken together with the Zagazig evidence, shows that this flow of coinage (seemingly limited now essentially to Athens alone) started up again after 460 and only with real purpose in the second half of the century.

A similar phenomenon takes place in Sicily. When the Gela hoard was buried, around 480, Athenian coins were plentiful. Some 10 to 20 years later, when the Monte Bubbonia hoard was buried, archaic Athenian coins are still found, but there are no new specimens of the wreathed variety. In this case it is not the Persian Empire but strong tyrannies and a closed coinage which may account for the change.[58]

Once the decadrachm hoard is subjected to more detailed analysis, greater precision on some of these questions may be obtained. On the positive side, however, we should not underestimate how much we now know about the chronology of archaic and early classical Greek coinage. It is exactly thirty years since Colin Kraay wrote his seminal article on the sequence of archaic Athenian owls.[59] Through his work and that of others, taken together with the Jordan, Asyut, and now the decadrachm hoards and the many new die studies, we may hope in the not too distant future to achieve general agreement on the dates of most of the major series.

[55] H. Dressel and K. Regling, 'Zwei ägyptische Funde altgriechischer Silbermünzen', *ZfN* 37 (1927), 1–138; and Kraay and Moorey (op. cit., n. 9), 208.

[56] C. M. Kraay, 'Archaic owls of Athens: new evidence for chronology', in H. Mussche, *Thorikos and the Laurion in Archaic and Classical Times. Miscellanea Graeca* I (Ghent, 1975), 145–60 (p. 147 ff.).

[57] Kraay and Moorey (op. cit., n. 9), p. 185.

[58] Kraay (op. cit., n. 28), p. 316.

[59] Kraay (op. cit., n. 6).

Lycian coins in the 'Decadrachm hoard'

JEFFREY SPIER

[PLATES VI–VII]

THE largest component of the 'Decadrachm hoard', and in fact the majority of the coins in the hoard, are Lycian. There are almost a thousand pieces of many different varieties, inscribed and not, and on several different weight standards, but nearly all are linked in some way—by die, inscription, or style—and must be closely contemporary. There is considerable die-linking and there are many die-duplicates. This situation, along with the excellent condition of the coins, which are to a large degree both uncirculated and corrosion-free, presents a rare opportunity for study. The original condition of the coins can be clearly seen, and the progressive state of the dies, along with their re-engraving or replacement, can be followed. It is of great importance that enough duplicates exist to allow a careful statistical study of the complicated weight systems used in Lycia. This will have wider implications. A number of known types are represented, including inscribed issues of dynasts, notably the best known dynast of this period, Kuprlli. However, there is an even greater number of entirely new types, new inscriptions, and even new dynasts' names.

It may be of value here to summarize briefly the state of our knowledge of Lycian coinage—which is meagre indeed.[1] In 1855 Sir Charles Fellows, best known for his writings on travels in Asia Minor and especially for bringing the Xanthos marbles to London, compiled a substantial list of Lycian coins in his *Coins of Ancient Lycia before the Reign of Alexander*. As he points out, these coins had previously been grouped as 'uncertain Cilicia', but Fellows, familiar with the topography, monuments, and inscriptions of Lycia, was able to lay the foundations for modern study. Other early pioneers were J.-P. Six writing in the *Revue Numismatique* for 1886 and 1887 and G. F. Hill, writing in the *Numismatic Chronicle* for 1895 in anticipation of his volume of the *British Museum Catalogue* which appeared in 1897. Around the same time (1893), there appeared E. Babelon's *Les Perses achéménides*, which published the Lycian coins in Paris. A short time later, his *Traité* dealt more comprehensively with Lycian coinage. It was at this time, also, that the inscriptions from Lycian tombs were being collected, notably in

[1] Cf. the summaries in O. Mørkholm, 'The classification of Lycian coins before Alexander the Great', *JNG* 14 (1964), 66 f. and O. Mørkholm and J. Zahle, 'The coinage of Kuprlli', *Acta Arch.* 43 (1972), 58.

Tituli Asiae Minoris, volume 1, by Ernst Kalinka, which appeared in 1901 and contained about 150 inscriptions, a near-corpus even now. The historical references were collected in 1887 by Oscar Treubner in *Geschichte der Lykier*.

Modern numismatic scholarship did not pick up again until the late 1950s, spurred especially by several new hoards and the appearance of the *Sylloge Nummorum Graecorum* volumes of the Berry and von Aulock collections, which included many new coins. The first new Lycian coin hoard, to which we will return, was published by Sydney Noe in the *ANS Centennial Publication* in 1958.[2] G. K. Jenkins examined possible mints in the *Numismatic Chronicle* for 1959.[3] A reexamination of the old material and new hoards was being made by several scholars, but most notably by the late Otto Mørkholm in Copenhagen. To date, the most important works on Lycian coins are his, including the von Aulock sylloge volume for Lycia (1964), 'The classification of Lycian coins before Alexander the Great' in *JNG* 14 (1964), and, with Jan Zahle, 'The coinage of Kuprlli', *Acta Archaeologica* 43 (1972) and 'The coinages of the Lycian dynasts Kheriga, Kherei, and Erbbina', ibid. 47 (1976). Also of great importance are the joint publication by Mørkholm and the linguist Günter Neumann, *Die lykischen Münzlegenden* (1978), which examines the inscriptions on coins in light of new linguistic work and recent finds, and Neumann's *Neufunde lykischer Inschriften seit 1901* (1971), which, despite its encouraging title, adds only 26 new inscriptions, mostly fragmentary, but also includes the highly important trilingual inscription (Lycian, Aramaic, and Greek) found by the French excavators at Xanthos.

Although excavations and archaeological work progress, the finds remain few that shed light on the history, politics, and personalities of Lycia, with least known about the first half of the 5th century, the period here under consideration. It must then be kept in mind that our knowledge of Lycian history and language is very poor, and that what we know of the coinage may also have many gaps, having been dependent on chance finds that so far have not provided much duplication. Every coin hoard may bring entirely new material, as this hoard has, but we are fortunate to have a hoard of such size and quality.

Mørkholm on several occasions called for the study of the extensive Lycian coinage, with careful attention to be given to the die-links, weights, and inscriptions, an additional incentive being that the study would shed light on the associated Greek coinage.[4] Our hoard allows much progress to be made. Attention here will be given to the basic types with particular attention paid to the inscriptions, weight standards, die-links, a few overstrikes, and relations to other hoards. The die-links are particularly revealing, and we are aided by the Lycian practice of disregarding the state of the dies, using them until they were worn out, and then summarily re-engraving them in an easily detectable manner.

The weight standards will first be considered. Six had already noted that the Lycians employed several standards,[5] but Mørkholm, through a careful statistical study which unfortunately depended on inadequate material, theorized that the

[2] S. P. Noe, 'A Lycian hoard', *ANS Centennial Publication*, New York, 1958, 543–51.

[3] G. K. Jenkins, 'Recent acquisitions of Greek coins by the British Museum', *NC* 1959, 32–41, 45.

[4] Mørkholm and Zahle, op. cit. in n. 1, 58 f.

[5] J.-P. Six, 'Monnaies lyciennes', *RN* 1886, 106.

different standards reflected geographical divisions, a heavy Lycian standard of just under 10 grammes being used in eastern Lycia, and a light standard of about 8·5 g in the West.[6] In addition, a few coins were struck on the Persian standard of about 11 g (double sigloi). He also detected an intermediate standard of around 9 g, used for some coins of Kuprlli as well as for uninscribed contemporary issues.[7]

The new hoard shows that his interpretation must be revised and that the situation was somewhat more complicated. The heaviest standard, at 11 g, was the Persian, known only from a few examples of the dynast Kuprlli, including four from the Asyut hoard. There are no examples in this hoard. The next standard, generally called the heavy Lycian, is just under 10 g (about 9·8 g), slightly heavier than Mørkholm supposed, and is known from boar protome obverse/incuse reverse types of the early 5th century (or earlier) and throughout the dynastic coinage until its end in the 4th century, with only minor variations from issue to issue.[8] The middle standard is somewhat elusive. There are in fact several middle standards, but it is not clear whether they existed at the same time, or whether there was a gradual reduction. In any event, there is clearly a standard of about 9·4 g (not exceeding 9·5 g). This is demonstrable only for the early issues in the hoard, which are related to the Noe hoard and to some examples in Asyut. These coins are linked to (and in some cases succeeded by) a slightly lighter standard at around 9·2 g, which appears to coincide with the introducion of the triskeles reverse (although these can also be on the heavy, 9·8 g standard).[9] The standard is further reduced to just under 9 g for several series issued by Kuprlli and others related to them. Coins of this standard had previously not been well attested, although Mørkholm perceptively recognized that a few such coins of Kuprlli did exist.

The middle standard in all its varieties disappears around the middle of the 5th century, replaced by the light Lycian standard of about 8·5 g, no doubt meant to correspond to the Attic didrachm. This light standard, which continues throughout the 5th century and into the 4th, is thus the further reduction of the middle standard, although this was not seen by Mørkholm. The total absence of light-weight coins from the hoard confirms that the weight change did not occur until around the middle of the century. This provides an extremely important chronological point, although a relative one, and allows the division of Lycian coins, most notably the extensive coinage of Kuprlli, by the introduction of the reduced weight, soon after the close of the hoard.

One other result of our analysis of the weights may be briefly considered. Mørkholm believed that coins of different weights could not have been struck at the same mint and could find only one die-link between coins of different weights.[10] This helped support his theory of cities striking coins according to their

[6] Mørkholm, op. cit. in n. 1, 69 f., and Mørkholm and Zahle, op. cit. in n. 1, 72 f.

[7] Mørkholm, op. cit. in n. 1, 70 n. 16, and Mørkholm and Zahle, op. cit. in n. 1, 72.

[8] N. Olçay and O. Mørkholm, 'The Podalia hoard', *NC* 1971, 22 f.

[9] A very early, if not the earliest, series of Lycian coins with lion's head on the obverse (as *SNG (von Aulock)* 4041–2) also appears to be on the 9·2 g standard.

[10] O. Mørkholm and J. Zahle, 'The coinages of the Lycian dynasts Kheriga, Kherei, and Erbbina', *Acta Arch.* 47 (1976), 54, a link between the dynasts Kuprlli and Kheriga.

own regional weight standard. However, the hoard now provides a number of examples of die-linked series of different standards, most likely from the same mint, which calls Mørkholm's idea into question. The reasons for the different standards must remain obscure.

The hoard contains few examples of early Lycian coins, and certainly none of the earliest. Among the earliest Lycian coins in it are those with boars (usually protomes) on the obverse and incuse punches on the reverse. A number of early Lycian hoards have appeared, including several in the 1970s, that contained coins of this type, but they are certainly of earlier date than this hoard. The relatively early Damanhur hoard[11] contained several examples, as well as some early two-sided types also absent from our hoard. Our hoard contained only three examples of the boar/incuse type, and these appear to be of the latest varieties of this series.

The next series of Lycian coins have devices, usually animals, on both sides and are usually uninscribed. Boars remain popular as obverse types, as do winged horses. The reverses may represent various animals, or their heads or protomes. Both Asyut and the hoard published by Noe are typical of this period. The coins in Noe's hoard, which was probably found in Lycia itself, all seem to be from one mint. They all have a winged horse on the obverse, and the reverses are either bull protomes, lion and bull protomes, or the peculiar hatched border with no device within. They are on the early middle standard of about 9·4 g. There is some overlap here with Asyut, which contains several of the same type.[12] Our hoard has die-duplicates and further die-links for this series, although only about 20 coins belong here, a very small percentage of the total and of clearly earlier date than the bulk.

Asyut has more variety than the Noe hoard, but must be of about the same date. Several other coins with boar obverse and various reverse devices are present, some of which link to the early material in our hoard. In addition, there are two boar types with reverse triskeles, probably among the earliest examples of this series,[13] both of which find duplicates in the new hoard. These types continue until the closing date of our hoard, and are well represented. They are eventually die-linked to a new inscribed coin of Kuprlli. Other dynasts, notably Kuprlli's contemporary Ẽkuwẽmi, also use the boar/triskeles type. They employ both the heavy and middle standards, and although no die-link between standards has yet been found here, the coins of different weight often look identical. The Kuprlli coins on the Persian standard found in the Asyut hoard have already been mentioned.

An example of the die-linking that our hoard has provided reveals connections between boar types with and without inscriptions and on different weight standards. It begins (**Pl. VI, 1**) with a stater on the heavy standard that has an already very worn obverse die of a boar walking left coupled with a reverse showing a griffin protome right with small triskeles in the field. There are two specimens in the hoard, die-duplicates that in turn match one now in Berlin from the Zagazig hoard,[14] which unfortunately can no longer provide a useful chronological point

[11] *IGCH* 1637. H. Dressel and K. Regling, 'Zwei ägyptische Funde altgriechischer Silbermünzen', *ZfN* 37 (1927), 69–72, nos. 117–24.

[12] M. J. Price and N. Waggoner, *Archaic Greek Silver Coinage. The Asyut Hoard*, 1975, nos. 755–8.

[13] ibid., nos. 765–6.

[14] *IGCH* 1645. Dressel and Regling, op. cit. in n. 11, 132, no. 247.

for our study since its burial date now seems to be *c.* 450 or later, rather than the previously supposed *c.* 470.[15] The obverse die then links to a different type of reverse die, an unusual type showing a sort of tetraskeles with a triskeles engraved in its centre, all within a dotted border (**Pl. VI, 2**). There are five examples in our hoard, on the middle standard of about 9·2 g. The reverse die seems to have been taken from a series with obverse boar protome left on the heavy standard known from a unique example in Paris[16] and not found in our hoard. Next (**Pl. VI, 3**) the obverse die is re-engraved, merely with the addition of a triskeles over the now barely distinguishable boar. The new reverse die is a triskeles with the letters *ku* for Kuprlli. There are 13 examples in the hoard, using two different reverse dies, all on the middle standard. Another series represented in the hoard (not illustrated here) similarly demonstrates these links between inscribed and uninscribed coins and between coins of different weight standards, again ending with the inscribed coins of Kuprlli.

Kuprlli is fairly well represented in the hoard with over 100 coins of at least 16 different types, half of them new.[17] This should not be too surprising in view of the large number of types collected by Mørkholm in his study and the long reign of the dynast, one of the few rulers known from the monumental dynastic inscriptions found in Lycia.[18] In fact, we have in the hoard only the beginnings of his coinage, which continues at least into the 440s, as can be seen by the advanced style of the later coin types and their reduced weight, as mentioned before.

Kuprlli's less well known contemporary Ẽkuwẽmi is also represented. There are 16 of his coins, all but one on the middle (9 g) standard and with considerable die-linking. One coin (**Pl. VI, 4**) is of special interest since the same obverse is used with both an uninscribed reverse and a reverse with the name of Kuprlli. The latter is not represented in the hoard, but is noted by Mørkholm.[19] That the two dynasts shared dies was already known from fractions, but this new example is welcome, as is the additional link to an uninscribed issue.

Some other dynasts are represented in only small numbers or single examples. Uele has 12 examples; Thibo 2; Zagaba (previously unknown except as a 4th-century dynast) 1[20]; Za... (Zagaba?) 8; and there are a few others that cannot presently be deciphered or are uninscribed. There is at least one further die-link to uninscribed issues.

Another series, although not especially well represented in the hoard with only seven examples, presents important evidence for relative chronology. It is an uninscribed series with boars on the obverse and turtles, similar to those on Aeginetan coinage, on the reverse. Mørkholm noted that nearly all are overstruck on other coins,[21] which is not unusual for Lycian issues, but several important overstrikes have been found. One example, in the British Museum, is twice

[15] Cf. C. M. Kraay, *Misc. Graeca* 1, Ghent, 1975, 147.

[16] Babelon, *Traité* I, no. 835, pl. 22, 17 = *Les Perses achéménides*, no. 462, pl. 12, 2.

[17] Previously known types of Kuprlli in the hoard include the following: Mørkholm and Zahle, op. cit. in n. 1, nos. 5, 17, 22, 24, 30, and 40, as well as staters of the types nos. 173 and 178, previously known only as fractions. There are additional links to previously known uninscribed issues.

[18] E. Kalinka, *Tituli Asiae Minoris*, vol. 1, Vienna, 1901, no. 44.

[19] Mørkholm and Zahle, op. cit. in n. 1, no. 35 (Kuprlli) and pl. II, D (uninscribed).

[20] Cf. P. Frei, 'Bemerkungen zu lykischen Münzlegenden', *SM* 17, 67 (1967), 86 f.

[21] Mørkholm, op. cit. in n. 1, 68 f. and n. 10.

overstruck, on another Lycian coin which had in turn been struck on a cut-down tetradrachm of Acanthus,[22] unfortunately not very useful in determining chronology. Many others are overstruck on early Lycian coins, but on two examples the undertypes can be seen to be inscribed Lycian coins, one of these clearly of Kuprlli.[23] Mørkholm notes this and points out that the series must therefore be of later date than was previously thought, perhaps continuing until after 450, although his date may be a little too late. A new coin from the hoard (**Pl. VI, 5**) shows an uninscribed boar / triskeles type clearly overstruck on a boar / turtle stater of the sort that was overstruck on a Kuprlli stater. Although the overstrikes must, of course, be later than the undertypes, the time difference in this case cannot be great, especially in view of the extensive overstriking on other closely contemporary Lycian coins. For reasons no doubt significant but unclear at present, Lycian coins of this period are more often than not overstruck on earlier, usually Lycian, coins.

We turn now to the bulk of the Lycian coins. All those previously mentioned, which include numerous varieties and dies, uninscribed and inscribed of various dynasts, represent only about 40 per cent. of the Lycian content of the hoard. The other 60 per cent. is composed of several issues that are closely die-linked and with many die-duplicates. Most of these coins were not previously known, or were known in only a few examples. Two main series are involved, one with a long string of die-links connecting different types and dynasts.

The other series is most unusual for the coupling of a single obverse die re-engraved several times with a single reverse die. All the coins are on the heavy standard, about 9·8 g, and there are about 120 examples in total. The first example (**Pl. VI, 6**) shows a goat with a triskeles symbol above. The reverse shows the triskeles and an inscription often read as *zẽt*, but which, as Mørkholm and Neumann point out, may be better read as *zẽ* with an accompanying symbol.[24] While the same reverse die is used, the obverse die, now somewhat more worn, is re-engraved (**Pl. VI, 7**). The triskeles is erased, and a letter or symbol *o* is substituted.[25] Traces of the triskeles are still visible. Next (**Pl. VI, 8**) this symbol is erased and a new one put in: the same symbol, resembling a T, that appears on the reverse.[26] Most of the coins in this series, nearly a hundred, are of this variety. Finally (**Pl. VI, 9**), a triskeles is added below the goat. The coupling of several obverses with one reverse is contrary to normal minting practice, in which reverse dies need replacing more often, and even in Lycia this is the usual case. For this issue we may interpret the re-engraving of different symbols as some sort of control system. The mint attribution will be discussed below.

The most revealing series, which eventually accounts for more than 450 of the coins in the hoard, links relatively early uninscribed coins with several dynasts and several weight standards. All the coins are die-linked or linked by inscriptions, and

[22] *BMC Lycia*, 4, no. 18, pl. 1, 15.

[23] Mørkholm and Zahle, op. cit. in n. 1, 76, nos. 15–18. One example of this type is in the hoard as well.

[24] O. Mørkholm and G. Neumann, *Die lykischen Münzlegenden*, Göttingen, 1978, M19. Cf. Mørkholm and Zahle, op. cit. in n. 10, 63, symbol No. 11.

[25] If a letter, it would be the Lycian *u*. A die-duplicate is *SNG (von Aulock)* 4117.

[26] A fraction of the series with the same obverse symbol is in Paris, Babelon, *Traité* II, no. 246 bis (1·27 g).

all are probably from the same mint. They have in common a winged horse or winged horse protome as an obverse type. The first coins show a winged horse obverse and lion head left reverse (**Pl. VII, 10**). The weight is the heavier 'middle' standard of about 9·4 g, and the coins are stylistically related to the Noe hoard, where the coins all have winged horse obverses and are on this same weight standard. There are no actual die-links to that hoard, however. Five reverse dies with lion head are used, but the obverse die, except in one example, is always the same. However, it is quickly worn out and undergoes several re-engravings. First, a T is added to the hindquarters of the winged horse, the same letter as seen on the winged horses in the Noe hoard, and which also appears on the neck of the lion on the reverse. The obverse die is recut four times, ending in a nearly unintelligible state. Then, unchanged, it is coupled with a new reverse, a triskeles with an inscription that I read as *esbehi*, certainly a name of an unknown dynast (**Pl. VII, 11**). An example from the same dies has been in Paris for some time and is illustrated in Babelon's *Traité*,[27] but the inscription is incomplete and was misread by Mørholm and Neumann, who confused it with a similar name, which will be considered shortly. The dynast *esbehi* is unknown, but the name does appear once on a brief tomb inscription from Limyra.[28] These coins are on the slightly reduced standard of about 9·2 g.

The die-links are lost at this point, but the new obverse and reverse dies on the next example are very similar and the name is the same (**Pl. VII, 12**), as is the weight standard. Now there is an important die-link. The same inscribed reverse die is linked with a new obverse that shows a winged horse protome with triskeles engraved on it and two letters (*kẽ* or *kg* retrograde?) of unclear meaning below (**Pl. VII, 13**). The new obverse die is used also for the next three reverses, and in all cases coins with this obverse are on the heavy standard of about 9·8 g. The next reverse (**Pl. VII, 14**) names a new dynast, previously unknown and with a name difficult to decipher. It is not clear at the moment in which order the next two dies come, but perhaps next is a short issue with no name, merely a symbol of a type paralleled on other Lycian coins, including coins of the dynast Ñaj like the ones that follow,[29] but with no clear meaning (**Pl. VII, 15**). Finally comes a large issue, with nearly 300 examples in the hoard, of the dynast *ñaj* (as Mørkholm and Neumann read it;[30] previously called Jña by Mørkholm) (**Pl. VII, 16**). The dynast is known through coins of similar type, although not die-duplicates, some of which were present in the Kaş (Antiphellus) hoard of 1961 (*IGCH* 1251), unfortunately not well recorded but mentioned several times by Mørkholm,[31] which must be at least a decade or so later in date than our hoard and which

[27] Babelon, *Traité* II, no. 161, pl. 92, 22.

[28] Kalinka, op. cit. in n. 18, 128, 1; cf. L. Zgusta, *Kleinasiatische Personennamen*, Prague, 1964, 176 no. 365, n. 90.

[29] Babelon, *Traité* II, no. 217, pl. 94, 25 and *SNG (von Aulock)* 4103 (same dies) for Ñaj; and Babelon, *Traité* II, no. 218, pl. 94, 26 for *zazthi*, with an obverse die-duplicate also in this hoard. Uninscribed issues with winged horse on shield and triskeles reverse, apparently from the Kaş hoard, also have this symbol, *SNG (von Aulock)* 4087–8. The symbol also appears on an unpublished type in the hoard with boar obverse / triskeles reverse. Cf. Mørkholm and Zahle, op. cit. in n. 10, 64, symbol No. 18, and similar symbols appearing on other coins and gems of this period, J. Boardman, 'Pyramidal stamp seals in the Persian Empire', *Iran* 8 (1970), 22 ff.

[30] Mørkholm and Neumann, op. cit. in n. 24, M103.

[31] Mørkholm, op. cit. in n. 1, 69, and Mørkholm and Zahle, op. cit. in n. 1, 75.

included a number of dynasts of the next generation, as well as some post-Starr group Athens tetradrachms. The coins of the dynast Ñaj, the most numerous type of the hoard, are also probably the latest coins in the hoard and might also give a clue in identifying the hoard's owner, if more were known about the history and personalities of Lycia at this time.

An issue that has elements in common with the last one must also be considered here. Another badly worn winged horse obverse, with T on the hindquarters, has a reverse inscription very similar to the first *esbehi* inscription (**Pl. VII, 17**), so similar that the coins must be looked at very carefully to distinguish the two, and in fact Mørkholm and Neumann confused the two in their publication.[32] The weights are the same, about 9·2 g. Mørkholm and Neumann read the inscription as *im̃ese*, although read the other way it may be *esem̃i* or *esehi*, very close to the *esbehi* inscription, although the *b* is clearly absent. It is possible, however, that the names are meant to be identical. Two examples of this otherwise unknown type are in Oxford; one, only fragmentary, having been cut in half, is from the Jordan hoard,[33] providing another link to that important hoard. Another unpublished example was recently acquired by the American Numismatic Society.

The next die-link is quite extraordinary. The same obverse is coupled with a new reverse (**Pl. VII, 18**) that has no triskeles, merely a dotted square with an inscription in Greek, not Lycian. It clearly reads *rhodion*, presumably for *nomisma rhodion*, a 'Rhodian coin'. These coins are on the same Lycian weight standard and were presumably struck for or by Rhodians in Lycia, perhaps as payments for mercenaries. Rhodian activity is well attested in Lycia since the 7th century or even before. Phaselis, on the eastern border of Lycia, was a Rhodian colony, and the Lycian city of Rhodiapolis perhaps bears witness to a Rhodian presence at some time. The coins, however, are a surprising and indeed unique document attesting Rhodian activity in Lycia in the 460s.

Finally, the subject of mints must be addressed. Two mints are named on the coinage of Kuprlli, Xanthos and Limyra (*zẽmure* in Lycian).[34] Phellos (*wehñtezi*) is known from coins of slightly later date. Our hoard includes a previously unknown type (**Pl. VII, 19**), on the heavy standard, with a dolphin on the obverse and a clear, neatly written inscription on the reverse reading *aprllazẽ*, which, according to Neumann[35] should be some form of the city name Aperlai. However, no other coins with this inscription are in the hoard.

There are several coins of Kuprlli inscribed with the name *zẽmure*, or Limyra.[36] Die-linked examples have reverses with either no inscription (**Pl. VII, 20**), or merely the single letter *z*, probably for *zẽmure*. Neumann suggested that the inscription *zẽt* on the goat staters discussed above may be better read as *zẽ* and a symbol, the *zẽ* perhaps standing for the place-name *zẽmure*. This theory becomes more likely in the light of the new material now available. The third sign is clearly

[32] Mørkholm and Neumann, op. cit. in n. 24, M22.

[33] *IGCH* 1482. C. M. Kraay and P. R. S. Moorey, 'Two fifth century hoards from the Near East', *RN* 1968, 188, no. 64, pl. 21.

[34] Mørkholm and Zahle, op. cit. in n.1, 75.

[35] Mørkholm and Neumann, op. cit. in n. 24, M108, M111.

[36] As Mørkholm and Zahle, op. cit. in n. 1, no. 22.

a symbol rather than a letter, as it is used on the obverse of one die.[37] The attribution of the entire group to Limyra is appealing, and it is also tempting to attribute the extensive run of winged horse coins of the various dynasts to this city or another close by, as the name *esbehi* appears on a tomb there.

There are both chronological and economic conclusions of relevance to this symposium that can be drawn from the evidence of this hoard, but unfortunately not as precisely as we would like. The date of the hoard, judging from earlier and later Lycian coin hoards, should be later than *c.* 470 and before *c.* 450, but this is less precise than the evidence given by the non-Lycian coins in the hoard. The economic implications are more far-reaching. Lycian coins do not seem often to have been struck on the Persian standard, and there are none in this hoard. On the other hand, we see a switch to the Attic standard (alongside the local Lycian standard) very soon after the closure of this hoard, certainly by 450, at a time when a number of nearby Greek mints appear to be closing, at least temporarily. Despite the lack of a good fixed chronological point, the information that the hoard adds to our knowledge of Lycian coinage—its weight standards, order of issues and relative chronology, inscriptions, and so on—is very great, and the forthcoming publication of the hoard in its entirety will discuss these aspects in more detail.

[37] Cf. the same symbol on a Lydian-Achaemenid gem in London, Boardman, op. cit. in n. 29, 23, symbol D18, and 42, no. 97, p. 4.

PLATE VI

PLATE VII

The coinages of the northern Aegean

M. JESSOP PRICE

[PLATES VIII–IX]

ONE of the excitements of working with coins is that there is a constant stream of discoveries which allows continuous reappraisal of traditional beliefs and more recent theories. The new Lycian hoard provides a wealth of evidence for the chronology of coinages in the third quarter of the fifth century, and I am indeed grateful to those responsible for the publication for this opportunity to delve into the hoard's consequences.[1]

Before plunging into the details of the coinages of northern Greece, I would like to make one or two general points which may have some relevance to the discussions. In dealing with coinage in the early fifth century it is important to remember that silver coinage was a relatively new phenomenon. The coinages that can be placed in the sixth century are relatively meagre, and there appears to have been an explosion of coinage in the early years of the fifth century. Several coinages exist from the late sixth and early fifth century with a well developed system of small denominations, but the vast majority of the pieces to have survived were of stater size or larger, and it is unlikely that these were designed for use in the market place. Silver objects surviving from the ancient world before the late sixth century BC are extremely rare. It may well be that improvements in the technology of processing silver from lead ores, linked with increasing contacts between East and West, led directly to increased mining and exploration at Laurion and other sources of silver-bearing lead ores, and that it was this that resulted in the coinage explosion. If silver was as rare, or rarer, than gold in the seventh century, there seems little doubt that its actual value must have been similar to that of gold. The silver produced in the late sixth and early fifth century in Greece found ready markets in the Persian empire and Magna Graecia, where clearly the value must have been greatly in excess of the falling value in the Aegean basin. By turning the silver into coins, the issuer was probably making a fair profit, and, even after absorbing that profit, the traders were happily transporting these little stamped ingots to areas where the price was still considerably higher.

The idea that tribute or taxes were the main reasons for the movement of silver

[1] I would particularly like to express my gratitude to Dr. Cornelius Vermeule for his continued generosity in sharing with me the details of the new Lycian find, and similarly I am most grateful to Miss S. Fried, Mr. J. Kagan, and Mr. J. Spier for generously making material available.

coinage[2] seems an unnecessary simplification. Any profit that may have accrued from turning raw silver into coins must have at once been lost in such payments, and since such sums would not have been paid as taxes by Macedonians to the satrapies of Cilicia, Abarnahara, or Egypt other reasons must have caused the movement of Greek coinage to a place such as Asyut-Lykopolis. However unfashionable such an idea may be today, I am convinced that movement of silver from such areas as north Greece to the eastern Mediterranean must have been conducted as a form of trade, and it is no surprise that a hoard such as that described in this volume, with contents of a type more normally associated with Egypt and Palestine, should have been found at one of the staging posts on the silver route.

The other subject of this debate is the effect of the Athenian currency decree. The stated purpose was to bring an end to local striking of coinage and to institute the use of Athenian coins, weights and measures throughout the confederacy. I would like to underline that very few inscriptions have survived which directly relate to the striking of coinage. There are however signs of confederate coinage agreements which survive in the coins themselves. The Boeotian League issues are a clear indication that confederacies thought in terms of uniformity in coinage without necessarily encroaching upon the sovereign autonomy of member states. One may imagine that for this coinage, and for the coinage of Corinth and her colonies, and for the well known symmachia coinage of *c.* 400 BC, there must have existed inscriptions set up in the member cities stipulating the particular weight systems and designs to be used.

The reason why Macedonia plays such a prominent part in the history of coinage in the late sixth and early fifth century is that the area was rich in silver mines. We have already seen some of the dramatic coinages from the Macedonian region found in the Lycian hoard. Of particular interest is the large number of octadrachms in the name of the Bisalti. Some of the latest examples display as a symbol in the field a helmet (**Pl. VIII, 1**), which may be linked with the appearance of this same device either as reverse design or as symbol on coinages of Alexander I, the Orescii, Derrones, Lete, and Laiai.[3] Alexander's own coinage is notably absent from this new hoard, a fact which provides only further complication to the debate over the presence of one of his octadrachms in the Asyut hoard.[4]

The new evidence confirms the statement made in the Asyut publication[5] that the coinage of the Bisalti must date after 480; and similarly the issues of Getas, king of the Edoni (**Pl. VIII, 2**), belong to the same period. This coinage is interesting because it consists of two varieties. One has the inscription on the obverse, as is normal on the issues of the Bisalti and other 'tribal' Macedonian coinages. The other places the inscription on the four sides of a shallow, linear, quadripartite square, and it is this arrangement of the reverse and its inscription that was to become the fashion of many Macedonian coinages in the middle of the fifth

[2] As for example in such statements as M. Vickers, 'Early Greek coinage, a reassessment' *NC* 1985, 1–44, p. 21.

[3] J. Svoronos, *L'hellénisme primitif de la Macédoine*, Athens, 1919, plates 1–3.

[4] I felt in the early 1970s that the Asyut hoard should be allowed to date the Alexander coin (*Asyut*, 39) and preferred not to see it as an item added twenty years later to the main deposit. This view won little favour and should be revised.

[5] *Asyut*, p. 39.

century. The beginning of this fashion, which is clearly under way during the striking of the issues of Getas and the Bisalti can be dated through the evidence of the new Lycian and Asyut hoards to around 460. It provides some confirmation for the dating of the octadrachms of Alexander I which in this particular feature stand out from the other Macedonian coinages in the Asyut hoard, and, as Dr. Kraay has shown, we must accept that the single piece of Alexander in that hoard was an addition to the original deposit.[6] The evidence of the new Lycian hoard would suggest that this issue is probably to be placed in the late 460s or 450s, with a *terminus ante quem* of Alexander's death in 451 (**Pl. VIII, 3**).

Alexander's coinage is not vast, and certainly does not reflect the story reported by Herodotus that he possessed a mine producing a talent of silver per day.[7] The octadrachms represent but one of the series of heavy ingot/coins produced by the Macedonian mining areas in the first half of the fifth century.

In contrast to the Asyut hoard, the new Lycian hoard contains, apart from the issues of the Bisalti, relatively few of the heavy Macedonian issues, confirming, perhaps, that most must date before the deposit of the Asyut hoard. However, it is important to note that the one coin of the Derrones present in the new hoard is of a variety with reverse design,[8] unlike the issues in Asyut, and this piece, with its prominent reverse square, is clearly the first of a new period of coining for the Derrones with reverse types triskeles or head of Athena (**Pl. VIII, 4**). This period of coinage must coincide with that of Alexander's octadrachms, and on the evidence of the new hoard may be placed in the late 460s or 450s.

Comparison of the contents of the Asyut hoard and of the new Lycian hoard will be particularly useful for the chronology of the issues of the Greek cities of the northern Aegean. The nine coins of Thasos present in the later hoard do not apparently display the features of the second phase—the classical modelling and splayed fingers[9]—and it may now be considered somewhat uncertain that this second group should be placed before the revolt from the Delian League in 465.

A clear pattern of development is visible at Abdera. May's period II, which had been dated 520/515–492, was the latest coinage of the city in the Asyut hoard.[10] The new Lycian hoard contains mainly the issues of period III, the latest being May nos. 83–5. The tetradrachms of period IV, which followed period III without a break, show the introduction of the fashion of placing the inscription around the reverse square (**Pl. IX, 5**).[11] These were not represented among the nineteen coins of Abdera in the new hoard. It is clear therefore that the new Lycian hoard confirms the evidence of the Asyut hoard and shows that period II at Abdera continued until 480 or later, and period III until after 460. Period IV, with twenty separate issues, must have continued uninterrupted into the 430's or even later.

The coinage of Ainos does not feature in the new Lycian hoard, but one of the

[6] C. M. Kraay, 'The Asyut hoard: some comments on chronology', *NC* 1977, 189–98, pp. 190–3.

[7] Herodotus 5.17.2, near Lake Prasias. The excellent account of the tribal coinages by N. G. L. Hammond and G. T. Griffith, *A history of Macedonia* II, Oxford, 1979, pp. 69–91 links the existing mine workings with some of the coinages. Lake Prasias is identified with Lake Butkova, ibid I, p. 194.

[8] See C. Sternberg, *SM* 137, Feb. 1985, 5.2 (from the new Lycian hoard).

[9] G. Le Rider, 'Les monnaies', in *Guide de Thasos*, 1968, 186–7.

[10] *Asyut*, pp. 36–7; cf. J. M. F. May, *The Coinage of Abdera*, 1966, pp. 67–81.

[11] Period IV is dated by May, ibid pp. 115–42, *c.* 473/70–449/8.

first dies of the goat reverse[12] was used to overstrike a coin of Abdera of period III belonging to an issue soon after the latest in the Lycian hoard (**Pl IX, 11**). It therefore seems very unlikely, on present evidence, that the coinage of Ainos began before the later 460s. It must have continued well into the third quarter of the century.

This pattern is repeated at Acanthus. The 38 coins of this city in the Asyut hoard belonged to the earlier phase of the first group. The 37 pieces in the new Lycian hoard continue to the end of period I, which Desneux had placed *c.* 480.[13] Most of the issues bear the rosette symbol, but a few examples bearing the letter A on the obverse were also present (**Pl. II, 13**). Period II, which introduces the fashion of placing the inscription around the linear square on the reverse (**Pl. IX, 6**), was wholly absent. Since there is no break in the relative sequence, it is clear that period II at Acanthus, as period IV at Abdera, continued well beyond the middle of the century.

At Mende we once again find the fashion of placing the inscription around the reverse on issues later than those present in the new Lycian hoard. The dramatic change of coinage, from the ass and incuse reverse punch to Dionysus reclining on the ass and reverse vine (**Pl. IX, 7**), took place well after the deposit of the Asyut hoard and most probably not before *c.* 460. A *terminus ante quem* for this change is provided by an overstrike on the later type at the mint of Gela[14] *c.* 450–440. The Kaliandra hoard shows that the new coinage continued uninterrupted,[15] most probably to the time of the siege and capture of the city in 423.

A city that lay on the other side of the peninsula from Mende provides particular interest for the comparison of the chronology of the coinages with the Athenian currency decree. Aphytis was one of the sites at which a copy of the decree has been found, and its silver coinage,[16] two issues of small denominations (**Pl. IX, 9**), both containing the vine design on the reverse, clearly dates after the introduction of the Dionysus type at Mende. One issue may belong to the 450s, but the other must be later, well into the third quarter of the century, and in apparent contravention of the decree.

Similarly, Maronea in Thrace introduces first an inscription around square, and then the vine as a reverse design[17] in a manner apparently adopted from Mende (**Pl. IX, 8,** cf. **7**), and thus provides an important coinage for the third quarter of the century. At Aeneia a coinage of small denominations with inscription around the shallow linear square (**Pl. IX, 10**) follows the fashion introduced towards the middle of the century, and is presumably itself a coinage of the third quarter of the century.

The currency decree stipulates not only that local coinages should cease, but also that Athenian coinage should be used. It is however a notable phenomenon that

[12] J. M. F. May, *Ainos*, Oxford, 1950, no. 9, dated 471/0–469/8, overstruck on a period III tetradrachm of Abdera, with symbol cock, May, *Abdera* group XLII.

[13] *Asyut*, pp. 40–2.

[14] G. K. Jenkins, *The Coinage of Gela*, Berlin, 1970, pp. 65–6.

[15] S. P. Noe, *The Mende (Kaliandra) Hoard*, *NNM* 27, New York, 1926, pp. 52–3.

[16] H. Gaebler, *AMNG* III.2, 44.

[17] A. B. West, *Fifth and fourth century gold coins from the Thracian Coast*, *NNM* 40, New York, 1929, pp. 55–77 = J. M. F. May, 'The coinage of Maroneia', *NC* 1965, 27–56, pp. 48–9, where a short gap *c.* 449 must be revised in the light of new evidence.

there are practically no hoards of Athenian coinage in the north Aegean area,[18] in stark contrast to areas of the eastern Mediterranean under Persian domination. This is hardly surprising. A currency decree, had it existed, might have had some influence on the circulation of the owls, but there can have been no commerical incentive for the coinage of Athens to have travelled to the north, an area rich in silver that had little need of more. There are two pieces of influence on design which may be remarked: the crescent moon behind the figure of 'Rhesus' on the octadrachms of Alexander[19] is too close to that on the owls of Athens to be coincidence. This is, perhaps, a further reason to place the octadrachms some time after 480. The head of Athena on the coinage of the Thracian Chersonese attributed to Miltiades[20] seems also to illustrate Athenian influence, but belongs to a period long before any currency decree.

From this brief résumé of some of the coinages of Macedonia and Thrace it should be clear that I find absolutely no reason to believe that an imperialist currency decree had any effect on the coinages of the north Aegean. If such a law had been passed by the 440s, it either had no effect or a lot of people were constantly being impeached for transgressing it. There is, however, one definite change in the mid-fifth century. The tribal issues, and particularly the large denomination ingot/coins which may be associated with them, disappear entirely. They are survived by tetradrachm coinages and issues of small denomination from the tributary states of the Delian Confederacy, such as Acanthus, Abdera, Mende, and Thasos, all of which had struck almost continuously from the early fifth century, and Ainos, which makes its appearance as a mint not long before the time when the currency decree would have precluded it.

Analysis of the lead isotope ratios in the metals of these coinages might show whether the source of silver before and after 460 was the same. The very meagre coinage from Aegae after Alexander's octadrachms proves with a fair degree of certainty that, although Alexander may have possessed an extremely rich mine at one point—possibly one of the mines that had produced one of the tribal coinages previously—this source of silver was not available after the middle of the century. Such a mine may have failed all too early. Veins of silver-bearing ores are not a widow's cruse. Availability of silver was a prerequisite for coinage, and its absence is one very cogent reason why a coinage might cease. There is every reason to believe that the sources of silver, which had given rise to the dramatic 'tribal' coinages of the early fifth century, had in the decade 460–450 run dry. This, rather than Athenian imperialism, was probably the cause for the change in coinage patterns in fifth-century Macedonia and Thrace.

Illustrations

Apart from Pl. VIII, 1 (1·6:1), all photographs are size 2:1. No. 1 comes from the new Lycian hoard. All others are from the British Museum.

18 Only the Athos hoard (*IGCH* 362), a mixture of Persian and Athenian coins, which is thoroughly untypical of circulation in the area, is the exception.

19 D. Raymond, *Macedonian Regal Coinage to 413 BC*, *NNM* 126, New York, 1953, plate VII, 55a.

20 C. T. Seltman, *Athens*, Cambridge, 1924, pp. 141–4.

1

2

2

3

4

PLATE VIII

PLATE IX

The Athenian Coinage Decree

D. M. LEWIS

THE organizers have marked the importance of the Athenian Coinage Decree for our subject by calling for two papers on it. I detect a suggestion that they hope for some degree of confrontation and that Lewis in 1986 is expected to hold the same views as Meiggs and Lewis in 1969. I shall say at once that I have no confidence that I know the truth about the problems and am merely trying to look at those facts with which I think I have some competence as straightforwardly as I can. I intend, if I can, to pretend that I know nothing about the coins.

In the *Birds* of Aristophanes, produced in spring 414, a Decree-Seller offers the inhabitants of Cloud-Cuckooland a clause providing that they should use the same measures, weights, and decrees as the Olophyxioi. What their relevance is no one knows, but the literal-minded, starting with Bergk[1], had long hankered after changing the decrees *(ψηφίσμασι)* into coins *(νομίσμασι)*. Amending what may be a joke is never safe procedure, but the joke has to have some foundation, and Wilamowitz in 1877[2] suggested that there might have been an Athenian law enforcing uniformity of coinage, weights and measures in the empire. He tells us that he was laughed at for the idea, but, totally unrecognized by anybody, a substantial fragment of such a law was already known, copied at Smyrna in 1855; no one has seen it since, and doubtless it perished in the burning of Smyrna in 1922. It was not until 1894, when a second fragment turned up on Siphnos, that Adolf Wilhelm confirmed Wilamowitz' suggestion, and even then no full publication followed until 1903.

It was on the ground of this publication that discussion began and that R. Weil[3] and Percy Gardner[4] started to contemplate the numismatic record in the light of the epigraphic text. They were fairly clear that at least two decrees were involved, since the text appeared to refer to 'the previous decree of Klearchos' (*τὸ προτέ]ρον ψήφισμα ὃ Κλέαρχ[ος εἶπεν*). They agreed that these decrees were late and that one of them at least was news at the time of the *Birds*, though their general impression of the coinage was that Athens had in fact tried to impose uniformity since the middle of the century. The epigraphists were not altogether

[1] In his Teubner edition of 1857, but I am not sure that he meant that the text was faulty; Blaydes and Van Leeuwen made the emendation.

[2] U. von Wilamowitz-Moellendorf, *Aus Kydathen*, Berlin, 1880, p. 30, *Reden und Vorträge*[3], Berlin, 1913, p. 52.

[3] R. Weil, 'Das Münzmonopol Athens im ersten attischen Seebund' *ZfN* 25 (1906), 52–62, 'Das Münzrecht der *Σύμμαχοι* im ersten attischen Seebund', ibid. 28 (1910), 351–64.

[4] P. Gardner, 'Coinage of the Athenian Empire', *JHS* 33 (1913), 147–88.

happy with a late date for the decree, and wanted to move it back at least a little to accommodate the more archaic form of the dative feminine plural, which appeared in the text and was held to disappear around 420; the epigraphic consensus tended towards putting the first decree early in the Peloponnesian War and the surviving texts around 422. Relatively little was added to the argument, as it stood then, by the recognition in 1924 of two fragments from Syme first published in 1922.

No question of epigraphic lettering had so far entered the argument. All the copies were in the Ionic alphabet, and did not seem to be at all closely datable. The situation changed in the late 1930s. A large fragment from Aphytis, in a competent, though rather anonymous, Ionic hand, was published in 1935, but very little progress had been made in assessing its contribution to the text when it was overtaken by a much more sensational discovery, a large fragment from Cos, first published in 1938. Unlike all the other copies, it was in Attic script, and Segre, who published it,[5] thought it was on Pentelic marble. Segre pointed out that the decree ordered each ally to publish it on stone and appeared to say that the Athenians would do it if they didn't. The Cos fragment was, he thought, imported from Athens and could be judged stylistically as an Attic text. It was therefore of the utmost significance that it used the three-bar sigma, of which there is no dated Athenian example after 446. By fairly general consensus, the whole decree was then moved to the early 440s and seen as a manifestation of Athenian imperialism in the period immediately after the Peace of Kallias. Stanley Robinson,[6] at least, saw very little difficulty in this from the numismatic point of view. Since we have already seen Weil and Gardner operating in the same direction, it would not be fair, even if we were talking of someone of lesser stature, to say that the numismatist was falling into line with the epigraphic orthodoxy.

The Cos fragment has not marked the end of new acquisitions. In 1933 the Odessa Archaeological Museum acquired a tiny fragment which it unloaded on to Odessa University. No one seems to have thought much of it, and, although its text was published in 1959 and it was recognized as a fragment of the Coinage Decree in 1960, the university seems to have lost it. There can be no certainty about its provenance. The only positive evidence is for Olbia, but this has been disputed, and, if I read the description of the stone, in Ukrainian, accurately, it was on finely granulated bluish marble, which doesn't seem normal for Olbia.

In 1961, Harold Mattingly opened his counter-attack,[7] and so we are celebrating, not merely the new hoard, but also the silver jubilee of the first of a long series of ingenious articles. Of course, although that first article was called 'The Athenian Coinage Decree', study of this decree is only one facet of a much broader approach to the Athenian empire on two levels. There is the technical level, in which challenge to the dogma about the date of three-bar sigma has been strengthened by careful investigations of epigraphic language and forms, and the historical level, which, roughly speaking, tends to the demonstration that much of what we think of as Athenian imperialism was a creation of the period of the

[5] M. Segre, 'La lege ateniese sull' unificazione della moneta', *Clara Rhodos* 9 (1938), 151–78.

[6] E. S. G. Robinson, 'The Athenian currency decree and the coinages of the allies', *Hesperia* Suppl. 8 (1949), 324–40.

[7] H. B. Mattingly, 'The Athenian coinage decree', *Historia* 10 (1961), 148–88.

Peloponnesian War and not of an earlier period. I am not sure that the arguments, on this level, have cumulative force, and I think I could find myself accepting a late date for, say, the Coinage Decree without changing my mind very much about the imperialism I see in the late 450s and early 440s.

Let me remind you briefly of what we have,[8] on the assumption that our fragments all go together to make a continuous text. Nothing useful survives of clause 1). Clause 2), very fragmentary, seems to provide that the *hellenotamiai* shall write up names of cities; if they don't do this correctly, they will be prosecuted. 3) provides that if any of the magistrates in the cities, citizen or foreigner, does not act according to what has been voted, he shall suffer heavy penalties. 4) provides that, if there are no resident Athenian magistrates, the local magistrates shall act. 5) would be crucial, but is in the worst condition. It is generally assumed that it describes what is to happen in the mint; references to 'not less than half', '*x* drachmae in the mina', and to 'changing' are all that is preserved, though some quite elegant Greek has been filled in in the gaps. There have been recent changes[9] in the interpretation of what I would now call 6), covering what has recently been 6), 7) and 8). To my mind, what is being said is that the surplus from the minting operations is to go into a special fund, which may have something to do with Hephaistos, and that any attempt or proposal to use it for anything else makes the offender liable to the death penalty. I am sure that the traditional interpretation, which makes proposals for the use of foreign money liable to the death penalty, is wrong. 7) (old 9) provides for the appointment of four heralds to announce what has been voted. One is to go to the Islands, one to the Hellespont, one to the Thraceward area; presumably the fourth is to go to Ionia. More was said about the method of their despatch, but we have lost a good deal. 8) (old 10) is the publication clause we have already referred to. 9) (old 11) seems to be an afterthought about what the heralds are to say. 10) (old 12) is fortunately very well preserved. The secretary of the Athenian council is to add the following to the bouleutic oath: 'If anyone mints silver coin in the cities and does not use Athenian coins or weights or measures but [foreign coins], weights and measures, [I shall punish him and fine him according to the previous] decree which Klearchos [proposed].' 11) (old 13) is quite hopeless, and about 12) we can really only say that the *epistatai* of the mint are to publish lists of something, for anyone who wishes to look at them. How far the text extended on either side of all this is anybody's guess; the small fragment from Syme could take us into ground otherwise not covered, and Mattingly has considered adding a large fragment of related subject-matter from Athens itself (*IG* I³ 90).

How do the epigraphic and historical arguments about the date stand? First, the find-spots. Smyrna was never a tribute-paying member of the empire, and it is in any case clear that the fragment formed part of a collection assembled from various

[8] For the text and its history, see *Athenian Tribute Lists* II pp. 61–8 D 14, *ML* 45, E. Erxleben, 'Das Münzgesetz des delisch-attischen Seebundes', *Archiv für Papyrusforschung* 19 (1969), 91–139, 212 (with commentary on the coins and the dating, ibid. 20 (1970), 66–132, 21 (1971), 145–62).

[9] D. M. Lewis, 'Entrenchment clauses in Attic Decrees', in D. W. Bradeen and M. F. McGregor (edd.), *Φόρος: Tribute to Benjamin Dean Meritt*, Locust Valley, 1974, 83–5; H. B. Mattingly, 'The protected fund in the Athenian Coinage Decree', *AJP* 95 (1974), 280–5; cf. R. S. Stroud, 'Three Attic Decrees', *Cal.Stud.Class.Ant.* 7 (1974), 280–2.

places. Odessa is also a place to which wandering stones have come, and the rather confused evidence that its fragment may have come from Olbia is matched not only by my doubts about the marble but by the absence of any other evidence that Olbia was ever subject to Athens; it will hardly do much to prove that the Decree postdates 425, the first year in which we know that Athens claimed tribute from the Black Sea area. Aphytis, paying tribute from at least 451, presents no problem. Siphnos starts appearing in the tribute lists from 449; it is to my mind overwhelmingly probable that this is her first appearance, whether because she had been contributing ships up to this point or because she had been through a period of disaffection.

As far as the Cos fragment is concerned, there is an initial doubt, since it was found in the modern city, which, on all reasonable evidence, was not the state centre of Cos until 366. Segre challenged that date, but there are preferable solutions. Cook and Bean[10] came down for the hypothesis that there was an Athenian naval base, at which this Attic copy was set up, but allowed the possibility that the stone had come from somewhere else. If that is so, the stone may not have been originally set up in Cos at all. Cos first appears in the tribute lists in 450. Again, it is unlikely that she had paid tribute earlier. Her tribute record for the next four years is chaotic, with many partial payments, and for 445 to 443 she is not attested at all. This provides an admirable context for us to set a city so uncooperative that she had to have a copy of the decree set up for her, but of course this is no more than suggestive; she has an unexplained short payment in 431 as well.

Finally, I come to Syme. It does not appear in the tribute lists until 433, and, when it does, it appears in a way which more or less proves it is a new arrival, under the heading of cities inscribed to pay by individuals, that is, on the best view,[11] by a party in Syme who were prepared to pay 1800 dr. a year to establish some claim to Athenian protection. It only gradually acquires a less anomalous status in the early years of the Peloponnesian War. Does this prove that 433 is the earliest possible date for the Coinage Decree?[12] One could weaken the force of the *terminus post quem* by saying that Syme might have up to that time paid through a larger group, and that she was in the empire enough to feel she had to exhibit the Decree. The alternative escape route is to suppose that a new member of the empire was required on its accession to exhibit a copy of the pre-existing Decree. These are possibilities, but clearly the argument that the Syme fragments prove a date after 433 is very strong and deserves a more prominent place in the argument than it generally gets; Mattingly did not produce it until 1966[13]; it is not mentioned in Meiggs and Lewis, Erxleben, Meiggs[14] or Schuller[15].

[10] G. E. Bean and J. M. Cook, 'The Carian Coast III', *BSA* 52 (1957), 124–5.

[11] W. Schuller, 'Über die *ΙΔΙΩΤΑΙ*-rubrik in den attischen Tributlisten', *ZPE* 42 (1981), 141-51.

[12] I now withdraw my early suggestion (*Towards a historian's text of Thucydides*, diss. Princeton 1952, pp. 44–6) that these *Συμαῖοι* were not from our Syme at all, but represented the fifth century name, appearing in Diodorus, of the Thracian city of Oisyme; Martin Price has obtained for me a photograph of the unique coin of Oisyme in Paris, and the full name is clear there.

[13] H. B. Mattingly, 'Periclean imperialism', in *Ancient Society and Institutions . . . Ehrenberg*, Oxford, 1966, 195–6.

[14] R. Meiggs, *The Athenian Empire*, Oxford, 1972, pp. 167–71.

[15] W. Schuller, *Die Herrschaft der Athener im Ersten Attischen Seebund*, Berlin, 1974, 211–7.

Next, the letter forms. All the fragments except for Cos are in Ionic. I must say, as a preliminary, that epigraphists are extraordinarily bad at dating classical Ionic texts and that the wildest differences of opinion are current. This may go back to a time when everybody's views were coloured by the belief that there were no Ionic inscriptions at Athens before 403/2, and there can still be considerable disagreement and muddle even as to whether a text is fifth or fourth century. This can happen even at Athens, where there is plentiful dated material. There has just been the extraordinarily embarrassing case of the Thorikos Calendar in Malibu, which Georges Daux has dated to 385–370, overlooking, I may say, one of those early feminine dative plurals. About this, I am only prepared to repeat what I have said in print,[16] that, had it not been for the authority of the editor, I would have unhesitatingly ascribed it to the decade 440–430. And, once one gets outside Athens, precisely dated material hardly exists anywhere, certainly not at Aphytis, Siphnos, or Syme. In the circumstances, it is folly, though it has been done, to worry at all about the fact that three Russians, inexperienced as epigraphists, two of whom do not appear even to have seen the stone, thought that the Odessa fragment looked fourth-century. No real argument, over the period 450–413, is going to come out of looking at the Ionic fragments, two of which are lost and two only available in terrible photographs. Smyrna was said to have shown the 'beautiful simple traits of the Attic period', Siphnos was certainly a fairly sloppy job, Syme not much better. Aphytis alone exhibits a decently professional, though rather anonymous, hand; if it had been an Athenian text, only some tendency to angularity in the rhos would cast doubt on the dating 430–410, and, to go outside Athens, it looks a shade later than a Milesian text which probably belongs to 435. If there were any justification for matching the texts against each other, it is the Syme text which one might have said looked earlier than Siphnos or Aphytis. All this is impressionistic; we cannot say that Ionic lettering moved at the same pace everywhere.

I now turn to the Cos fragment. Let me say at once that, after the work of Meiggs[17] and Walbank[18] stimulated by Mattingly's assault, I remain more than ever convinced of the essential correctness of conventional Attic epigraphic dating. I haven't yet discussed it with him, but one of his better cases has just taken a hard knock. Just after the best demonstration he has yet given[19] that the first decree for the priestess of Athena Nike (*ML* 44) should belong to the 420s and not the early 440s, it has been shown[20] that its stonecutter was the same man who cut the accounts for Pheidias' statue of Athena Promachos. I don't know whether he will argue that the Promachos is later than we had supposed or that the accounts are for something else or that a fifth century Athenian stonecutter might be recognizable over a twenty-five year period. I remain convinced that, for public inscriptions, any attempt to date a well-attested letter form like three-bar sigma outside its attested range starts with a serious handicap.

[16] D. M. Lewis, 'A new Athenian Decree', *ZPE* 60 (1985), 108 n. 3.

[17] R. Meiggs, 'The dating of fifth-century Attic inscriptions', *JHS* 86 (1966), 86–98.

[18] M. B. Walbank, 'Criteria for the dating of the fifth-century Attic inscriptions', in *Φόρος* (see n. 9), 161–9 (= id., *Athenian Proxenies of the Fifth Century* B.C., Toronto, 1978, 31–51).

[19] H. B. Mattingly, 'The Athenian Nike temple reconsidered', *AJA* 86 (1982), 381–5.

[20] S. V. Tracy, 'Hands in fifth-century B.C. Attic inscriptions', in *Studies Presented to Sterling Dow* (Greek, Roman and Byzantine Monograph 10), Durham N. C., 1984, 281–2.

All this could of course be described as a malicious digression, only tangentially relevant to the Cos fragment. Segre's original observation, that the marble was Pentelic and the stone was therefore imported already carved from Athens, cannot survive the petrographic analysis given by Georgiadis.[21] The marble was not Pentelic, although inspection of Georgiadis' data by Jack Zussman, Professor of Geology at Manchester, confirms my suspicion that he has not shown that it was Parian, merely that it was more like Parian than any of the other samples scrutinized in that particular article. Parian marble was of course available at Athens, but it is not likely that it would be thought economical to use it. If the stone was not carved at Athens, it can be and has been maintained[22] that the script, Attic though it is, need not be judged in the same way as one would judge a text from Athens. On this, Meiggs and Lewis commented: 'But why should a mason, whether Coan or Athenian, working in Cos use an Attic sigma that had been obsolete for more than twenty years, when none of his other letters suggests that he was old-fashioned? The epigraphic argument may be a little weakened, but it remains strong.'

I can think of various possible answers to our question, notably one arising from the fact that Athens had, for a considerable time, been virtually unique in the Attic-Ionian world in using three-bar sigma; even Cos, not technically part of that world, had the fourth bar. Even some time after Athens had abandoned it, a foreigner might think that he was giving the proper flavour by using it; the Spartan text from Delos of 402–400 (Tod *GHI* II 99) is very unlike anything we know of from contemporary Laconia. I can only say that our text does not strike me as the work of a non-Athenian or even an amateur. To put the matter in its context, it is worth looking at some other Athenian public or semi-public texts carved or exhibited abroad in the fifth century. There are two other decrees, both in Ionic. I have not seen the Delos text (*ZPE* 60 (1985) 108); presumably its script was like the fifth century accounts from Delos, which are straightforwardly Ionic and were surely carved there. Squeezes of a lost decree from Karpathos (Tod *GHI* II 110), long thought to be fourth century, have now turned up in Berlin; it turns out, Ionic though it is, to be carved by a respectable Athenian professional, probably in the 430s; taking the script together with the fact that an epigraphist with far broader experience than Segre thought the stone Pentelic suggests that we have one case here of an Athenian text being shipped a very long way. Of the two inventories drawn up by Athenian cleruchs on Aegina, one (*IG* IV 1588) is an amateurish mess in mixed script and the other (*IG* IV 39) fairly straightforwardly Ionic. There are public dedications from Delphi (*Fouilles de Delphes* III 4, 190) and Dodona (*SIG*[3] 73) which use four-bar sigma unexpectedly early. Only a group of rather mysterious *leges sacrae* from mid-century Delphi (Sokolowski, *Lois sacrées des cités grecques, Supplément* 40) are anything like pure Attic of their period. All this suggests to me that, if whoever was responsible for putting up the Cos text had to get it done locally, he was unusual in stipulating for an Attic text and fortunate to find someone who was capable of turning out so good an imitation of an

[21] A. Georgiadis, 'The Koan fragment of the monetary decree', *BCH* 89 (1965), 400–422.

[22] W. K. Pritchett, ibid. 425.

Athenian text. It cannot of course be determined whether this cutter was still in the main stream.

I shall say little about the other dating points which have been adduced. The argument about the long plural datives still holds up more or less. It may be interesting to observe that there are two in texts which almost certainly belong to the Athenian recodification of the laws in 410–404 (*IG* I³ 236.37, 237 *bis*.4); I have attributed that to their appearance in the originals which were being recopied. On the extremely copious literature on the heralds' journeys, I propose to say next to nothing. The argument was originally tied up with Pericles' Congress Decree, which is no longer a respectable text; I have never seen any necessary connection between the journeys and the way that tribute lists and assessments are organized; I am perfectly prepared to contemplate the possibility that the Athenians varied their procedures and word-order without there being any particular significance to the variations.

Before I come on to more general matters, there is one tiresome point to mention, the 'previous' decree of Klearchos. The restoration depends only on Baumeister's copy of the Smyrna fragment; he read *ρον*. *πρότε*]*ρον* goes back to Wilhelm; *δεύτε*]*ρον* and *ὕστε*]*ρον*, suggested by Segre, would not alter the implication that Klearchos proposed two decrees. The authors of *ATL* denied that implication, saying,[23] not very convincingly: 'There was, we hold, no other such decree, for the provisions and penalties which each councillor swore to enforce must have been those of the present text. It is just possible that Klearchos, in phrasing the oath, called his own decree *πρότερον*, because for the future swearer the decree would be "earlier" than his oath'. They did not really like that themselves, perhaps wrongly, as we shall see, and continued 'but we note the possibility that the letter read by Baumeister as *Π* was really *N*; this would allow the restoration [*γενόμε*]*ν̣ον*'; the advantage of that restoration would seem to be that it means nothing. I would also reject the other attempt to break away from the two decrees. Erxleben suggests *ἡμέτε*]*ρον*, 'our', but I doubt whether the Athenian Council would describe a decree of the Athenian Assembly as 'our decree'.

I will leave it to Mattingly to expound his ideas about *IG* I³ 90, which may or may not be relevant, but, of course, if Klearchos moved two decrees about coinage and related matters, most of our effort in trying to date our fragments has been a waste of time. It would remain perfectly possible to hypothesize an earlier attempt to enact these or similar provisions and date this whenever your view of the coins suggests. Empires, as a short look at the Roman *Digest* will show, sometimes have to repeat themselves when measures do not work, and the Athenians, who certainly made more than one attempt to regularize the delivery of tribute, can have made more than one to tidy up this question. I have in the past considered distributing our fragments between two decrees. If the second decree incorporated large parts of the first, it would, I think, be just possible to keep Cos in the early 440s, to keep us orthodox epigraphists happy, and make everything else later, but I am not recommending this line very strongly.

[23] II p. 67.

There is also the other possibility, suggested by Tod,[24] that 'Klearchos' earlier decree' was not about these matters at all, but about legal procedures to be followed in imperial offences. If you are used to looking at combined texts, you may think that that would be a rather cryptic reference, but there probably was room on the Smyrna fragment to add a word or two to define the content of the decree, and that would certainly make things easier. Compare the closest parallel, *IG* I³ 107. 6–8:

> *καὶ τ]ἆλλα α[ὐτ]οῖν ἕναι κατὰ [τὸ πρότερον ψήφ]-*
> *[ισμα ὃ . . . ιπ]πος ε[ἶ]πε περὶ τῶν εὐεργ[ετῶν τô δήμο τ]-*
> *[ῶν πρότερον] ἐξεληλυθότων ἐκ τῶν πό[λεων.*

It is maddening that *πρότερον* is even more restored here than it is in our text, since it looks as if it would provide a much needed parallel for *ATL*'s suggestion that it need mean no more than 'previous to the present time'. Perhaps the evidence for there having been two Coinage Decrees is not all that strong.

It is more than time to assess the general motivation of the Decree. Wilamowitz, who started it all, was giving a ceremonial lecture on the Athenian Empire to celebrate the Kaiser's birthday in 1877, and saw the Athenian empire as an enlightened forerunner of the new German Empire. In making the suggestion that there was a Coinage Decree, he saw Athens as stimulating general economic progress, as well as profiting herself from the gain involved in reminting a multitude of strange currencies into her own. The two strands of this have had numerous successors. On the one side, some have almost thought of the Decree as part of Athens' attempt to create a sort of free trade area. On the other, there has always been a school of thought with a keen eye on the profits to be made by reminting and in other ways; there has been a very recent article[25] arguing that hardheaded calculations about economic advantage always played an essential role in Greek coinage. Both strands, of course, tie in to the major division among modern scholars about ancient economics, that between modernists and primitivists. Those who hold that the ancients did not necessarily think about economic matters in modern capitalist ways have poured scorn on the idea that the main motive to the Coinage Decree can have been anything which we would call either macro- or micro-economic. Moses Finley, of course, has been the main exponent of this view, and we can consider one of his statements of it in full:[26]

> Equally political was the fifth-century B.C. Athenian decree which laid down the rule that Athenian coins alone were to be current for all purposes within the Athenian empire ... The political element is unmistakable: the unprecedented volume of Athenian military and administrative payments, at a time when foreign tribute was the largest source of public revenue, was much facilitated by a uniform coinage, and Athens was now able and willing to demonstrate who was master within the empire by denying the subject-states the traditional symbol of autonomy, their own coins. The Athenians may

[24] *GHI* I, p. 166.

[25] H. Engelmann, 'Wege griechischer Geldpolitik', *ZPE* 60 (1985), 165–76.

[26] M. I. Finley, *The Ancient Economy*, 1973, pp. 168–9; see also *2nd International Conference of Economic History, Aix-en-Provence 1962*, Paris and the Hague, 1965, I, pp. 22–5.

also have aimed at mint profits, but we shall not know until the missing bit of the text stating the mint charge for re-coining is found.

It is also held that there was a commercial motive, a desire to give Athenian merchants the advantage over others.[27] The logic escapes me. Everyone had been equally the victim of a profusion of mints; had the Athenians been able to enforce their decree for a sufficient number of years, everyone within the empire would have benefited slightly but equally, the Athenians no more than the others, questions of pride and patriotism apart. Only the money-changers would have been the losers, and no one has yet suggested that such a powerful decree was passed just to hurt them.

I do not think that anyone seriously holds now, if they ever did, that the Athenians were trying to benefit their merchants[28], but the tide certainly seems to be turning against this fairly pure political explanation. The political explanation, of course, does not explain the apparent exclusion of electrum; one could only suggest that the value of electrum coinages to Athens in the Black Sea trade forced their exclusion. What is far more serious is that the political explanation, however it might work for coins (and Robinson too[29] speaks of the mass of Aeginetan money still circulating being a continual reminder of Aegina's former greatness and a continual irritation to Athens), becomes progressively weaker when applied to the weights and measures, which are after all in the decree, though they may not interest numismatists very much.

There is surely much in what Finley himself says about the unprecedented volume of military and administrative payments being much facilitated by a uniform coinage. The point was taken up by Starr[30], who found reason to suppose that Athens recoined the treasury of the Delian League when it arrived in Athens, by Will[31] and by Schuller[32]. The great advantage of this line of thinking, it seems to me, is that it will readily accommodate the weights and measures as well. I had written a short piece along these lines for *CAH* V, but I have now been overtaken by Thomas R. Martin.[33] Martin's main concern, of course, is to debunk the link between coinage and sovereignty, but he has a good treatment of this point too. I am not suggesting that anyone responsible for Athenian legislation knew or cared what length of foot the builders used on Samos, to take our well-known local example. Martin concentrates on the revenue aspect of the measures, the need to have an agreed standard for taxing the imports of, say, Thasian wine. I am more concerned with the needs of Athens' administrative and military machine. Twice in the early years of the Peloponnesian War (*IG* I³ 61.34–41, 62.1–5), states are given the privilege of drawing *x* thousand *medimnoi* of corn directly from Byzantium. The type of *medimnoi* does not need to be stated (contrast Tod *GHI* 140.80 ff., where the Delphic *naopoioi* have to convert from Pheidoneian to Delphic *medimnoi* before putting a cash value on a gift of barley); something must have been done to make sure that everyone knew that they were talking about the

[27] I think the allusion may be to C. H. V. Sutherland, 'Corn and coin', *AJP* 64 (1943), 145 with n. 3, which does not mention the Decree at all.

[28] Meiggs, op. cit. (n. 14) 172, rather vaguely, comes close to it.

[29] op. cit. (n. 6) 325.

[30] C. G. Starr, *Athenian Coinage 480–449* B.C., Oxford, 1970, pp. 69 f.

[31] E. Will, *Le monde grec et l'orient*, I (1972), pp. 207 f., 209 f.

[32] op. cit. (n. 15) 216.

[33] T. R. Martin, *Sovereignty and Coinage in Classical Greece*, Princeton, 1985, pp. 203–4.

same measure. And what about the needs of the Athenian fleet, by far the greatest economic complex of ancient Greece? Quite apart from the imports for original construction, it must constantly have been buying supplies of all kinds of commodities, from nails to paint, all over the place. Would it not make life a great deal easier if some kind of standards could be arrived at, so that haggling could be done about mutually understood quantities? That it would make life a great deal easier all round if coinage was uniform and of clear value is of course common ground, though surely our emphasis should be on state, not private, transactions.

If we continue to think along these lines, there are perhaps a few more chronological pointers to be gleaned by looking around. We have already seen that *medimnoi* of corn needed no definition by 426. Weights of bronze, certainly, and perhaps tin were qualified in some way in the 450s (*IG* I^3 435.69–71, 101–5), not in the years after 421 (*IG* I^3 472.139 ff.). That does not get us far. Let us return to coinage.

It is well known that electrum was, at any rate originally, an acceptable way of paying Athenian tribute. The first Athenian list, of 453, had a postscript which divided Athena's sixtieth into silver and Cyzicene staters (*IG* I^3 259. postscript 6–13), though the total tribute paid in Cyzicenes cannot have been even as much as 10 per cent. of the whole and was probably a good deal less. The lists contain various odd amounts of tribute. Some of them appear to be official, that is to say, with tributes actually assessed in terms of electrum and showing a fair amount of consistency. Others do not. For many years I kept notes on these, wondering whether the odd sums recorded might represent situations where the allied state was tendering coinage in the belief that it had a particular value, but the Athenian *hellenotamiai* were only prepared to tariff them at a lower value. I made periodic attempts to write them up, but repeatedly came to the conclusion that my arithmetic was getting fancier and fancier, that I could not myself draw the line between plausible and implausible cases, and that other people were likely to draw the line far less charitably. But an article was needed and was eventually produced by Eddy in 1973.[34] It is certainly vulnerable in some of the ways which I feared, but it is nevertheless interesting reading. The most solid result seems to be that the irregular amounts more or less disappear between 446 and 430, only starting up again during the Peloponnesian War. Eddy suggests that this was the period when Athens really was insisting on uniformity of coinage, brought it into line with Robinson's chronology for allied coinages, and arrived at a date for the Coinage Decree. 'If we apply the evidence in the quota lists strictly, and if we can believe that the Athenian ban on minting silver coins discouraged the use of electrum, then we might date the decree exactly to 446 B.C.'

As stated, this is not likely to convince any one, I fear. The Decree does not mention electrum. My suspicion, however, is that Eddy may still be on the right track, but is paying the penalty for explaining too many of his anomalous payments in electrum. Some of my fancier unpublished arithmetic involves silver coinages instead. And there is this to be said. It is not only these uncertain sums in the quota lists which suggest that Athens went through a long period of avoiding

[34] S. K. Eddy, 'Some irregular amounts of Athenian tribute', *AJP* 94 (1973), 47–70.

the official use of electrum. It is a well-known fact that in 447 someone succeeded in unloading on the Parthenon commissioners 74 Lampsacene staters and 27 Cyzicenes (plus a *hekte*) and that this electrum remained unspent for the next fifteen years. If we leave out some odd bits of foreign money owned by various gods in 429/8 (*IG* I³ 383 *passim*), it is not until 418/7 that we find electrum playing any part in official Athenian accounts.[35] Of course, it can very simply be said that they will use Attic coin for convenience as long as they have it and only draw on other coinages when they do not. Eddy's line of thought, by which it is the period 446–430 in which uniformity is aimed at, could, I suppose, be matched by a supporter of a late dating for the Decree. It could be maintained that a purpose of the Decree was to restore the circulation of Attic owls and to bring back into the system supplies which had been draining from it.

I conclude by considering the principles on which the epigraphic and numismatic evidence should be brought together. As a result of the conference, I accept that there could be numismatic evidence which might date the Decree, though the apparent continuity of northern coinages points in a different direction from the unexpected appearance of electrum at Chios. What I remain very doubtful about is whether an independent dating of the Decree would or should make any serious difference to correct numismatic operations. You will have gathered that I find it helpful sometimes to go back to the history of a question, and in this case I did look to see how the great historians of the first part of the century had reacted to the discovery that Wilamowitz' suggestion had been correct. I have not yet discovered that the greatest of them all, Eduard Meyer, took any note of the matter at all, but it is, I think, well worth looking at the 1908 treatment by Cavaignac,[36] largely independent of Weil. For Cavaignac, it was merely the position of Athens and its administrators in the Delian League after 478 which inevitably reduced the need, as well as the utility, of coinage for the allied states. The reduction and disappearance of their coinages which he saw rested, he thought, on the facts of the situation. That the Athenians eventually attempted to regulate the matter by decree was a sign of weakness, not of strength, as rival coinages, starting from the successful revolt of the Chalcidian confederacy, began to challenge the primacy of Athenian coinage. It is not totally clear to me what Cavaignac, who had laid proper emphasis on administrative considerations, meant by saying that Athens wanted to preserve her *privilège monétaire*, but I think I do want to know how a numismatist studying a particular coinage is to distinguish between a cessation of coinage imposed from outside and a simple stop because there is no need to coin. That, incidentally, is what Martin's book is about, in relation to fourth-century Thessaly. The cities, he thinks, stopped, not because Philip destroyed their autonomy, but because they could not afford to coin and had no need to. The difference in our case is that we do have evidence for external action, but I am not sure how, in the circumstances, we really expect that the Decree can do anything to date any coinage.

35 *IG* I³ 370.13; several instances thereafter.

36 E. Cavaignac, *Histoire financière d'Athènes au Vᵉ siècle*, 1908, 177–87; J. Beloch, *Griechische Geschichte*² II 1, 92 is dependent on this.

The Athenian Coinage Decree and the assertion of Empire

HAROLD B. MATTINGLY

I WAS tempted, when planning my contribution, to indulge in some such delusive mathematics as David Lewis feelingly described—to follow Eddy in extracting from anomalous part-payments of tribute reckoned in Attic drachms evidence for round payments in non-Attic silver. But, though I also agree that non-Attic payments *do* occur, I share the fear of exposing numismatic or mathematical incompetence. All that I would stress here is that such odd payments occur even in the late 430s (Berge; Kos) and not just before 446 and after 431.[1] Perhaps some numismatist, now that we have both aired the question, will investigate all the evidence systematically. Mixed payments in electrum and non-Attic silver, in non-Attic and Attic silver, or in one or more silver coinages and darics should not be ruled out. I hope too that experts on the amphora series now securely identified will come up with a wider spread of fifth-century capacity-measurements than are as yet available. It should then be possible to ascertain when Thasos, Mende, Samos, and Lesbos moved over to the Attic standard as required by the Coinage Decree, which, as David rightly emphasized, was concerned just as much with imposing Attic measures and weights.[2] This evidence has the advantage over coinage in that change from local to Attic standards must surely imply the ban, whereas breaks in coinage—even prolonged breaks at major mints—may have other causes and were not necessarily dictated by Athens.

I found myself very much in agreement with David's persuasive presentation of the Coinage Decree as a political and imperial manifesto, a clear declaration of intent by Athens. He acutely showed also that, while the material gains of a unified coinage would be shared equally by Athens and allies, unifying measures and weights would prove convenient to the Athenian state in myriad ways—some of them seemingly trivial, but in bulk cumulative. Here Athens was asserting its will, with no pretence of consultation, on the innermost territory of *polis* autonomy.[3]

[1] See D. M. Lewis, above, pp. 53 ff. I must thank him here for kindly letting me see a fairly final draft of his paper in advance of the Symposium. I was relieved to find that we had independently decided on neat dove-tailing of our contributions. For the tribute part-payments see S. K. Eddy, 'Some irregular amounts of Athenian tribute', *AJPh.* 94 (1973), 47–50. I commented on his views in 'The Second Athenian Coinage Decree', *Klio* 59 (1977), 83–100, at pp. 90–2. For Berge see *IG* I³ 277, col. VI.30; 279, col. II.51; 280, col. II.43. For Kos see 280, col. I.36.

[2] In 'Coins and Amphoras—Chios, Samos and Thasos in the fifth century BC', *JHS* 101 (1981), 78–86 I applied the limited evidence known to me in this connection.

[3] See Lewis, above, pp. 60 ff. and compare the stand taken by M. I. Finley in *The Ancient Economy*, 1973, 168 f.

The language of the Coinage Decree and of the tribute regulations proposed by Kleinias is overtly imperial and the closest parallels come from the 420s and the next decade, though that alone cannot obviously exclude them from the early 440s.[4] That they are contemporary with each other is not axiomatic and they should be examined separately and strictly on their merits. When Meritt published the tribute decree in 1937, the text was very gappy and defective. He put it shortly before Kleonymos' decree of 426/5, which established boards of tribute-collectors in the cities. The arguments for this priority were necessarily defective also.[5] A new fragment found in 1938 revealed the proposer's name, revolutionized reconstruction—lines 15 to 77 had 40 letters only, not 57—and threw unexpected new light on the Decree's content and scope.[6] In the same year Segre published the Kos fragment of the Coinage Decree with its *Attic* text and three-bar sigmas. It was known, of course, to Meritt and his collaborators some time *before* 1938 and in *ATL* I (1939) the composite text of the decree as given by Segre was published under the dating 449.[7] Kleinias' decree appeared in *ATL* I in its old defective form, numbered D 7—a sign, as Wade-Gery admitted years later, that they then thought it not long before Kleonymos (D 8). There was just time to acknowledge the new fragment's existence as *ATL* I went to press, by a note appended to the Introduction.[8] Finally the Kleinias Decree was republished by Hill and Meritt in 1944 and definitively dated 448/7. Its proposer would be Alkibiades' father, who died at Koroneia. This was the logical consequence in their minds of moving back the Coinage Decree from the 420s. No-one has really been able to claim that there is a powerful, independent epigraphic argument for the shift. The text of D7 has four-bar sigma and mainly developed Attic lettering, though there are some oddities and the spacing is cramped[9]

It may be instructive, as well as amusing, to speculate. The new fragment of D 7 could easily have been found *before* it was known that Segre had found his Attic copy of the Coinage Decree at Kos. It was after all photographed *in situ* in 1936, lying face-down and serving as part of a replacement in the southern jamb of the Parthenon's east doorway. The other top fragment of D 7, which almost joins it, had been found similarly in 1926—built into repair masonry in the Parthenon's west doorway. With this knowledge freely available someone might have noted the stone sooner, though its original thickness had been cut down to fit the area of

[4] For the texts see *ATL* II, D 14 (*ML* 45) and *IG* I³ 34 (*ATL* II, D 7: *ML* 46). For the 420s and later see *IG* I³ 61.41–7 (*ML* 65: Methone); 78.30–6 (*ML* 73: Eleusis first-fruits); Thuc. 5, 18.7 f. (Peace of Nikias) and 6, 84.2 f. and 85.2 (speech of Euphemos of Athens) with 7, 57.4–7.

[5] See B. D. Meritt, *Documents of Athenian Tribute* (*DAT*), (Cambridge, Mass., 1937), 43–60. For Kleonymos see *ATL* II, D 8 and the better text in *IG* I³ 68 (*ML* 68), incorporating a new fragment.

[6] See G. P. Stevens, 'The Setting of the Periclean Parthenon', *Hesperia* Suppl. 3 (1940), 78: B. Hill and B. D. Meritt, 'An early Athenian decree concerning tribute', *Hesperia* 13 (1944), 1–15. Compare *ATL* I, D 7 with II, D 7!

[7] See M. Segre, 'La legge Ateniese sull'unificazione della moneta', *Clara Rhodos* 9 (1938), 151–78: *ATL* I, 1939, p. 579, T 69.

[8] See *ATL* I, p. xl: H. T. Wade-Gery, 'The question of tribute in 449/8 BC', *Hesperia* 14 (1945), 216 n. 10.

[9] See Hill and Meritt, op. cit. n. 6. As early as 1938 (*JHS* 58, 108) A. M. Woodward, reviewing Meritt, argued that on epigraphic grounds D 7 should be dated considerably earlier than D 8; but it is uncertain whether he was unaware of the new fragment and its import. His judgement was at least probably swayed by knowing of the Kos fragment of the Coinage Decree. Both factors underlay A. E. Raubitschek's determined efforts to find epigraphic reason for putting back D 7 to the early 440s ('A new fragment of *ATL* D 8', *AJPh*. 61 (1940), 475–9).

replacement. A missing slab of around the same size in the northern jamb of the east doorway could well have come—so Meritt shrewdly guessed—from the lower left part of the Kleinias stele.[10] How might the evidence of the new fragment have been evaluated in 1934–6? With the Coinage Decree still safely in the 420s, the close resemblance of mood and language now revealed in D 7 might have anchored it too firmly in the same decade. Certainly no Kleinias from Scambonidai can be found then, but, though the name is rare in Athens, it is found in families other than Alkibiades'. Kleinias son of Pedieus, a handsome youth of the 450s, could have been a Councillor a generation later. Kleinias, father of the general Kleopompos (431 / 0), is another possible candidate. He would have been in his sixties then, but as Rhodes rightly noted, there was no official retiring age at Athens. Sokrates was Councillor in 406 / 5 at the age of sixty-three.[11] Meritt's original order of Kleinias and Kleonymos might have perhaps been challenged, even reversed.[12]

Is this sheer speculation? We cannot recover the innocent eye, however hard we try. But possibly some of our students have never lost it. Four years ago a young finalist from Canterbury wrote to me out of the blue. In an Athenian Empire seminar it suddenly occurred to her that the Kleinias clause on the 'cow and the panoply' presupposed the existence of the second decree of Thoudippos of 425 / 4. Kleinias laid down that "if anyone commit an offence concerning the offering of the cow and the panoply, he shall be prosecuted and punished exactly as for offences concerning tribute". Thoudippos ordained that "those cities for which tribute has been assessed under the Council whose first secretary was Pleistias in the archonship of Stratokles shall all without exception offer a cow and a panoply at the Great Panathenaia". My correspondent noted '*the* offering', '*the* cow', '*the* panoply' in Kleinias and the omission of the article by Thoudippos. If he was simply extending or reaffirming a long-standing obligation, why did he not use the article himself? Now here was someone who had read *none* of the learned arguments deployed on this topic—least of all my own, to which I had to direct her—someone unburdened by all the ingenuity and sophistication which beset us. She had merely had a hard look at the evidence, at what stands on the stones and at what perhaps it ought to be allowed to mean.[13]

I said earlier that the Coinage Decree and that of Kleinias are not self-evidently contemporary. So perhaps some might be prepared to concede a 420s dating for Kleinias, whilst retaining the Coinage Decree in 449 because of the three-bar sigmas in the Kos copy. That copy, I agree, should be treated exactly as any

[10] See Hill and Meritt, op. cit n. 6, 1–3 and figs. 1–3; Meritt, op. cit. n. 5, 43–60; Woodward, loc. cit. n. 9.

[11] See *PA* 8502–12; Beazley, *Attic Red-Figure Vase Painters* vol. 2, p. 1549 f.; Thuc. 2, 26.1 and 58.1. On 'retirement age' see P. J. Rhodes, *The Athenian Boule*, 1972, p. 1 f. and J. H. Oliver, *The Athenian Expounders of the sacred and ancestral law* (Baltimore, 1950), p. 55 f. (asserting the opposite without argument).

[12] Among reviewers of *DAT* only H. Nesselhauf (*Deutsche Liter. Zeit.* 69 [1938], 1033 f.) evidently suggested that D 7 should be put *after* D 8; Raubitschek, op. cit. n. 9, p. 477, n. 9, dismissed his view too cavalierly, implying that it rested on a now superseded text of D 7.

[13] See *IG* I³ 34.41–3, [...] [... *καὶ ἐ]άν τις περὶ τὲν ἀπα[γογὲ]/ν τε̂ς βοὸς ἒ [τε̂ς πανhοπλία]ς ἀδικε̂ι, τὰς γραφὰ[ς ἒνα]/ι κατ᾽αὐτὸ κ[αὶ τὲν ζεμίαν κ]ατὰ ταὐτά*; *IG* I³ 71.55–7, *hοπόσ[εσι πό]λεσι φόρος [ἐτάχ]θ[ε ἐπὶ τ]ε̂ς [βολε̂ς hε̂ι Πλειστί]ας προ̂τος [ἐγρα]μμάτευε ἐπὶ Στρατοκ/[λέος] ἄρχοντος βο̂[ν καὶ πανhοπ]λ[ίαν ἀπάγεν ἐς Παναθ]έναια τὰ με[γάλα] hαπάσας*. For my first treatment of this point see 'The Athenian Coinage Decree', *Hist.* 10 (1961), 144–84 (p. 153).

document from Athens or Attica and not be made a special case.[14] As Lewis noted, I have always argued on a wide front and not made the Kos copy an isolated survivor into the 420s. Other three-bar sigma documents should join it. Some masons arguably continued to use three-bar sigma and other earlier Attic letter-forms for an appreciable period after 445. The epigraphic criterion should never have been made so absolute. In 1961 I argued that there was a strong case for down-dating on historical grounds five other documents with three-bar sigmas.[15] Stephen Tracy seems now to have demolished my first example by demonstrating that the mason who cut the first Athena Nike decree also cut the accounts for the Athena Promachos, surely not long after 450. This is an unexpected blow and I cannot see an easy escape. I may simply have been wrong about Athena Nike.[16] Fortunately it was never crucial to my main case, since it is in no way an overtly imperialistic measure.

But what can we say if there really is no *dated* example of three-bar sigma after 446? I can object immediately that one possible example was dealt with drastically long ago by Kirchoff. Finding the archon Euthynos in the text of the Miletos Decree he was not content to date it 426/5 with its first editor. Because of its three-bar sigmas and curved upsilons he proposed emending 'Euthydemos' in Diodoros 12.3 (450/49) to 'Euthynos' and the Miletos Decree was thus put back twenty-five years without any support from MSS variants in Diodoros.[17] Supporting evidence for a revolt by Miletos in the late 450s has since been sought and found in the early Quota Lists. But it no longer looks so good as once. A new fragment of List 1 seems to show that Milesians from the city paid in spring 453, together with Milesians from Leros and Teichioussa.[18] Miletos certainly paid in 451 and 449, in close geographical association with Latmos and Myous.[19] We may perhaps discern another pattern of association for Miletos in 453 and 452, with Miletos appearing in the same general context as Samothrace and Astypalaia.[20] Only for 450 do we lack any evidence for Miletos, but—as Earp long ago pointed out—the absence may be purely fortuitous and due to the gappy state of the list. There is plenty of room, with some 45 missing entries, and, if Kameiros *is* followed by Latmos in col. II.16, Miletos could well have followed in the ensuing gap before the four Thracian names led by Singos (line 26). Ionic-Caric names predominate in col. I.29–33 and the surviving two-thirds of col. II.[21] There is thus in fact no

[14] For the 'special case' see W. K. Pritchett, 'The Koan fragment of the monetary decree', *BCH* 89 (1965), 425 and for an effective rebuttal see *ML* p. 115 (no. 45) and D. M. Lewis, above, pp. 57 ff.

[15] op. cit. n. 13.

[16] See S. V. Tracy, 'Hands in fifth-century BC Attic inscriptions' in K. J. Rigsby (ed.) *Studies presented to Sterling Dow* (Durham, N. Carolina, 1984), 277–82, and Lewis, op. cit. n. 1 above.

[17] See *IG* I^3 Suppl. (1891), 22a, p. 7. Kirchhoff there argued that the Diodoran MSS gave 'Euthydemos' for the correct 'Euthynos' in 426/5 (12, 58.1); but there is no force in this argument for 450/9.

[18] See B. D. Meritt, 'The tribute quota list of 454/3 BC', *Hesperia* 41 (1972), 403–17: *IG* I^3 259, col. III, 18–20. *IG* I^3 gives Meritt's ingenious supplements in the text, which dispose of Miletos. I follow essentially M. Pierart's alternatives ('Milet dans la première liste de tributs', *ZPE* 15 [1974], 163–7), which are recorded in the lemma: *ΝΕΟΠΟ[ƲΙΤΑΙ: ...]/ ΜΙƲΕ[ΣΙΟΙ: ...]/ ΑΚΡ[...6...]Ι: ΗΗΗ*. For Leros and Teichioussa this year see col. VI, 19–22 and D. W. Bradeen and M. F. McGregor, *Studies in Fifth-Century Attic Epigraphy* (Oklahoma, 1973), p. 68 f. (aware of new fragment); R. Meiggs, *The Athenian Empire* (Oxford, 1972), p. 112.

[19] See *IG* I^3 261 (List 3), col. II.28–30 and 263 (List 5), col. V.18–20.

[20] In *IG* I 259 (List 1) Miletos in col. III.19 would follow the other two in lines 13 f.: in 260, cols. V, 9–12 we could read *[ΜΙƲΕΣΙ]ΟΙ/ [...5...]ΕΣ/ [ΑΣΤΥΠΑ]ƲΑΙΕΣ/ [ΣΑΜΟΘΡ]ΑΙΚΕΣ*.

[21] See T. J. Earp, 'Athens and Miletos *c.* 450 BC', *Phoenix* 8 (1954), 142–7, at p. 143 n. 4. As the photograph in *ATL* I shows (fig. 22: see pp. 20 and 172), the stone unluckily allows no chance of decid-

evidence from the early Quota Lists of a revolt and recovery of Miletos *c.* 450.

The Miletos Decree itself is so poorly preserved that not much consecutive sense can be won and there is little chance of finding firm internal dating evidence. We really do not know what circumstances lay behind it.[22] Most tantalising are the military provisions in lines 10–15. We find hints of 'triremes', 'troop transports', 'hoplites and servants', 'four obols pay'. Do the lines provide for Milesian hoplites supporting Athens in Greece? Or for the Athenian garrison (lines 75 and 82) that was to back the five Athenian *archontes* established by this decree? Oliver, the *ATL* editors, and Meiggs opted for the first alternative. Lewis urged the second as early as 1954. More recently he was followed by Bradeen and McGregor and by Meritt and McGregor in *IG* I³ 21.[23] The passage is cruelly broken, but [... ? *'Αθέν]αζε τοῖς στρ[α] τιό[τεσι]* "to Athens? to [or 'for'] the soldiers"—is very tempting in line 15 and it would be an exact pendant to *'Αθέναζε τοῖς ἐπιμελετ[ε̂σιν]*—"to Athens to [or 'for'] the *epimeletai*—in line 40. There the decree has clearly moved to Athens and the *epimeletai* who function there. So the direction of troops in line 15—on this formal ground—would seem to be contrary to that required by Lewis's theory.[24] But it is still all uncomfortably conjectural.

I turn briefly to another decree with three-bar sigma, where the internal dating evidence seems still clear to me and most damaging to the accepted high dating. This may advance the problem of the archon in *IG* I³ 21. *IG* I³ 32, 7–13 provides that *epistatai* shall be appointed annually for the Eleusinian funds on the model of the Acropolis building boards: "and they shall superintend the funds of the Goddesses as those in charge of the Acropolis works superintended the temple and the cult-image."[25] We need the innocent eye again. The imperfect tense of *ἐπεστάτουν* should first be allowed its natural force. Then the innocent might conclude that the decree was passed *after* the boards for the Parthenos and the Parthenon had gone out of office. The earliest possible date would be 432.[26] There *was* another great statue of Athena on the Acropolis—the Promachos dedicated *c.* 450—but no other temple surely was 'built' there in Perikles' time than what we call the Parthenon and the Eteocarpathians in the late 430s termed 'the temple of Athena Queen of Athens'.[27] No objection to this dating can be derived from the decree's failure to mention the Propylaia board. With its five annually elected *epistatai*, it is superficially the most like the Eleusinian board—but it is the least

---

ing between *Ɣ* (Latmos) and *I* (Ios: the one alternative here).

22 This remains true even after the heroic efforts of Bradeen and McGregor (op. cit. n. 18, pp. 24–70).

23 See J. H. Oliver, 'The Athenian decree concerning Miletos in 450/49 BC', *TAPA* 66 (1935), 177–98, at 190 f.; *ATL* III (1953), p. 256; Meiggs, op. cit. n. 18, pp. 139, 179, 222. For a garrison see D. M. Lewis, 'Notes on Attic inscriptions', *BSA* 49 (1954), 17–50, at 24 n. 19; Bradeen and McGregor, op. cit. n. 18, pp. 40 and 62; H. Bengtson, *Staatsverträge* II, 1961, pp. 60–4, no. 151; *IG* I³ 21 (p. 29).

24 For line 40 see the perceptive commentary of Bradeen and McGregor, op. cit. n. 18, p. 40.

25 I quote just lines 10–13: *τούτο/[s] δὲ ἐπισ[τε̂]ναι [τ]οῖς χρέμασι [τ]οῖς τοῖν θ/[ε]οῖν καθάπερ hoι ἐπὶ τοῖς ἐμ πό[λ]ει ἔργ[ο/ι]s ἐπεστ[ά]το[ν] τôι νεôι καὶ τôι ἀ[γ]άλματι.*

26 Meritt and Wade-Gery ingeniously argued for an idiomatic use of the imperfect here, 'The dating of documents to the mid-fifth century II', *JHS* 83 (1963), 100–17, at 111–4—"as they were to supervise"—but they seem to have won little support. The last accounts of the boards are of 438 and 433/2 respectively (*IG* I³ 460 and 450).

27 For the Promachos accounts see *IG* I³ 435. For the reference of *IG* I³ 32.10–13 to the Promachos and a supposed restoration of the Polias temple see C. Picard, *CRAI*, 1933, 10–14: R. Vallois, *REA* 35 (1933), 196 f.: Raubitschek, op. cit. n. 9, 478 n. 11. For the Eteocarpathian decree see Tod II, no. 110 and Lewis, above, p. 58.

relevant. The Athena boards formed the proper model—*epistatai* cooperating closely with the traditional custodians of the sacred funds, Athena's treasurers. At Eleusis the *epistatai* would have to work in the same close harmony with the Goddesses' *hieropoioi*.[28]

We may now return to Miletos. The one certain archon Euthynos held office in 426/5 and in summer 425 Thucydides records Milesian hoplites serving under Athenian command in Greece, as *IG* I³ 21.10–15 *may* have arranged.[29] Is this pure coincidence? Or could Kirchhoff have been wrong in suggesting emending Diodoros 12.3? Euthynos is an extremely rare Attic name and I would reckon the chances of its twice coming up by lot for the archonship at Athens rather small.[30] It is true that Thucydides does not even hint at a revolt of Miletos in 426/5 and this must give one pause. But he omitted the *stasis* in Kolophon and the loss of the city to Persia in 430. He recorded it only in connection with the story of how Paches rescued Notion from a similar fate three years later.[31] Moreover Aristophanes makes two slightly ominous allusions to Miletos in spring 424 (*Knights* 361 and 927–34). There is threat in the air. Miletos may face further trouble from Athens, unless Kleon is kept happy with a talent's bribe for pushing a decree in Miletos' favour through the assembly. Might this be some revision of the regulations passed in the previous archonship?[32]

It now seems that there are strong grounds for putting both the Miletos Decree and that for the Eleusinian *epistatai* much later than the accepted dates, despite their three-bar sigmas. There is really no commanding epigraphic reason why the Coinage Decree should still be dated 449, when historical and numismatic arguments support a comparable down-dating.[33] Proxeny decrees with the language of Empire—'the cities which the Athenians rule' [or 'dominate']—may equally be put down to the 420s.[34] Without them there is not really any clear evidence for the language or the existence of Empire in the early 440s.[35]

What finally shall we make of *IG* I³ 90, the 'second' Coinage Decree from Athens? I still think that this was cut on the lower part of the large stele outside the Mint, which carried the Athenian text of the Coinage Decree itself. Its position would closely parallel that of the Halikyai Treaty cut below the Egesta alliance or the second Neapolis decree cut below the first of 410/09.[36] *IG* I³ 90 then should be seen as a supplement to the major Decree imposing Athenian coinage, weights, and measures, and interestingly it seems to cover gold/electrum as well as silver and to

[28] For the Propylaia board see *IG* I³ 462–6. It had no close association with any one treasury, but drew funds from a wide area.

[29] Thuc. 4, 42.1. This is the first allied help on land recorded in the war, though 2, 9.5 has been taken to mean that it could be counted on from the start—perhaps wrongly.

[30] This point quite escaped Kirchhoff and later scholars. It struck me first only in the late 1970s. See 'The Athenian decree for Miletos: a postscript', *Hist.* 30 (1981), 113–17 and *AJPh.* 105 (1984), 347 f. (Review Discussion of *IG* I³ [1981]).

[31] See Thuc. 3, 34.

[32] A. W. Gomme noted the first reference (*A Historical Commentary on Thucydides* [Oxford, 1945–6] III, p. 489), but failed to use the fuller, later passage or to see any link with the presence of Milesian hoplites in Greece. They served again in the year 424/3 (Thuc. 4, 54 f.).

[33] See M. J. Price, above, p. 47, for the damaging evidence from the north Aegaean mints.

[34] See *IG* I³ 19.7–11 (Acheloion) and 27.13–17.

[35] Few, I fancy, would want to put much trust in Plutarch's *Pericles* or in Diodoros' unsupported narrative.

[36] See my earlier treatment in Mattingly, op. cit. n. 1, 83–9. For Halikyai and Egesta see *IG* I³ 11 and 12: for Neapolis *IG* I³ 101 and *ML* no. 89, pp. 271–3.

deal with clay storage containers (*kerameia*).[37] The mason who cut it has an elegant, distinctive hand. As Michael Walbank has shown, he also cut the Athenian copy of the Eleusinian first-fruits decree and some dated decrees of 421/0.[38] There is no problem then. The Coinage Decree itself can go in 425/4 with Kleinias, probably also after Thoudippos. Within a year or two, since further regulations proved desirable, they were embodied in a new Decree. All the fragments found in allied territory come from the main, substantive measure. The considerable remains of the Decree from Athens have no point of contact at their start with the end of the composite allied document and that clearly makes consecutive sense throughout.[39]

In the Eleusis first-fruits decree of the late 420s the allies are ordered to send offerings annually to Eleusis, but other Greeks' cooperation is invited; the choice of verbs is instructive. "The Council shall also approach all the other Greek states", the text runs, "in whatever way it judges possible, informing them of how the Athenians and their allies are offering first-fruits—not ordering them, but encouraging them to make such offerings if they wish ... ". When it was needed, the Athenians could still show some finessse and tact, though the *allies*' subordination is not glossed over.[40] The same insensitivity on this point is shown in the Coinage and Kleinias Decrees. It was hardly tactful to ban the allies from striking or using non-Attic silver, whilst arranging seals with them for identification for the tribute-records sent to Athens. Those seals would most naturally in most cases carry the very coin-types which Athens had just prohibited. It would appear a quite unnecessary affront, however useful administratively as a check on provenance.[41]

[37] See *IG* I^3 90.10 and 21 f.

[38] In *Studies presented to B. D. Meritt* (1974), n. 21 on p. 169.

[39] Comparison of the text of *ATL* II D 14 (*ML* 45) with *IG* I^3 90 will make this abundantly clear.

[40] See *IG* I^3 78.30–3 (*ML* 73: *c.* 422?): note *ἐκέ[νοι/s] δὲ μὲ ἐπιτάττοντας, κελεύοντας δὲ ἀπάρχεσθαι, ἐὰν βόλονται.*

[41] See *IG* I^3 34.11–3: *χούμβολα δὲ π[οιέσα]σθαι π/ρὸς τὰς πόλες, hό[πος ἀ]μ μὲ ἐχσ/êι ἀδικêν τοῖς ἀ[πάγο]σι τὸμ φ/όρον.*

The 'Regal' Coinage of the Persian Empire

IAN CARRADICE

[PLATES X–XV]

THE coins usually identified as the 'regal' issues of the Achaemenid Persian Kings are the pieces with 'royal-archer' obverse types and incuse reverse, conventionally termed gold *darics* or silver *sigloi*, and also the gold and silver lion-and-bull type coins, conventionally referred to as *croeseids*, though now attributed, at least in part, to the Persian conquerors of Lydia. The purpose of this paper is to look again at these well known, though little understood, coinages, and in particular to investigate their chronology and circulation pattern in the light of the evidence provided by coin hoards.[1]

THE CROESEIDS

The *Κροίσειος στατήρ* is mentioned in ancient literature as a significant gold coin.[2] On the assumption that a gold coin came to be known in ancient times as a croeseid because it was believed to have been issued, and presumably inaugurated, in the reign of King Croesus of Lydia (*c.* 561–547), the gold coins that are recognized to be the earliest, and indeed probably the only gold coins that can be given a sixth century date, have been identified with the term *Κροίσειος στατήρ*:[3]

Obv. Confronting foreparts of lion, facing right, and bull, facing left.
Rev. Two approximately square incuse punches.

These types also appear on parallel silver issues, and a similar obverse but with lion and bull foreparts depicted back-to-back can also be seen on very rare electrum

[1] I wish to express my gratitude to Martin Price and to other colleagues and friends who have contributed helpful ideas, comments or criticisms. Sole responsibility is, however, accepted for all opinions expressed.
The following abbreviations have been used:
Asyut = M. J. Price and N. Waggoner, *Archaic Greek Coinage: the Asyut Hoard*, 1975.
ACGC = C. M. Kraay, *Archaic and Classical Greek Coins*, 1976.
Les Perses = E.Babelon, *Les Perses Achéménides*, 1893.
Hill = G. F. Hill, *Catalogue of the Greek Coins of Arabia, Mesopotamia and Persia (British Museum Catalogue vol. 28)*, 1922 = *BMC*.
Noe = S. P. Noe, *Two Hoards of Persian Sigloi*, ANSNNM 136, New York 1956.

[2] Pollux, *Onomasticon* iii. 87, ix. 84; for other literary references see P.Naster, 'Remarques charactéroscopiques et technologiques au sujet des Crésé-ides', in *Atti Congresso Internazionale di Numismatica Roma 1961*, Rome, 1965, 25–36 (p. 26, n. 2).

[3] "there is no other plausible candidate than the Lydian gold . . ." (Kraay, *ACGC*, 30).

pieces.[4] All these issues derive from western Asia Minor and they can with confidence be attributed to the Lydian region. However, opinion has in modern times divided on the question of their date and specifically on how much of the croeseid coinage could actually be attributed to the time of Croesus himself. The most popular early view was that all the issues of croeseid-type coins were produced in the reign of Croesus.[5] But the fact that the coinage series which was acknowledged to have succeeded the croeseids, namely the Persian darics and sigloi, could not be given a starting date earlier than the reign of Darius (521–486), caused difficulties for this view because it required the belief that there was a significant gap in production of 'regal' coinage under Cyrus and Cambyses.[6] Consequently, the idea that production of croeseids probably continued in to the Persian period following the overthrow of Croesus gradually gained ground, and is probably now the orthodox view.[7] More recently, it has been suggested that all croeseids were issued under the Persians.[8]

No major detailed study of the croeseids has yet been published, which is surprising in view of their prominence among the early issues of Greek coinage. However, it seems that although the croeseids as a whole form a single series, probably all from the same mint (which is presumed to be Sardes, whether under Lydian or Persian control), there are clear differences in weight, style, and use of denominations, which enable some pieces to be described as 'early' and others as 'late'.

The 'early' croeseids include two groups.[9] One group has a gold stater weighing about 10·9 g (heavy standard), a silver stater of the same weight, and numerous fractional denominations in both gold and silver. The second early group has a lighter gold stater, weighing about 8·2 g. On these 'early' croeseids the style in which the design of the types is executed can be quite varied. The size of the lion and bull foreparts ranges from very large, on the heavy gold staters and associated silver, to small and 'nervous' on the light-weight gold, though always the figures are cut in a quite fine, naturalistic manner. The 'later' croeseids, on the other hand, form a single group. They exist only in two denominations: a 'light' gold stater, weighing about 8·2 g and a silver half stater (also called a half-shekel or siglos) of about 5·4 g. They also have only one style for the depiction of the lion and bull, which can be described as crude and stylized.

4 L. Weidauer, *Probleme der frühen Elektronprägung* (= *Typos*, vol. 1) (Fribourg, 1975), p. 30, no. 133. A silver piece with lion and bull foreparts back to back, though of a style quite different from the electrum, has recently been published by M. J. Price, 'Croesus or Pseudo-Croesus? Hoard or Hoax?' in *Studies in Honour of Leo Mildenberg*, Wetteren, 1984, 211–21 (p. 215). This coin was in the controversial Odemis hoard which some believe to be a hoard of modern fakes.

5 e.g. H. P. Borrell, *NC* 1840, 216–23; Babelon, *Les Perses*, p. ii–iii; B. V. Head, *HN*², p. 647.

6 Babelon, *Les Perses*, p. iii; cf. Price, op. cit. n. 4, p. 212.

7 This was the earlier view of B. V. Head (*The Coinage of Lydia and Persia*, 1877, p. 23)—cf. n. 5 above. Naster, op. cit. n. 2, p. 32–4, divided the coinage between Croesus and the Persians on the basis of stylistic differences and, most significantly, a change in weight. His views were accepted by Kraay (*ACGC* 30–1).

8 M. Vickers, 'Early Greek coinage, a reassessment', *NC* 1986, 1–44 (p. 8–9), who believes the 'croeseid' coinage was introduced by Darius. Price, op. cit. n. 4, p. 221, had earlier suggested that 'the gold and silver coinage of this type was more probably struck after the fall of the Lydian royal house than in the lifetime of Croesus'.

9 For a more detailed description and discussion of the separate groups of croeseids see Naster, op. cit. n. 2, 30–32. Naster concluded that the 'early' croeseids were Lydian, and the 'later' croeseids were Persian; cf. J. H. Jongkees, 'Kroiseios en Dareikos', *Vooraziat-Egypt. geselschap.; Jaarber* 9 (1944), 163 ff.

The two groups of 'early' croeseids seem to have circulated together,[10] and dies are shared between examples with different styles and weights, and between gold and silver pieces. These coins are all obviously closely connected. By contrast, the 'later' croeseids are never found mixed together in hoards with 'early' croeseids; they are clearly a separate issue of coinage, and they are not only separate, but also they must be later, because it is the silver half-staters of this group alone which are found, frequently, in hoards together with Persian sigloi.

THE DARICS AND SIGLOI

The term *daric* was used from the fifth century by Greeks as a descriptive term for Persian coins, especially in gold.[11] Its earliest appearance in literature is in Herodotus 7, 28, where we read the story of the meeting between King Xerxes and the wealthy Lydian, Pythius, who claimed to possess nearly four million *στατήρων Δαρεικών (χρυσίου)*. It is now generally accepted that the word *daric* derives from the name of Darius I, as Pollux explicitly states.[12] Darics are mentioned frequently on surviving Greek inscriptions, but the earliest references date only from 429/8.[13] It is also worth noting that the term 'croeseid staters' appears on an inscription from Athens dated 439/8.[14] If we accept that the terms *croeseid* and *daric* were used by Greeks in the fifth century to refer to two different varieties of 'oriental' gold coin,[15] we must be careful to consider exactly what these objects could have been. It is normally assumed that the term *croeseid* always refers to lion-and-bull type coins and that *daric* identifies the royal-archer type coins which succeeded the lion-and-bull issues. Later literary references, which mention both terms together, certainly imply a distinction of this sort, but what of the fifth-century references? There is no real difficulty in accepting that lion-and-bull coins could have survived in circulation till the 430s, even if they had been replaced in the reign of Darius by the royal-archer coins. What is perhaps more surprising is that there are no references to the term *daric* earlier than the 430s (Herodotus) or early 420s (inscription). The absence of surviving documentary evidence from the first half of the fifth century may be an explanation, or perhaps the term *daric* only gradually came into general use to describe these coins. A further complication to the argument is the suggestion, recently made, that the term *daric* could refer to lion-and-bull type coins.[16] This is possible, particularly in an early-fifth century context, but if the term *daric* was still being used in the 430s to describe lion-and-bull coins, what coins were understood by the term *croeseid* in the

[10] A mixture of styles can be seen in the S. W. Turkey hoard (No. 1 in Table A); cf. also the loose finds of croeseid silver pieces in the Persepolis excavations (E. F. Schmidt, *Persepolis II, Contents of the Treasury and other discoveries*, Chicago, 1957, p. 111, nos. 3–9).

[11] For silver darics see Plutarch, *Cimon* 10. In the nineteenth century the term *daric* was used for Achaemenid Persian coins in general, whether gold (gold daric) or silver (silver daric).

[12] *Onomasticon* III, 87. Alternative explanations have been put forward; see E. E. Herzfeld, 'Notes on the Achaemenid coinage and some Sasanian mint names', *Trans. Int. Numismatic Congress, London 1936* (1938), p. 416, for the theory that *daric* derives from an Old Persian word meaning 'gold'.

[13] *IG* I³ 383, 17–18, 43–44, 110–111 (*Δαρεικό Χρυσίο στατέρες*). I am grateful to David Lewis for helpful comments and advice on inscriptional evidence for darics and croeseids.

[14] *IG* I³ 458, 29. This concerns the acquisition of gold for Pheidias' statue of Athena Parthenos.

[15] The Greeks of this period did not always draw a clear distinction between gold and electrum, so electrum issues should not be ignored.

[16] Vickers, op. cit. n. 8, p. 8. The suggestion is made in the context of a discussion of the Persepolis finds from the period of Darius / Xerxes.

Athenian inscription of 439/8? Early Lydian electrum coins would be the only obvious candidates, though surely not many of these would still have been in circulation that late. It is clear that the chronologies of the lion-and-bull and royal-archer coin series cannot be fixed by documentary evidence alone; that is why the evidence provided by the coins themselves must be looked at in detail.

Perhaps all 'Persian' gold coins, whether of lion-and-bull or royal-archer types, could at one time have been covered, in some areas at least, by the term *daric*.[17] By the early fourth century, however, the connection between Persian gold and the royal-archer coin type was unambiguous. When Agesilaus withdrew from the Troad in 394, claiming that he had been driven from Asia by the King's thirty thousand archers, he was referring not to Persian troops but to the gold coins used by Artaxerxes to raise revolt against Sparta in Greece.[18]

The Greek word *σίγλος* (or *σίκλος*) is the same as the Hebrew *shekel*. The word *shekel* was in use long before the invention of coinage, referring to a weighed amount of silver. It later came to be used for a denomination of silver coin. The term *σίγλος* first appears on inscriptions dating from the last years of the fifth century,[19] though the type of coin there referred to, assuming that it is the royal-archer, can be shown to have been in circulation long before that date. The low value of the individual siglos piece is probably one of the reasons why it is seldom mentioned in Greek literature; silver is usually referred to in very large amounts that can only be expressed in weights (minae or talents). In 400 the siglos is said to have been valued at 7·2 Attic obols.[20]

Though other coins with 'Persic' weight and oriental types no doubt came into the possession of Greeks, it was the coinage with the royal archer design alluded to by Agesilaus that became in Greek minds the definitive 'Persian' gold or silver. The royal archer obverse type[21] appears in four major varieties. Three of these can be seen in parallel issues of gold darics and silver sigloi. With so few typological changes and no inscriptions the royal archer coins are notoriously difficult to date with any precision. The chronological sequence now accepted for the issue of the separate obverse types results from the work of S. P. Noe[22] and E. S. G. Robinson[23] in the 1940s and 1950s. Using the evidence of newly discovered hoards they were able to overturn the chronologies earlier proposed by others, notably E. Babelon and G. F. Hill.[24] The four major varieties numbered according to Robinson's proposed sequence,[25] are as follows:

Obv.

I Half-figure, bearded, facing right and wearing crown, holding two arrows and a bow. Siglos (5·4 g).

II Crowned figure, bearded, kneeling/running right, with quiver at shoulder, drawing bow. Daric (8·35 g); siglos (5·4 g); gold and silver fractions.

[17] See J. R. Melville Jones, 'Darics at Delphi', *RBN* 125 (1979), 25–36, for the use of the term daric in the later fourth century for gold coins of Philip II.

[18] Plutarch, *Artaxerxes* 20.

[19] *IG* II², 1384.

[20] Xenophon, *Anabasis* I, 5, 6.

[21] For a discussion of this type and its interpretation see H. Seyrig, 'Le roi de Perse', *Syria* 36 (1959), 52–6; P. Naster, 'Les sicles persiques à la demi-figure', *BSFN* 17, 6 (1962), 170–1.

[22] See n. 1.

[23] 'A hoard of Persian sigloi', *NC* 1947, 173–4, 'The beginnings of Achaemenid coinage', *NC* 1958, 187–93, 'Two Greek coin hoards', *NC* 1960, 31–6.

[24] See n. 1.

[25] *NC* 1958, 188 (see n. 23).

III Crowned figure, bearded, running right, with quiver at shoulder, holding transverse spear and bow. Daric (8·35 g); siglos (5·4–5·6 g).

IV Crowned figure, bearded, running right, with quiver at shoulder, holding short sword/dagger and bow. Daric (8·35 g); siglos (5·6 g); gold and silver fractions.

Rev.

A single oblong incuse with irregular ground (all issues).

Babelon had assigned these principal types to the Achaemenid reigns as follows:

III(various styles)	: Darius I (521–486), Xerxes (486–465), Artaxerxes I (465–425), Darius II (424–405), Cyrus (401).
III and II	: Artaxerxes II (405–359)
III and I	: Artaxerxes III (359–338)
(Babylonian issues under Alexander) and IV: Darius III (337–330)	

Hill adopted the following arrangement (including his own stylistic subdivisions):

III Styles A–E	: *c.* 521–400
Style F	: Cyrus
Style G	:
Styles H–K	: *c.* 400–333
IV Styles A–D	: to about 400
Style E	: 4th century
II	: 4th century
I	: 4th century

Two of the important 'fixed points' in both these earlier chronologies were, it seems, false clues. Firstly, the infamous Athos hoard (*IGCH* 362) of type III gold darics and silver Athenian tetradrachms, which was made the basis for putting the types in order, was dated far too early. The early date was based on a mis-interpretation of the description of the Athenian coins, which caused them to be dated as archaic instead of fourth-century,[26] and on the curious assumption that the burial of the hoard in the bed of Xerxes' canal at Athos dates it to the period of the canal's construction.[27] The second false clue was the identification of the beardless king on a type III daric (*BMC* 61 - Hill group F) as Cyrus the Younger. This identification was always questionable, and certainly needs support from other evidence. A comparison with other darics suggests to me that the type may have been re-cut from a regular, bearded type III royal-archer. Whether this alteration took place to the die or to the coin could only be established by a close inspection of all the surviving examples of this exceedingly rare coin type. In any event, the coin should not be used as a dated fixed point for tracing the stylistic development of type III.

Babelon and Hill both recognized that type III was under production for a very long time, and they were both able to distinguish correctly between some of the

26 I prefer to regard the descriptions as unusable and the identifications as unreliable; the hoard cannot therefore be dated by its Athenian coins.

27 For a comprehensive demolition of the 'traditional' date for this hoard see C. M. Kraay, *Greek Coins and History*, (1969), pp. 49–51.

early and later varieties within this type. However, many of the sub-groups they devised are not relevant in terms of chronological classification and some are probably illusory.[28] Perhaps the most important subdivision of type III was recognized more recently by C. M. Kraay, who observed that a few examples can be distinguished from the rest by the inclusion of two pellets beside the beard of the crowned figure.[29] All sigloi with these pellets (**Pl. XI, 14–15**) appear to be of the same, lower, weight as sigloi of types I and II (and the Croeseid silver half-stater), and they tend to be found in the earliest hoards that contain type III sigloi. It is clear that in the now-accepted sequence of issues these form an early variety of III, which can conveniently be referred to as IIIa. The remaining varieties of type III can therefore be labelled IIIb.

Type I

Type II

Type IIIa

Type IIIb (early)

Type IIIb (late)

Type IV (early)

Type IV (late)

CHRONOLOGY: THE EVIDENCE OF HOARDS

In his attempt to tackle the chronology of the darics and sigloi Hill recognized the importance of evidence from hoards: 'It would seem that the only direction in which a solution is to be expected is the recording of finds of darics or sigloi with other coins susceptible of being dated.'[30] When Hill wrote this he could make use of only a limited number of hoards. Many more have since been recorded and, of course, the order of issue of the major daric/siglos types has been reorganized as a direct consequence. The purpose of the present study of hoards is to look again at the evidence provided for both the croeseid and the daric/siglos series, bringing together many more hoards than have hitherto been considered.

[28] Hill himself noted the difficulties in distinguishing between his groups A and B of type III and I would also add his style D to this group. Also within type III a gold daric in group C (*BMC* pl. xxiv, no. 25) has the same reverse die as the daric illustrated as style F (pl. xxv, 14), and a siglos of group B (pl. xxiv, 18) seems to have the same reverse die as several in group C bis (pl. xxv, 2–6).

[29] *ACGC* 33; *NC* 1977 (full ref. n. 38 below), 193–4.

[30] Hill, p. cxxxi.

TABLE A

Hoards including croeseids, darics, sigloi

AR = ◇ AV = ◆ Cr: A = early; B = late ( ) = number of examples recorded
(in hoards 8, 11, 12 and 13 number gives total of types IIIa and IIIb together)

	IGCH or *CH* reference		approx. date	CR	I	II	IIIa	IIIb	IV
1	–	SW Turkey, 1982	520	◇A (77)					
2	1162	Sardes, Turkey, 1922		◆A (30)					
3	1632	Egypt, 1900		◆ (5)					
4	1637	Damanhur, Egypt, 1900	500	◇A (1)					
5	1639	Sakha, Egypt, 1897	500	◇ (1)					
6	1166	Bairakli, Turkey, 1951	500	◇B (2)	◇ (1)	◇ (3)			
7	1789	Persepolis, Persia, 1933	490	◆B (8)					
8	1175	W Asia Minor, 1961	? 480	◇B (6)		◇ (1)	◇ (38)	◇	
9	1178	Çal dag, Turkey, 1945		◇B (475)	◇ (98)	◇ (537)	◇ (310)	?	
10	1177	S Turkey, 1961	480				◇ (1)		
11	1644	Asyut, Egypt, 1968	475			◇ (1)	◇ (17)	◇	
12	*CH* VI, 4	Antilebanon, Syria, 1978	475			◇ (1)	? (3)	◇	
13	1183	Colophon, Turkey, 1962	455			◇ (1)	? (1)	◇	
14	*CH* I, 14	N Syria, 1974	? 450			◇ (1)			
15	1197	Smyrna, Turkey, 1948						◇ (271)	
16	*CH* II, 26	Asia Minor, 1975						◇ (350)	
17	1247	Gordium, 1957						◇ (110)	
18	1483	Massayaf, Syria, 1961	425					◇ (1)	
19	*CH* I, 15	Black Sea, 1970	425					◇ (13)	◇ (7)
20	1255; *CH* I, 21	Cilicia, 1957	400					◇ (1)	
21	1230	Miletopolis?, Turkey, 1919						◇ (8)	◇ (4)
22	*CH* I, 36	Asia Minor, 1973						◇ (16)	◇ (8)
23	1791	Persia, 1895						◇ (5)	◇ (5)
24	–	Lebanon, 1983						◇ (57)	◇ 93)
25	*CH* I, 34	Asia Minor, 1965						◇ (160)	◇ (41)
26	1224	Ionia, Turkey, 1915						◇ (14)	◇ (38)
27	*CH* I, 35	Asia Minor, 1960						◇ (4)	◇ (11)
28	*CH* II, 32	Asia Minor, 1975 } same						◇ (9)	◇ (58)
29	*CH* II, 38	Asia Minor, 1974 } hoard?						◇ (39)	◇ (11)
30	*CH* IV, 24	Asia Minor, 1977							◇ (19)
31	1201	Durasalar, Turkey, 1956	390					◇ (72)	◇ (28)
32	1747	Babylonia, 1900	385					◇ (6)	◇ (1)
33	1259	Cilicia, Turkey, 1914	380					◇ (28)	◇ (10)
34	1278	Vouni, Cyprus, 1928	380					◆ (4)	
35	1830	Tchaman-i Hazouri, Afghanistan, 1933	380					◇ (8)	
36	*CH* I, 26; V, 19	Isparta, Turkey, 1960	375					◇ (1)	◇ (24)
37	2122	Avola, Italy, 1914	370					◆ (43)	
38	2124	Avola, Italy, 1888	360					◆ (4)	
39	1748	Warka, Babylonia, 1923	330						◇ (1)
40	*CH* I, 38	Babylonia, 1973	320						◇ (1)
41	1792	Susa, Persia, 1932	315						◇ (2)
42	1831	Bhir Mound, Pakistan, 1924	300						◇ (1)

The approximate dates of burial listed for the above hoards are usually no more than the approximate dates of issue of the latest coins (excluding the darics/sigloi) in each hoard, which may not always be reliable. Also, the dates of the Persian coins may not necessarily be very close to the approximate burial dates of the hoards. It is worth noting that the sigloi in many hoards are often noticeably more worn than many of the other coins they were buried with. However, hoards do provide *termini ante quem* for the introduction of the various types and classes of darics/sigloi, and even if we must accept that the contents of a hoard can only give a general, rather than a precise, date for groups of coins, a survey of the contents of mixed hoards which include sigloi can be expected to provide an overall view of the development of the latter. A more detailed picture of the composition of most of the early silver hoards can be found in the publication of the Asyut hoard.[31] Here I intend only to summarize the pattern of association of the Persian issues with certain 'key' coinages, but many more hoards will be brought into consideration and I shall also be looking into style—and into die-links between groups of darics and sigloi from different hoards.

Croeseids and early darics and sigloi (hoards 1–12)

The early hoards provide confirmation of the now generally accepted sequence of typological development from lion-and-bull croeseid to royal-archer types I and II, then types IIIa and IIIb. These are the 'Persian' coin types of the archaic period.

Croeseid silver coins first appear in a hoard from Asia Minor (1) (**Pl. X, 2–5**) alongside the earliest known silver issues of Caria, which have obverse type with lion forepart (**Pl. X, A–B**).[32] A few coins of other cities from Asia Minor, including Miletus, have also been connected with this, as yet unpublished, recent find, though some of these coins are suspected of being intrusive. The hoard contains similar quantities of croeseid and Carian coins, and many fractional denominations of both series are included. All of the croeseids are of 'early' style, and some pieces show definite signs of wear. On the Carian coins wear from circulation is less evident, though many of these pieces have been weakly struck and therefore have a 'worn' appearance. The hoard is obviously very important for the date of the 'early' croeseids. Though the oldest coins in the hoard, on the evidence of wear, seem to be some of the croeseids there is no obvious difference in condition between the majority of croeseid and Carian coins. The two coinages must be regarded as roughly contemporary, and therefore, as similar Carian coins have been found in later contexts,[33] this hoard supports a down-dating of the early croeseid series.

Of the hoards containing gold croeseids, neither (2), from Sardes, which contained only 'early' issues, nor (3), from Egypt, which is inadequately recorded, can be dated. The much discussed hoards (7) discovered in the excavations of the Apadana at Persepolis contained unworn 'late' croeseid gold staters together with late-sixth century coins of Aegina and Abdera (north-east deposit) and coins of

[31] *Asyut* fig. 1, pp. 14–16.

[32] Usually attributed to Mylasa; see E. S. G. Robinson, 'A hoard of Archaic Greek coins from Anatolia', *NC* 1961, 114–5.

[33] Hoards (10) and (11) in Table A.

Cyprus tentatively dated to about 500 and to the 480s (south-east deposit).[34] The croeseids in each of these two deposits are identical in both style and condition. If the group found with the Cypriot coins was laid down not earlier than about 490, then the other group can hardly have been buried much earlier. Therefore, even allowing for imprecision in the dating of the Cypriot coins it seems impossible to support the early date, of about 515, which has sometimes been suggested for the deposition of these hoards. A date early in the fifth century becomes much more likely.[35]

Attention has always been focused on the eight gold croeseids from these two 'foundation deposits' but the loose finds of croeseids from the Persepolis excavations are also interesting. A total of seven pieces was recorded: one 'late' gold stater belonging to the same series as the 'foundation deposit' pieces, and six 'early' silver croeseids (3 staters and 3 halves). Only one half-stater was recorded in close association with other coins (one Lydian electrum third, one Milesian diobol and one archaic silver piece attributed to Ephesus). The significance of these finds is not especially that they show 'early' croeseids in an archaeological context that dates to the period Darius/Xerxes. That is a point worth noting, but it cannot be proved that the coins were of recent manufacture when deposited. It is perhaps more significant that no 'late' croeseid silver nor any darics or sigloi were found on the site.

In the earliest mixed hoards from Egypt (4, 5) silver croeseids appear alongside very early Aeginetan and Corinthian issues, Athenian 'Wappenmünzen', the earliest Macedonian and Thracian coinages, and early issues of various Ionian cities. Each of these hoards contained only one croeseid, but it is perhaps worth noting that the only well recorded example (in the Damanhur (4) hoard) is in 'early' style.

The next three silver hoards (6, 8–9) contain a mixture of croeseids, all of which are invariably of the 'late' style, and early siglos types. These hoards were all found in Asia Minor. The huge Çal hoard (9) is crucial for the internal chronology of the early siglos issues, but it contained no non-'Persian' coins. The Bairakli (6) and Asia Minor (8) hoards, on the other hand, contained, in addition to their 'Persian' issues, coins from Miletus and Cyzicus (8 only), and 'uncertain Ionia' (Smyrna or Phocaea?) (6 and 8).[36]

The next group of hoards comprises the great Asyut find from Egypt (11) and the Antilebanon hoard (12), which both contained a mixture of siglos issues down to type IIIb but no croeseids, together with the south Anatolian hoard (10), which contained one siglos of type IIIa. These hoards also included the following sorts of coins: 'Samians at Zancle', 'unwreathed' Athenian owls, early and 'skew' Aeginetan issues and 'Athena head' Corinthians, as well as many other 'archaic' coinages.

If we consider all the early silver hoards together (Nos. 1, 4–6, 8–12), it is clear

[34] E. F. Schmidt, op. cit., n. 10, p. 113–4. For discussion of date see E. E. Herzfeld, loc. cit. n. 12, 413 and M. Vickers, loc. cit. n. 8, p. 4–9.

[35] See D. Stronach, 'The Apadana: a signature of the line of Darius I', in *De l'Indus aux Balkans, Recueil Jean Deshayes* (1985), 433–45 (esp. 443–4).

[36] Hoard (8) is wrongly described in *IGCH* (no. 1175) as containing 14 silver fractions of Cyzicus. According to the file photographs of this hoard it contained 1 fraction of Cyzicus and 13 fractions of 'uncertain Ionia' with female head obverse type (as in the Bairakli hoard). However, it should be noted here that there is some doubt that all the various issues recorded with this hoard actually derived from the same find. For another mention of this hoard see M. J. Price, op. cit. n. 4, p. 215, n. 13.

that they provide some interesting clues for the chronology of the croeseids and for the transition from croeseid to siglos coinage. As it can be assumed that the earliest hoards containing croeseids that we are ever likely to meet will be hoards found in their area of origin (Asia Minor), rather than areas to which they were exported (e.g. Egypt), important new evidence for the development of this coinage can be expected to emerge when hoard (1) is published in detail. It is worth emphasizing that the two groups of croeseids, 'early' (A) (e.g. **Pl. X, 1–7**) and 'late' (B) (**Pl. XI, 8–9**) are never found hoarded together, even though they had the same types and included denominations of exactly the same weight. This strongly suggests that they were separated by a significant gap in time; 'early' and 'late' croeseids are both found in the same areas so they were obviously not separated geographically. But dating this gap is not easy. If we accept the 'Asyut' dates for various archaic Greek coinages which, according to hoard evidence, may be contemporary with croeseids, then the gap between them would seem to lie in the late sixth century, perhaps about 520–505. These were the first fifteen years of the reign of Darius I and dating a gap in 'regal' coinage to such a period may be thought objectionable, but on the other hand at this time there was scarcely a necessary link between currency changes in western Asia Minor and dynastic, political, or even economic developments in the Achaemenid Empire as a whole.

The earliest Egyptian silver hoards suggest that at first croeseids found their way to that country alongside other, presumably contemporary, silver coins from the Greek world, such as Athenian 'Wappenmünzen' and early Aeginetan 'turtles', but by the time the Asyut hoard was buried it would appear that croeseids had largely disappeared from circulation in Egypt. On the other hand, no Persian sigloi appear in the earliest Egyptian hoards,[37] but by the time of Asyut coins from several phases of the siglos sequence had not only been produced, but had been circulating long enough to show, in some instances, signs of wear. Some, also, had been mutilated, though it was no doubt possible for a coin to acquire a chop mark quite soon after its date of issue if it was quickly exported to an area in which all silver coinage was treated simply as bullion.

The overall composition of the earlier Egyptian silver hoards (4, 5) is clearly very different from that of Asyut and it is obvious that the difference in date between these hoards is crucial for the chronology of the early sigloi (and darics). If we accept the suggested approximate dates of 500 for the burial of Damanhur and Sakha, and 475 for Asyut we have a royal-archer coinage replacing the croeseids in Egypt early in the fifth century. But can we accept these dates?[38] They are based on the pattern of archaic hoard finds as discussed in the Asyut publication. Does a closer examination of the 'croesids' and darics/sigloi in the early hoards from

[37] In the Mit Rahineh hoard (*IGCH* 1636), which has a similar overall composition to Damanhur and Sakha, some type III sigloi were recorded as being connected with the find, but these coins must be intruders.

[38] C. M. Kraay, 'The Asyut hoard: some comments on chronology', *NC* 1977, 189–98, and H. A. Cahn, 'Asiut: Kritische Bemerkungen zu einer Schatzfundpublikation', *SNR* 56 (1977), 281–2, both pointed out problems in accepting a burial date of 475. Largely because of the presence in the hoard of a certain coin of Alexander I of Macedon they p-roposed a lower date. See also M. Vickers, op. cit. n. 8, p. 39–41. At the Oxford symposium Martin Price agreed that the Alexander I coin was anomalous, but that this did not necessarily affect the chronologies as argued for many other coinages in the Asyut publication.

elsewhere support these dates? The Bairakli hoard was, according to the excavators, 'found in a stratified deposit belonging to the early years of the fifth century'.[39] The first royal archer types appear in this hoard mixed with 'late' croeseids. This is not inconsistent with the evidence of the Egyptian hoards. The absence of royal archer darics or sigloi from the Persepolis deposits containing croeseids also fits this pattern if a date not much later than 500 is accepted for the relevant areas of the excavations.

The presence in the Asyut hoard of sigloi from type IIIb was regarded by Kraay as a problem.[40] Certain varieties in Asyut seemed from the evidence of other hoards to belong to the second half of the fifth century, though this 'dating' was influenced by an alleged, but I believe erroneous, reverse die-link between a coin in Asyut (no 731) and the latest group (F) in the Smyrna hoard (15—which Noe dated to about 400).[41] However, the low weights (about 5·30–5·39 g) of the Asyut type IIIb coins suggested to Kraay that they might have belonged to the first issues of this variety, minted before the adoption of the higher weight standard more usually associated with IIIb (about 5·55–5·60 g). He postulated that two mints may have been in operation at the same time, one producing coins with pellets (IIIa) and another coins without pellets (IIIb), until the former mint closed and the latter, which then continued in production, increased its weight standard. This theory cannot yet be proved. Some of the type IIIb coins in Asyut seem worn, so it may be dangerous to place too much reliance on the evidence of weights when dealing with limited numbers of coins and small differences in apparent weight standards. In any case, there is still the problem of the early introduction of IIIb sigloi suggested by Asyut. If the Asyut hoard was buried about 475 type IIIb sigloi must have been in production at least as early as 480, taking into consideration the condition of the coins. Even if, as many have now suggested, the burial of Asyut should be down-dated by a few years,[42] these sigloi are still appearing earlier than would formerly have been expected. But is this really a problem? If we accept that Darius I introduced the daric/siglos coinage very early in the fifth century, and if we also accept that types I and II can be dated very close together, or even that they might have begun at the same time but at different mints,[43] then it is not difficult to imagine a rapid development through to types IIIa and IIIb. Reverse die-links are very common within, though never between, types I, II, and IIIa. It seems that not many dies were used so it is indeed likely that these coinages were not in production for many years.

The Asia Minor 1961 hoard (8 in Table A) would seem to provide further confirmation of the rapid succession of early siglos types, though it must be treated with great caution because of its somewhat unlikely composition.[44] The South Anatolia (10) and Antilebanon (12) hoards contain too few sigloi to make a really

39 *NC* 1960, 31 (see n. 23).

40 *NC* 1977, 193–4 (see n. 38).

41 Asyut coin 731 shows, I believe, the same reverse die as nos. 12 and 13 in the Smyrna hoard (15). These coins were regarded by Noe as belonging to an earlier group than the coins of his group F.

42 See n. 38 above.

43 C. M. Kraay, *ACGC* p. 32–3, *NC* 1977 p. 194 n. 15 (see n. 38).

44 See n. 36 above. The 'hoard' also included Lydian electrum as well as the silver issues already mentioned. Though recorded in *IGCH* (1175) as a single entity, Kraay chose to ignore the hoard when he discussed the chronology of the early sigloi (op. cit. n. 38, 193), even though he must have been well aware of it.

significant contribution to the discussion, but they present no obstacles to the theory that type IIIb first emerged as early as the 480s; indeed, the Antilebanon hoard provides rather impressive confirmation of the Asyut pattern. As the Antilebanon hoard is dated on the basis of Asyut there is obvious circularity in this argument, but at least the Antilebanon hoard did not contain any anomalies as difficult as the Asyut Alexander I coin.[45]

Type IIIb siglos dominant (silver hoards 13–19)

In the period following the 'time of Asyut' there are further difficulties in the daric/siglos chronology, caused principally by the shortage of mixed datable hoards. It would, of course, have been helpful if the new 'decadrachm hoard' of silver had contained sigloi, but, rather interestingly, it did not. In Table A the two hoards tentatively dated to the 450s (13, 14) contained together only three sigloi. Two type II sigloi survive apparently well into the type IIIb period but these figures are hardly worth dwelling on.

The next mixed hoards which include sigloi are those from Massayaf in Syria (18), which had a single piece from type IIIb, and Samsun in central northern Turkey (19), which contained examples of types IIIb and IV. Among the non-Persian coinages from these hoards are 'wreathed' Athenian tetradrachms, Aeginetan 'tortoises' and the earliest issues from the Phoenician cities of Sidon and Tyre. These coinages clearly belong to a later period than the issues which appeared alongside sigloi in the earlier comparable hoards, and indeed neither hoard could have been buried before about 425, perhaps some fifty years after Asyut.

It does not follow, however, that all the sigloi in these hoards have to date from the second half of the fifth century. In fact the condition of many of the sigloi suggests that they may have been in circulation for many years before the hoards were buried. The single piece in the Massayaf hoard is cut and apparently quite worn. It may date, like many coins in this hoard, from the late archaic period. In the Samsun hoard not only are many of the type IIIb pieces worn, but also, and perhaps more significantly, the type IV pieces show, in many cases, signs of considerable wear. This suggests that type IV sigloi were probably in circulation as early as the middle of the fifth century.[46] These earliest type IV sigloi have a distinctive 'stiff' obverse figure with a shapeless body completely lacking a waist, and the reverse incuse often contains a symbol (e.g. **Pl. XIII, 33–5**).[47]

At this point we should consider also the 'siglos-only' hoards. Three hoards, all from Asia Minor (15–17), which contain only coins of type IIIb, and which are, on the basis of shared dies and style, closely related to each other, can also be die-linked to the Samsun hoard and to hoards from the earlier period (8, 11, and 12). Together these three un-mixed hoards contained over 700 sigloi. The absence of any types earlier than IIIb suggests that they should belong to a later period than the 'Asyut' group, but these hoards also lacked any type IV coins. Either they were buried before type IV came into wide circulation, let us say around 450, or they were assembled and buried, perhaps later, in an area where type IV coins were not at the

[45] See n. 38 above.

[46] C. M. Kraay and P. R. S. Moorey, 'A Black Sea hoard of the late fifth century BC', *NC* 1981, 1–19 (p. 9).

[47] See *Hill* p. cxxvii, cxxxiii.

time available. The latter explanation would be more plausible if these two types were produced at separate mints, and this is a distinct possibility. Although they were minted to the same weight standard the 'dagger' type is often struck on irregularly shaped flans,[48] or across the axis of ovoid shaped flans, whereas IIIb coins are almost invariably ovoid with the obverse design struck upright along the axis. It can be shown that the chronologies of these two types involve a considerable period of overlap, so either a single mint was switching between production of the two types or there were separate mints. Only one reverse die-link has ever been observed between obverse types IIIb and IV.[49] The link may, in fact, not exist; but even if it does I believe it belongs to the very earliest phase of type IV, in which case it might pre-date a separation of mints. The theory of two (or more?) mints could only be confirmed by a detailed study of the circulation pattern, as well as the chronology, of these coinages, and a shortage of reliably provenanced finds renders this a difficult objective at present.

Type IIIb and IV together (silver hoards 20–33, 35–6)

The next group of silver hoards in Table A includes few that can be dated, because most of the hoards contain only sigloi. The main feature of these hoards in general is the increasing occurrence of type IV sigloi.

The first mixed hoard, from Cilicia (20), contained only one recorded siglos, of type IIIb. One isolated piece in such a large hoard can provide little information. Much more useful is the Durasalar hoard (31). It contained a mixture of sigloi from both types IIIb and IV. They show considerable variations in degrees of wear, suggesting that some were in circulation much longer than others before the hoard was buried. The hoard also included some quite closely dated Greek issues from Asia Minor, notably Samos, but also Cyzicus, Ephesus, and Rhodes. The presence of these coins, some of which appear virtually uncirculated, allows the hoard to be dated with some confidence. Many of the reverse dies on the Durasalar sigloi of both types can be observed on sigloi from other hoards, both mixed and unmixed. It is more difficult to recognize obverse die links, but changes in obverse style, often associated with the appearance of new reverse dies, can be detected in Durasalar and paralleled in the large unmixed hoards. Durasalar thus becomes a key hoard for siglos chronology. It provides, for instance, a *terminus ante quem* for the appearance of perhaps the most significant development in the design of type IIIb. This is the change in the rendering of the drapery of the royal archer figure, from showing the *kandys* folded over the advanced left knee (there are many variations in detail but in general this gives a more naturalistic impression of the running figure) to showing the lower drapery as a broad semi-circular sweep from the left knee back to the right heel (e.g. **Pl. XIV, 37–8**). The latter style is certainly a late development; it continued into the period of the double-darics under Alexander and it is a feature which can serve to distinguish 'late' IIIb from 'early' IIIb.

[48] Martin Price has pointed out to me that the only other mint which frequently used such mis-shapen flans as type IV sigloi is the mint for Cyzicene electrum. Was there then a 'dagger' mint in N. W. Asia Minor?

[49] E. S. G. Robinson, *NC* 1958, 192–3 (see n. 23).

The hoards from Babylonia (32), Cilicia (33), and Tchaman-i Hazouri (35) also included non-Persian coins, thus enabling their dates of deposit to be estimated, but most of the sigloi in these hoards are very worn and often mutilated with cuts or counterstamps, suggesting that they could have been circulating for a considerable time before burial. The Isparta hoard (36) contained only one type IIIb siglos, with twenty-four type IV sigloi. This hoard can be dated approximately according to the issues of the other authority represented in the find, the city of Aspendus. Again, many of the sigloi in this hoard appear worn and heavily countermarked, but others, notably a group of nine type IV pieces all struck from the same reverse die (**Pl. XIV, 45**), seem much fresher and therefore were no doubt produced more recently.

The many siglos-only hoards in this part of Table A (21–30) can be connected with the mixed hoards through similarities in obverse style, or reverse die-links. They have been placed together in a block in Table A before hoards 31–5 because they cannot yet be dated with any precision. Although most contain issues of sigloi that are, on the basis of comparisons with Durasalar and other hoard coins, later than any of the worn sigloi contained in the Babylonia and Tchaman-i Hazouri hoards, this does not prove that they were buried later. It seems that the distribution between types IIIb and IV gives a rough guide to chronology. Hoards in which type IV are dominant over type IIIb seem generally to be later than hoards in which type IIIb are commoner. The datable non-Persian issues in the mixed hoards suggest that the period of burial of all these hoards was the first quarter of the fourth century, though the sigloi contained within them include issues which could have been produced anything up to 100 years earlier.

Fourth-century darics (hoards 34, 37 and 38)

There are very few hoards of Persian gold coins included in Table A. After the three hoards containing gold croeseids (2, 3, 7) there is a long gap. Darics of types II and IIIa exist, but none have so far been recorded in hoards. Only a handful of dies have so far been recorded for darics of type II, and type IIIa darics are also very rare. These are the issues of darics that should have been in circulation at the time of Pythius (Herodotus 7, 28) but it is difficult to connect these apparently meagre issues with the riches reported in that story.

A number of hoards of type IIIb darics are known, though only three are included in Table A (34, 37, and 38) because the others are all either insufficiently well-recorded or are daric-only hoards. The following table lists these other daric hoards, all exclusively of type IIIb, to show how they can be linked to the Vouni hoard and the Avola hoards from Table A.

TABLE B

Hoards containing darics (all III b)

IGCH or *CH*		Date	Darics recorded	
362	Athos, Macedonia, 1839		300	linked together by shared reverse dies or stylistic similarities
1278	Vouni, Cyprus, 1928	380	4	
CH VII, 27	Isthmia, Corinth		3	
CH VI, 12	Uncertain		30	
1194	Vourla, Asia Minor, 1875			die-links or similarities in style
2122	Avola, Italy, 1914	370	43	
2124	Avola, Italy, 1888	360	4	
CH VI, 13	Kiti, Cyprus		6	
32	Athens, 1929			
32?	Athens? (Vierordt coll.)			
43	Elis 1918		12	
–	Iran 1982		7	
63	Eretria 1855	340		details not available
1654	Damanhur 1896	330		
1656	Garbieh 1896	330		
1822	Oxus 1887 — darics included in mixed hoard(s)			
1222	Pirli bey 1870 — ? 1,000 darics reported, not identified			
1241	Mudanya 1969— ? 2,000 darics reported, not identified			

The absence of any hoards containing darics from the fifth century is obviously a severe handicap to a study of chronology from hoard evidence. All Table B can show is that at least two separate groups of type IIIb darics can be identified. Sub-groups within these major divisions could certainly be identified from a detailed study of obverse styles and reverse dies, but for the present, because of the lack of datable fixed points, it is intended only to highlight the differences which enable these two major groups to be distinguished. The earlier group, which is represented in the Vouni hoard, but not in either Avola hoard, is characterized by a neatly drawn obverse figure (**Pl. XIII, 27–31**). The reverse is a rough pattern, similar to that on the majority of type IIIb sigloi. One notable member of this group is the reverse die (**Pl. XIII, 28–9**) found with the 'beardless king' obverse, traditionally attributed to Cyrus the younger. Though no darics of this major group have yet been recorded in a context that can be dated earlier than about 380, stylistic comparisons with sigloi suggest that the group as a whole is probably fifth-century. One obverse style (**Pl. XIII, 27–8**), again linked by a reverse die to the 'beardless king', can be compared closely with sigloi that have appeared in hoards from as early as the 470s (cf. **Pl. XII, 18–19**).

The second group, which can safely be termed fourth-century, has an obverse figure which is broadly similar to that on 'later' type IIIb sigloi. There are stylistic variations within this group (**Pl. XIV, 39–42**) but a typical obverse shows a large, formal, royal archer figure, neatly drawn, but somewhat stylized (**Pl. XIV, 40**). The semi-circular curve of drapery is particularly noticeable. The reverse design of this 'period' is the usual roughly-cut pattern within an oblong incuse. Another group of darics, not identified as yet in any hoard, though with the same 'formal' obverse figure as has just been mentioned, has a reverse design (**Pl. XV, 50–1**) that is developing towards the 'horizontal-bands' pattern characteristic of the Babylonian 'double-daric' coinage of Alexander (**Pl. XV, 53**). It is logical to assume that darics with these reverses succeeded the 'Avola' group in a chronological development which culminated in the 'double darics'. This does not mean that we should seek a Babylonian mint for mid-fourth century darics (though this is not entirely out of the question). The Alexander double-darics obviously copy earlier daric prototypes, but their fabric, which is chunky and straight-edged, is clearly different from any of the fourth-century darics.

The last sigloi (hoards 39–42)

The four remaining finds listed in Table A provide the latest contexts for sigloi in hoards. The Warka hoard (39) contained one type IV siglos together with three silver staters of the satraps Pharnabuzus and Mazaeus. The coins of Mazaeus date the hoard to the period just before Alexander the Great's conquest of the Persian Empire. The siglos is not particularly worn and it has a rather well drawn royal archer figure, quite different from the crude figures which appear so often on type IV sigloi in earlier hoards. It is also characterized by a semi-circular sweep of drapery between the figure's legs, similar to that on 'late' type IIIb sigloi and darics.

The hoards from Babylonia, Susa, and the Bhir Mound (40–2) included coins of Alexander and of Philip III (Bhir Mound only), and their few sigloi are all of type IV.[50] The single siglos in the Babylonia hoard (40) is so mutilated by cuts and countermarks that it is almost unrecognizable. The two sigloi in the Susa hoard seem quite worn; in style they look comparable to type IV sigloi encountered in earlier hoards. The single siglos in the Bhir Mound hoard (42) looks fresher, and its style is comparable to the Warka siglos. There are, of course, limits to what one might deduce from such a small number of coins, but, such as they are, these few sigloi from datable late contexts tell a consistent story. They suggest that at least one variety of type IV siglos, which can be distinguished from others on stylistic grounds, can be dated probably to as late as the second half of the fourth century.

A hoard which should have contained a good sample of late sigloi was the Calymna (1823) hoard (*IGCH* 1216). This hoard is said to have contained thousands of sigloi, as well as a number of fourth-century coins from the region of Caria. The presence of coins of Pixodarus of Caria (340–334) dates its deposit to the period immediately prior to the arrival in the area of Alexander, since no coins of Alexander were recorded in the find. Borrell, who published a note on the hoard in the *Numismatic Chronicle*,[51] reported that, 'unfortunately, nearly nine-tenths of the whole were consigned to the crucible, not from ignorance, but on account of their degraded preservation. They were useless for any scientific purpose'. We must assume that the great majority of the coins that were melted down were sigloi, and that therefore these 'thousands' of sigloi were mostly very worn. In fact they probably looked quite similar to most of the sigloi that have turned up in hoards since that date, that is, worn, cut, and possibly countermarked as well. Would they

[50] On the Susa hoard, G. le Rider, *Suse sous les Seleucides et les Parthes*, 1950, pp. 222, 243, says that one of the two sigloi (no. 609, 1) belongs to type III, but from the illustration on pl. xi the coin appears more likely to be a type IV piece.

[51] H. P. Borrell, 'Unedited Greek Coins', *NC* 1847, 143–172, at 165–6.

then have been fourth-century sigloi? It must be doubted whether many could have been. To have become so 'degraded' the vast majority were probably fifth-century issues similar to the pieces in most of the known large hoards of sigloi considered earlier (e.g. hoards 15–33).

CIRCULATION PATTERN

Of the 36 hoards containing silver croeseids/sigloi in Table A, 22 hoards are mixed, while 14 contained only croeseids and/or sigloi.

The 22 mixed hoards were discovered in the following regions:

Croeseids	: Asia Minor 1*, Egypt 2
Cr., sigl. I, II, III	: Asia Minor 2*
Sigl. II, III	: Asia Minor 3, Egypt 1, Syria 3
Sigl. III, IV	: Asia Minor 4*, Persia/Babylonia 1*, Bactria 1
Sigl. IV	: Persia/Babylonia 3, Bactria 1

In the eight hoards marked with an asterisk the croeseids/sigloi constituted a major element.

The 14 unmixed hoards originated as follows:

Croeseids, sigl. I, II, III	: Asia Minor 1
Sigl. III	: Asia Minor 3
Sigl. III, IV	: Asia Minor 7, Syria 1, Persia/Babylonia 1
Sigl. IV	: Asia Minor 1

If we add together the 14 un-mixed hoards and the eight mixed hoards in which croeseids/sigloi made up a major element we arrive at the following regional distribution: Asia Minor 19; Syria 1 (Lebanon ?); Persia/Babylonia 2. This pattern may be distorted slightly by the fact that Asia Minor is the expected area of origin, so any completely unprovenanced finds of sigloi are liable to be labelled 'Asia Minor'. On the other hand, Asia Minor would still be the dominant source of siglos hoards even if all the imprecisely located hoards were excluded.

For the 21 hoards from Table A and B which included gold croeseids or darics, the following find-areas have been recorded:

Croeseids	: Asia Minor 1, Egypt 1, Persia 1
Darics III b	: Asia Minor 3, Cyprus 2, Egypt 2, Persia 1, Bactria 1, Greece/Macedonia 6, Italy 2, Uncertain 1.

These results confirm the observations made by Schlumberger,[52] when he investigated the circulation pattern of Persian coinage as revealed by a much smaller number of hoards in 1953. He concluded that, whereas the gold daric was an 'Imperial' coin current throughout, and indeed in use far beyond, the Persian Empire, the siglos was a local coin of Asia Minor, that travelled to other parts of the Persian Empire, such as Egypt or Syria, only in the same way as other silver coinages, such as the Greek issues of the Aegean area. It is perhaps worth noting that later siglos types appear more frequently in Persia/Babylonia than earlier

[52] D. Schlumberger, 'L'argent grec dans L'Empire Achémenide', in R. Curiel and D. Schlumberger, *Trésors monétaires d'Afghanistan*, 1953, 3–62.

types. I believe that although the vast majority of fifth-century sigloi were produced in, and probably remained in, western Asia Minor, it is nevertheless possible that certain later groups were produced in eastern Asia Minor, or indeed further East. When Alexander inaugurated the double-daric coinage to serve as a local currency in Babylonia he presumably felt that the earlier royal-archer coinage on which it was based had a local relevance.

CONCLUSIONS

The following catalogue sets out the sequence of issues of croeseids, darics, and sigloi as revealed by the study of the hoards. It is intended to be only an outline catalogue, illustrating major stylistic developments and dies which typify the various groups into which the coinages can be divided. The dates are only approximate, and are reliant on the dating of contemporary Greek issues. The fine details of the coinage issues within this basic framework will only be revealed by a die study of all the issues. There is a pressing need for a die-study of the croeseids, and a similar study of the early daric/sigloi of types I–III a would be both welcome and relatively straightforward. A die study of the sigloi of types III b and IV would be a daunting task because of the massive amount of available material and the awful condition of so many of the coins. However, it is not difficult to find reverse die-links within these types, so that project is by no means beyond possibility. It is worth noting that reverse dies for darics/sigloi often seem to have been used for a considerable time, so that features change until they often become almost unrecognizable,[53] but as long as the die can still be identified this aspect of production can be used to our advantage. A worn siglos die can provide an important chronological link between different obverses and between separate hoards. Another technical point worth noting is that the die-axis of darics and sigloi seems always to be regular,[54] which greatly facilitates the recognition of reverse dies.

Regarding the hoard study it is clear that such a study can only yield worthwhile results if plenty of well-recorded hoards are available. In the case of the sigloi there is no shortage of hoards as a whole but for certain periods there is a shortage of datable hoards mixing Persian and non-Persian material. For darics the situation is much worse. The total number of hoards is unimpressive; more significantly, few hoards can be dated, and none at all can be dated to the fifth century. There also seems to be a contradiction between the evidence of the daric and siglos hoards. III b daric types which can be linked stylistically with fifth-century sigloi do not appear in any datable hoards before about 380. If we used the same broad principles of dating for the gold as the silver coins we would have apparently parallel issues of darics and sigloi being produced 50 to 75 years apart. Can either the silver hoards or the gold hoards be relied upon? I believe that the evidence of the silver hoards is reliable, or at least is more reliable than that of the gold coins in hoards. In the fifth century gold coins were a great rarity. They were not as a rule produced by any Greek cities, and they should therefore not be expected to behave like 'normal' coins in circulation. Even in the Hellenistic period

[53] E. S. G. Robinson, *NC* 1958, 191–2 (see n. 23).

[54] *Noe* 15.

when gold coinage was much more familiar one can find relatively unworn gold coins in hoards whose burial date must be at least 100 years later than the date of issue of the coins.[55] I therefore believe that darics can be dated more accurately by comparison with related siglos issues than by the evidence of their appearance in hoards.

The worn condition of many sigloi has frequently been mentioned. It is, of course, essential to take this into consideration when attempting to attach dates to groups of sigloi appearing in hoards. The royal archer coins were unlike most contemporary series of coinage in that they were issued under the authority of an Empire, and each successive issue was struck with virtually the same designs and to the same weight standard. In such a coinage system issues do not become obsolete with age as would, for instance, the issues produced by Greek cities with frequently changing political or economic circumstances. The silver coinage of Athens, with its unchanging Athena head/owl designs, and the very common archaic coinage of Aegina both circulated long enough to become as worn as sigloi, but it is generally true that surviving examples of ancient Greek coinages are often relatively unworn compared with many of the sigloi that are found today. This must be because the Greek issues were much more frequently de-monetized, melted down, and re-struck, whereas sigloi carried on circulating year after year, getting steadily more worn. There are certain similarities between the currency systems and political circumstances of the Persian Empire of the fifth and fourth centuries BC and the Roman Empire of the first and second centuries AD, and it is worth noting that in silver denarius hoards firmly dated to about AD 200 there is no shortage of worn coins more than 100 years old.

The numerous countermarks which are encountered so frequently on sigloi, especially on types III b and IV, also provide evidence of circulation and not just of the period, but also the area of circulation.[56] It is reasonable to expect that a detailed study of the countermarks on sigloi and other contemporary coinages would produce evidence for refining the chronology and circulation pattern of many issues.

Regarding the chronology of the croeseids, darics and sigloi, as revealed by this study, the following main points can be singled out:

1 The 'early' croeseids include issues that were probably contemporary with early Greek coinages such as Athenian 'Wappenmünzen' and the first Aeginetan issues and also the earliest coinage of Caria. The hoard study provides no conclusive evidence for dating the introduction of these croeseids, though none of the finds considered here points to a date as early as the reign of Croesus. If the lion and bull coins really are what fifth century Greeks knew as 'croeseids' then the use of the term is the best, if not the only, evidence supporting the early date. It is to be hoped that a complete die-study of the croeseids would help, in that it might provide

[55] e.g. *IGCH* 866 (Anadol, Ukraine), gold coins of Philip II in hoard of *c.* 220; *IGCH* 958 (Marasesti, Romania) Philip II and Alexander gold coins in hoard of early first century BC; *IGCH* 1404 (Gordium), Philip II gold in hoard of *c.* 223.

[56] On countermarks on sigloi see, e.g., J. G. Milne, 'A hoard of Persian sigloi', *NC* 1916, 1–12, *Hill* p. cxxxvi ff., Kraay, *ACGC* 286.

information for an estimate of the time span for this series.

2 The 'later' croeseids are close in date to the earliest sigloi (types I, II, and III a). Together these coinages, which were probably all introduced under Darius I, belong to the period of the archaic Athenian 'owls'.

3 Sigloi of type III b began to appear in about the 480s.

4 Siglos type IV was introduced by about 450.

5 The vast majority of surviving sigloi seem to date from the fifth century, even though many of the examples now found in hoards may have still been in circulation in the fourth century.

6 There are no hoards of gold darics which can be dated to the fifth century. Darics of types II, III a, and fifth-century issues of III b do exist, but not in large numbers. Die studies would probably reveal that daric issues earlier than the end of the fifth century were probably very limited.

7 In contrast, there are few issues of sigloi that can be given a fourth-century date, and those that can are stylistically quite separate from the typical fifth-century issues.

8 It is likely that siglos types III b and IV were produced by different mints in the fifth century, and still more mints may have been producing the fourth-century issues.

It is left only to consider whether this outline of the Achaemenid coinage can be related to what we know of the history of the period. Our Persian history is largely dependant on Greek sources and is therefore Greek-orientated, but this bias is not so much of a problem because the Achaemenid coinage was in any case confined mostly to the westernmost, Greek-influenced areas of the Empire. It could be argued that the Persians needed coinage, as opposed to bullion silver, only when they were in contact with coin-using peoples (mostly Greeks). The European campaigns of Darius and Xerxes are obvious occasions to look for large issues of Persian coinage, not for the payment of Persian troops, but for logistical and diplomatic expenses and the hire of mercenaries. Thus the earliest siglos/daric types I–III a may have coincided with the suppression of the Ionian Revolt and Darius' invasion of Greece. If type III b was introduced in the 480s then many of the issues of this large coinage might have been struck in preparation for Xerxes' invasion of Greece and in the period while hostilities continued in the 470s, 460s, and 450s. Persian intervention in the later stages of the Peloponnesian War, the expedition of Cyrus, and various campaigns in the early fourth century, when many Greek mercenary armies fought in the pay of Persian generals, provide further obvious occasions for coinage production. It seems certain that many of the gold darics must have been issued within this period,[57] and also the 'later' type III b sigloi. There were also numerous occasions in the mid-fourth century when coinage

[57] Note the comment of Agesilaus mentioned earlier (p. 76 and n. 18).

might have been required by the kings or satraps (now mostly fighting each other rather than the Greeks), but although there is no shortage of daric issues that could be dated to this period there are not so many sigloi that can comfortably be placed here. Why is this? The obvious answer is that payments could be made in other silver coinages, and it is certainly noticeable that increased production of 'local' silver coinage within the Persian Empire after about 400 (e.g. satrapal issues from Cilicia and coinages in Phoenicia) coincides with the apparent fall in the production of sigloi. This rather sweeping observation and the suggested relationships between coinage issues and historical events is no more than speculation. It may be argued that the search for links between Achaemenid coinage output and Greek wars is both futile and misguided. One might attempt a commentary based more on administrative/economic considerations, or it might be wiser for the present to resist entirely the temptation to speculate on occasions of issue. Certainly there is still much more work to be done on Achaemenid 'regal' (croeseid, daric and siglos) coinages and on the many 'local' (satrapal and city) issues produced within the Empire.

CATALOGUE: ILLUSTRATIONS, PL. X–XV

All the coins are shown enlarged to twice their natural size.

AR = ◇ AV = ◆

pl. X, A Caria ◇ stater 10.83g (hoard 1)
pl. X, B Caria ◇ sixth 1.79g (hoard 1)

Early croeseids (hoards 1–4; *c.*550(?)–520) Pl. X

1 ◆ stater 10.71g Ars Classica sale 17, Geneva 1934, 581
2 ◇ stater 10.69g (hoard 1)
3 ◇ half 5.30g (hoard 1)
4 ◇ third 3.54g (hoard 1)
5 ◇ twenty-fourth 0.44g (hoard 1)
6 ◆ stater 8.03g *BMC* 33
7 ◆ third 2.70g *BMC* 36

Late croeseids (hoards 6–9); *c.*505–500 Pl. XI

8 ◆ stater 8.06g *BMC* 34
9 ◇ half 5.38g BM 1904-8-3-23

Darics/sigloi types I–IIIa (hoards 6, 8–11; *c.*500–485) Pl. XI

10	◇ Siglos I, 5.36g	BM 1948-7-12-15 (hoard 9)
11	◆ Daric II, 8.30g	BM 1976-11-2-1
12	◇ Siglos II, 5.32g	*BMC* 190
13	" " II, 5.37g	BM 1948-7-12-18 (hoard 9)
14	" " IIIa, 5.36g	*BMC* 69
15	" " IIIa, 5.38g	*BMC* 67

Sigloi IIIb group A (dies or styles in hoards 8–12; *c.* 485–470) Pl. XII

16	◇ Siglos 5.23g (? low weight, rev. die in Asyut)	*BMC* 56
17	" " 5.43g	BM 1929-10-13-536
18	" " 5.58g	*BMC* 23 bis
19	" " 5.49g	*BMC* 44

Sigloi IIIb group B (hoards 15–19); *c.*475–420) Pl. XII

20	◇ Siglos 5.52g	*BMC* 46 ter
21	" " 5.47g	*BMC* 36 bis
22	" " 5.55g	*BMC* 24
23	" " 5.70g	BM 1976-2-1-1 (hoard 16)
24	" " 5.44g	*BMC* 11
25	" " 5.49g	BM 1920-9-7-63
26	" " 5.51g	*BMC* 31

Darics IIIb, groups A–B (fifth century) Pl. XIII

27	◆ Daric 8.28g	*BMC* 43 (obv. style, cf. 19, 20 above)
28	" " 8.30g	*BMC* 42 (obv. style, cf. 19, 20 above)
29	" " 8.33g	BM 1927-4-2-1 (obv. style, cf. 21–26 above)
30	" " 8.36g	*BMC* 1 (obv. style, cf. 21–26 above)
31	" " 8.36g	*BMC* 20

Darics/sigloi type IV group A (hoard 19; *c.*455–420) Pl. XIII

32	◆ Daric 8.28g	*BMC* 109
33	◇ Siglos 5.41g	BM 1931-12-4-1
34	" " 5.48g	*BMC* 124
35	" " 5.55g	*BMC* 111

Darics/sigloi IIIb group C (hoards 24–36; *c*.420–375) Pl. XIV

36	◇ Siglos 5.52g	*BMC* 62
37	" " 5.54g	*BMC* 88
38	" " 4.78g	*BMC* 90
39	" " 5.59g	(hoard 24)
40	" " 5.58g	(hoard 24)
41	" " 5.48g	(hoard 24)
42	◆ Daric 8.32g	*BMC* 58

Sigloi IV group B (hoards 24–36; *c*.420–375) Pl. XIV

43	◇ Siglos 5.53g	*BMC* 146
44	" " 5.49g	*BMC* 159
45	" " 5.53g	*BMC* 158

Sigloi IV group C (? late, *c*.375–340) Pl. XV

46	◇ Siglos 5.36g	*BMC* 176
47	" " 5.39g	(hoard 39)
48	" " 5.39g	*BMC* 175
49	" " 5.34g	*BMC* 177

Late Darics IIIb and IV (? mid-fourth century) Pl. XV

50	◆ Daric IIIb 8.37g	*BMC* 78
51	" " IIIb 8.33g	*BMC* 84
52	" " IV 8.31	*BMC* 171

Double Darics (period of Alexander and later) Pl. XV

53	◆ 16.68g	*BMC* Alexandrine Empire 4
54	◆ 16.47g	*BMC* Alexandrine Empire 1

PLATE X

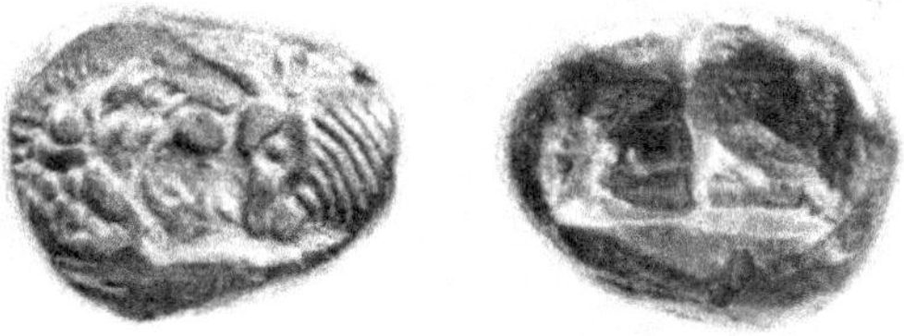

8

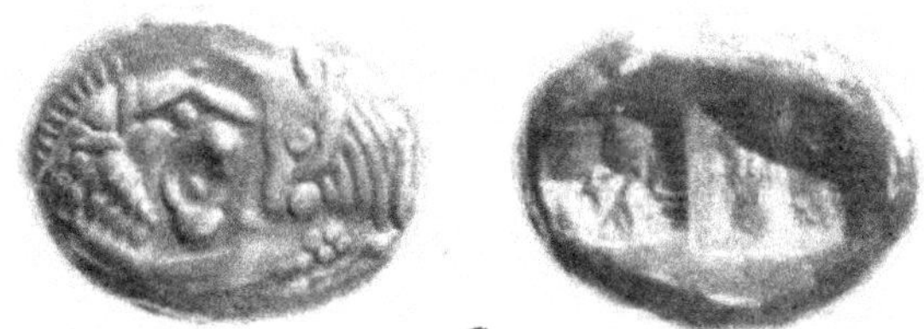

9

10 11 12 13

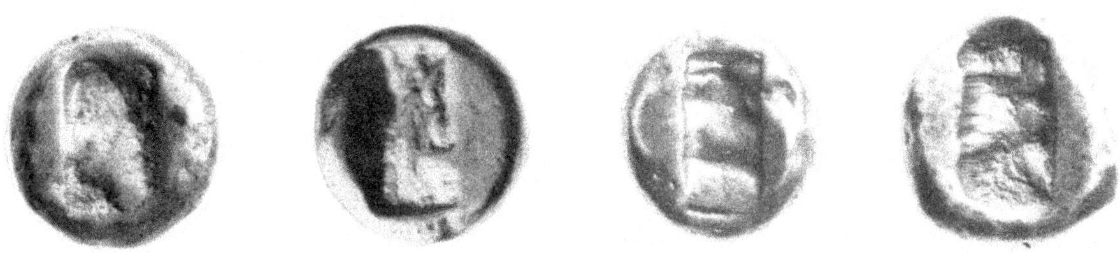

14

15

PLATE XI

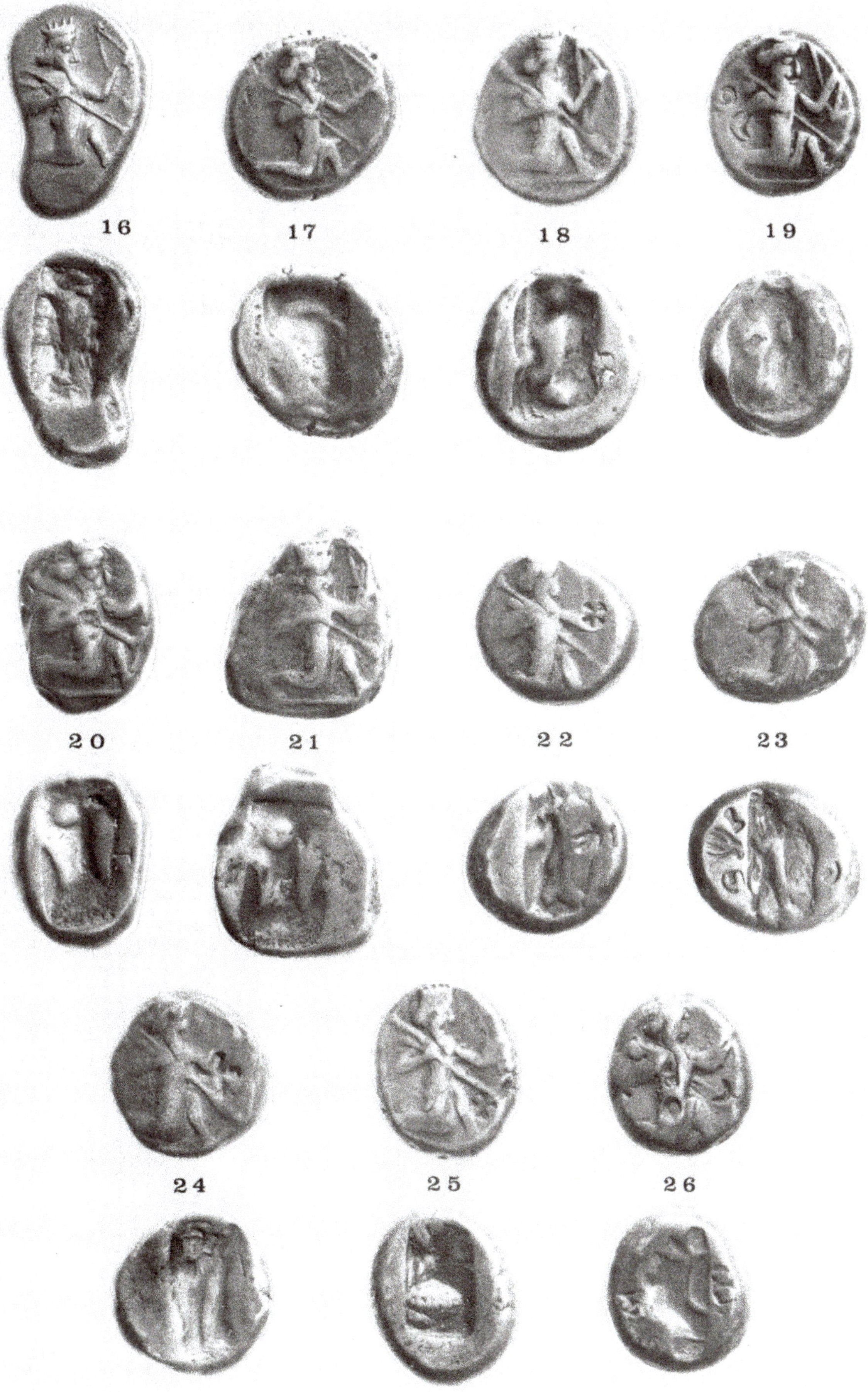

PLATE XII

27

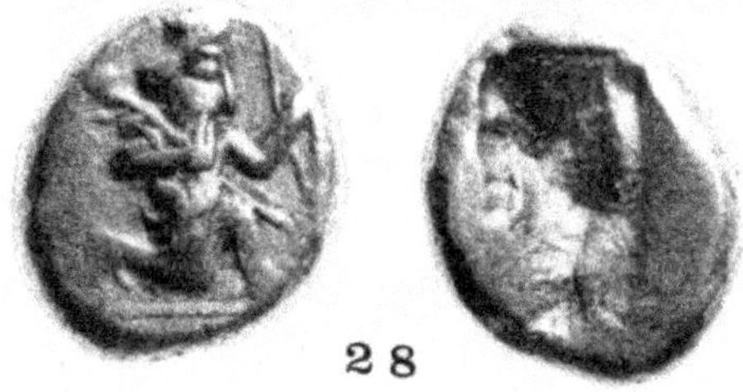

28

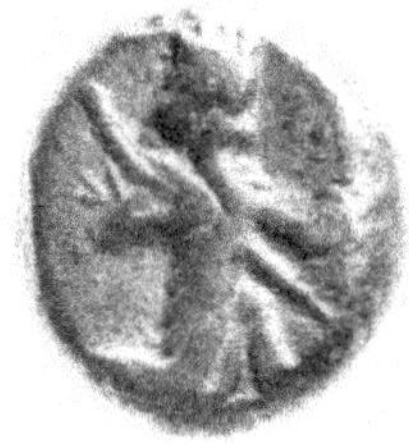

29 30 31

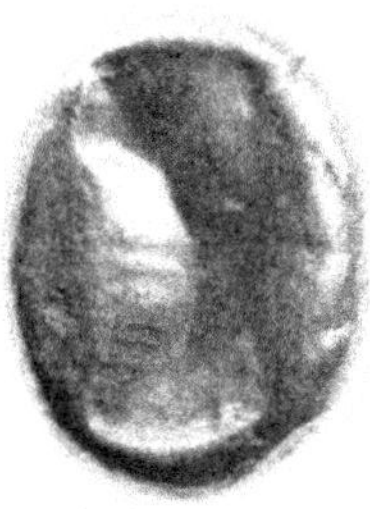

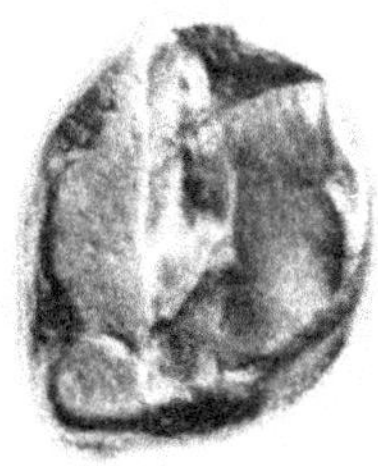

32 33 34 35

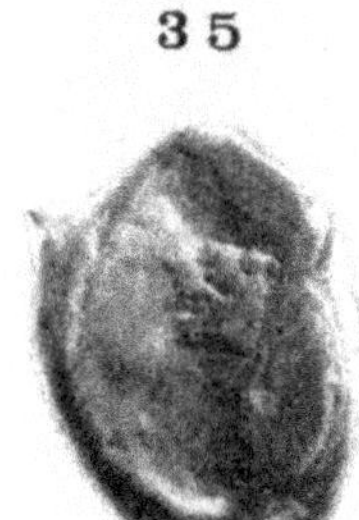

PLATE XIII

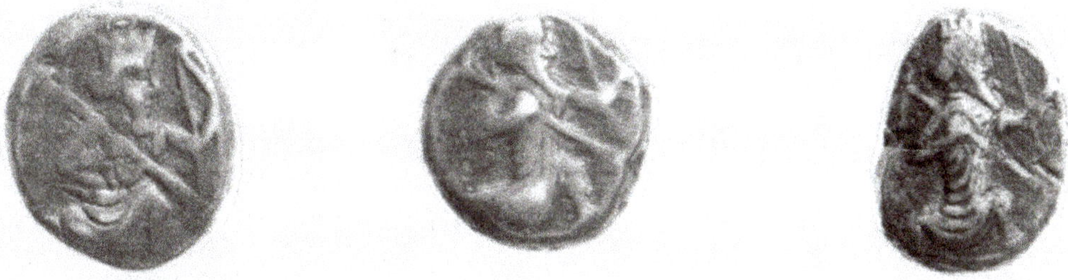

36 37 38

39 40 41 42

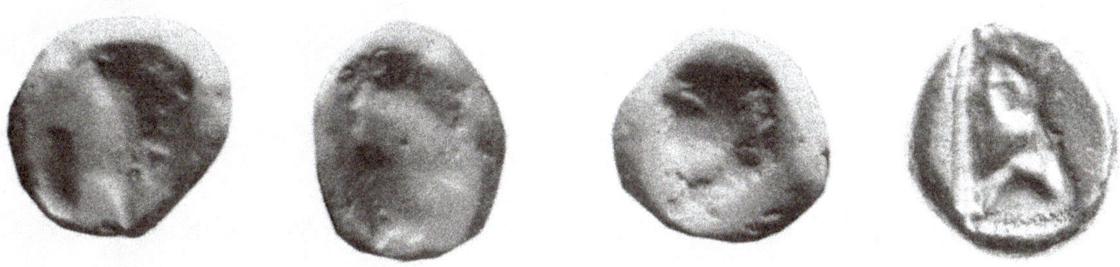

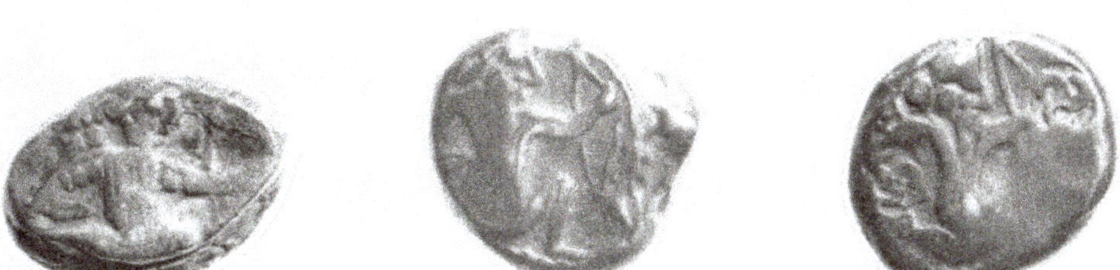

43 44 45

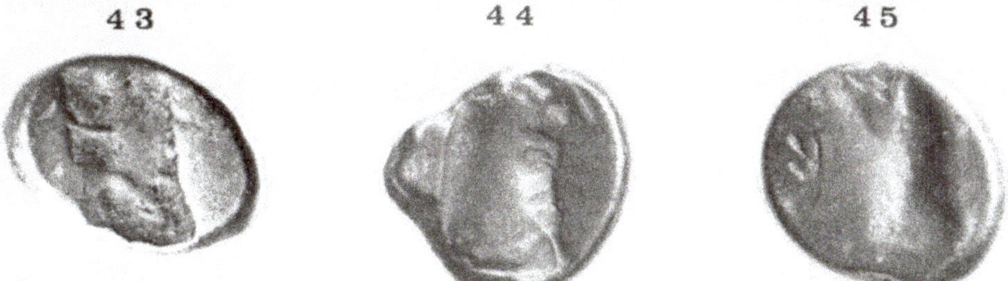

PLATE XIV

PLATE XV

The Administration of the Achaemenid Empire

CHRISTOPHER TUPLIN

INTRODUCTION

IMPERIAL administration concerns above all two things: the extraction of profit for the ruling power and the maintenance of control (and hence of the possibility of exploitation). The former presupposes structures for collecting tribute or exploiting resources more directly (e.g. by reallocation of ownership); the latter is partly a matter of eradicating or (better) manipulating high status local interest groups and taking advantage of low status groups' indifference to the identity of the ruling power (administratively speaking both favour maximum use of existing structures) and partly a matter of force—the threat of large scale reprisal for revolt and the permanent presence of garrisons—of which the second at any rate is a standard administrative feature. The purpose of the present paper is not to reveal any particularly new interpretation of its subject but to provide a (doubtless far from complete) conspectus of relevant material, some of it not perhaps very familiar to Greek historians and numismatists who have not made special study of the Achaemenid empire. To find a convenient arrangement of the material is not easy and I have chosen to use two approaches: delineation of some geographically defined administrative units of the empire and description of the tribute system.

I begin with three preliminary points. Bureaucratic tendencies were highly developed in the Persian empire. This is reflected even in literary sources. *Ezra* speaks of archives where royal edicts might be consulted.[1] The particular case in question is somewhat controversial (Cyrus' decree about the Jerusalem temple). No copy could be found at Babylon (the expected location) but one did turn up at Ecbatana. (The possibility of a Persepolitan copy is not even considered). Taking things at face value this suggests that storage was rather haphazard and the bureaucracy far from perfect. Alternatively one could wonder whether the decree (or at least the copy) was not after all spurious. But even so the imposture presupposes the existence of a document-oriented bureaucracy of some sort. The same perhaps goes for the belief of Ctesias (688F1 = Diod. 2.22.5, F5 = Diod. 2.32.4) and the authors of *Ezra* and *Esther* in various Persian 'historical' chronicles (though the status and subject matter of these is debatable).[2] And the statement in

[1] *Ezra* 5.17, 6.1–2 (cf. *I Esadr.* 6.21 f., Joseph. *AJ* 11.94, 98). According to *Ezra* 6.1 the Babylonian archive was in a treasury.

Note: for Abbreviations and Bibliography see end of article.

[2] *Ezra* 4.15, 19 (*I Esdr.* 2.21 f., Joseph. *AJ* 11.24 f.) refers to the 'annals of your (i.e. Artaxerxes I) predecessors' which tell of the history of Jewish rebelliousness: these are certainly meant to include neo-Babylonian records and that may be all that is involved. Ctesias consulted *basilikai diphtherai* 'in which the Persians, in accordance with a law, had a

Esther (1.22, 3.12, 8.9) that royal edicts were sent 'to each province in its own script and each people in its own language', though doubtless hyperbolic (especially since the author takes there to be 127 provinces), does reflect a multilingual empire with which central authority communicated in writing and not exclusively in Persian. Hellanicus' observation (687A F7) that Queen Atossa 'invented' the transmission of royal decisions through *epistolai* and *bibloi* belongs in the same category: people knew that the empire was a literate system, and Greeks loved to have a *prōtos heuretēs*. (The clearest example of a royal text communicated to all parts of the empire in various tongues is Darius' Behistun narrative: his own statement 'This inscription I sent off everywhere among the lands/peoples (*dahyāva*)' (DB 70) is confirmed by an Aramaic fragment from Egypt (Greenfield & Porten 1982) and an Akkadian one from Babylon (Voigtlander 1978:63).)

But it is the evidence revealed by archaeology that makes the point about bureaucracy most emphatically: the caches of Achaemenid *bullae* which are all that remain of such administrative centres as Dascyleium (Balkan 1959) or Memphis (Petrie 1910:xxxv, xxxvi, Bresciani 1958:182)[3] and the Elamite tablets from the Persepolis administration,[4] which reveal, for example, the bureaucratic aspect of the Royal Road.[5] What Greek sources have to say should already have suggested that a considerable organization was needed to keep 111 *stathmoi* between Sardis and Susa in commission for royal despatch riders.[6] But their tendency to concentrate on the latter distracted attention from the generality of travellers (except for a few stories suggesting that such people could expect police surveillance).[7] We now see that there was a system of travel authorizations by king, satrap, or other high official, which entitled the traveller to draw provisions at daily stopping places and we can understand what lies behind Alcibiades' need to

compilation of ancient events' (F5): the claim appears at the start of the *Median* history, and the *basilikai anagraphai* of F1 concern Memnon's actions in the Assyrian period. By contrast in *Esther* 2.23, 6.1 f. (cf. Joseph. *AJ* 11.208) a contemporary event is recorded in royal chronicles: cf. the benefactors-list in Thuc. 1.129, Hdt. 8.85, Wiesehöfer 1980: 10.

[3] These cases are only special because of large concentrations at one site: Achaemenid seals are found in small numbers all over the empire, as are non-Achaemenid seals and seals displaying varying degrees of influence from pure Achaemenid style. The large caches are generally associated with finds in these latter categories, so all sorts of design might evidently be found in any given administrative centre and we may e.g. legitimately regard the provenances of the pyramidal seals in Boardman 1970 as reflecting Sardis' role as administrative centre.

[4] Texts: Cameron 1948, 1958, 1965; Hallock 1969, 1978. Many Elamite texts remain unpublished. The Treasury archive contains one Akkadian tablet (PT 85). The Fortification archive contains 700 unpublished Aramaic tablets, one Akkadian tablet (Stolper 1984), one Greek text (Hallock 1969: 2) and one Phrygian text. It is assumed that what survives is an unbalanced cross-section of the archives' original contents because of the total disappearance of Aramaic texts on perishable material (Hallock 1973), and that the total absence of tablets after 458 indicates that the administration went over totally to such Aramaic records. Studies: Hallock 1960, 1977, 1985; Hinz 1971; Koch 1980, 1981, 1983; Lewis 1977:4 f., 1984:592 f.

[5] See especially Hallock 1985, Lewis 1977:4 f., 1984:596 f. Hallock 1978:114 discerns officials concerned with maintenance and measurement of roads in the *dattimara* and 'spear-bearers' found in some texts.

[6] The basic source is Hdt. 5.52; cf. also id. 3.126.2, 8.98, Xen. *Cyr.* 8.6.17, *Esther* 3.13 f., 8.9 (all on despatch riders). Substantial 'royal *stathmoi*' are mentioned in Plut. Artox. 25 (Median/Cadusian border), Hdt. 6.119.2 (Cissia); and cf. Ael. *VH* 1.32, *NA* 15.26. *The* Royal Road (Sardis-Susa) is not the only 'royal road': cf. Ps. Ar. *Oec.* 1348a25 (Lycia), BP 3.8, 10, 4.10, 12.19 (Elephantine), P. Louvre E. 2430 (Thebes), VS 3.153, 156, 158, 160, 165, 5.110 (Dilbat), FP 18, 30, 44, 63, Ball 1892:167 (Babylon), VS 4.98 (Borsippa), YOS 7.136 (Uruk), TCL 13.203 (Nippur), Dar. 140.

[7] Hdt. 5.35, 7.239 (secret messages), Xen. *An.* 1.9.13 (roads in Cyrus' provinces 'kept safe'), Diod. 11.56.6, Plut. *Them.* 26 (travel in *purdah* to avoid surveillance).

have Pharnabazus 'arrange' a projected trip to the king.[8] Nor was this the only way to travel. The Egyptian satrap Arsames issued an Aramaic passport to his personal estate-manager allowing him to get provisions from counterparts in Babylonia, Assyria, and Syria (AD 6). But Arsames' estates did not run continuously from Susa to Memphis, so the manager presumably carried other provision authorizations as well.[9]

Secondly, the Persian approach to administration did not involve abolishing existing structures and replacing them with a unified Persian one. There could be interference, of course: the bow-fief system in Babylonia (below, pp. 153 f.) was a Persian innovation and must have involved considerable dislocation of the previous *status quo*, and this would no doubt be generally true of landholding throughout the empire. Surveillance of the appointment of *lesonis* priests in Egypt belongs in the same category, since they were temple presidents concerned with financial administration[10]—though even in native practice they would theoretically be (and perhaps were actually) royal appointees (Lloyd 1983:303). But equally typical is the continued functioning of the Elders and the 'popular' assemblies of Babylonian temple/city communities which had jurisdiction in various sorts of property dispute (Dandamayev 1976:473 f., 1977:590 f., 1982:38 f.) or the Jewish community assembly at Elephantine (AP 15.22, 26, BP 2.7, 7.2: also a judicial body) or similar foreign community institutions in Babylonia (Eph'al 1978:76, Dandamayev 1982:41, 1984a:339) and maybe even Persis (Stolper 1984:309) or (of course) the Phoenician or Cypriot or Anatolian Greek city-state.[11] The Persians might interfere in the political matter of which individual or class controlled a particular city-state; they might visit enslavement, deportation, and destruction upon the population and buildings of a rebel *polis*, but they did not eradicate the institution (even in the latter cases),[12] and did not necessarily object to the union of several cities in leagues or the like.[13] It is also typical that Achaemenid rulers were eager to adopt the titles and status of some of the monarchs whom they displaced[14] and that viewing pre- and post-Persian conquest native documentary evidence

[8] Diod. 14.11.2 f., Plut. *Alc.* 37 (Pharnabazus would authorize safe passage and provide a *hodegos*)—Naveh 1975 suggests that some Arad ostraca reveal the place to have been a way station. For Achaemenid roads and associated way stations in the Persepolis/Pasargadae region and on the road to Susa cf. Stronach 1978:166 f., Kleiss 1981, Sumner 1984:17.

[9] Briant 1982a:311, n.d.(a) thinks the text more strictly comparable to Persepolis travel documents, identifying the officials as 'intendants qui gèrent les Magasins royaux', not private estate-managers; but that Arsames speaks of his *byt'* (house) not *bg* (domain) is of little significance (the terms being used interchangeably of personal estates) and the uneven distribution of the managers over the area through which the passport-holder was travelling favours the traditional interpretation.

[10] P. Ryl. 9.2/8, P. Berlin 1359–40 (Spiegelberg (1928)), 13572, 23584 (Zauzich 1978). On *lesonis* priests cf. Jelínková-Reymond 1955:55, Lloyd 1983:306. P. Cairo 50060 (Jelínková-Reymond 1955:33 f.) exemplifies their functions in the early Persian period.

[11] The continued existence of city-states hardly requires proof; there are inscriptions recording public acts and coinage to supplement the literary evidence.

[12] e.g. Miletus (Hdt. 6.18.1, 20.1, 25.2), other Ionian rebels (id. 6.9.4 f., 32), Eretria (id. 6.101, 119, Strab. 747), Barca (Hdt. 4.204). For continued existence of Ionian cities after 494 cf. Hdt. 6.42, 43.3.

[13] Phoenicia: Diod. 16.41.1 (Tripolis, a Phoenician *synhedrion*). Ionia: Tod 113 (Strouthas delegates initial arbitration of border-dispute to Ionian league). Bryce 1983:33, 35, 41 suggests the Persians actually promoted a Lycian federation under Xanthus, but this is decidedly speculative.

[14] cf. Cambyses (Posener 1936:no. 1) and Darius (Winlock 1941:7) in Egypt, and all Kings up to Artaxerxes I in Babylonia (Cameron 1941: with additional, later information in Kuhrt & Sherwin-White n.d.). Ackroyd n.d. argues that Achaemenid kings also saw themselves as Kings of Judah, successors to the Davidic line.

from Babylonia or Egypt as a whole one is conscious of considerable continuity, especially in the fairly immediate vicinity of the Persians' arrival. (In Babylonia more than a generation passes before changes in legal practice and terminology begin to manifest themselves: Meuleau 1969:381, Dandamayev 1984:332, Kuhrt n.d.). In short, it was the Persian way to use existing institutions and seek to harness the energies and interests of native dominant classes to their own ends. Hence just as Asiatic Greek cities always contained those who looked to Persia (and might flee 'to the Mede' if things went wrong), so in Egypt we encounter not only the notorious Udjahorresnet (Posener 1936:no. 1, Lloyd 1982) and Somtutefnekhet (Tresson 1931) but also Khnemibre (chief of works and military commander) and Ahmose (another military commander) (Posener 1936:nos. 6–7 and 11–23). Their titles may in the last analysis have been empty (Briant n.d.(b)) but their status was maintained and they are the sort of people who make up 'the Egyptians who did not join the rebellion' (Thuc. 1. 104) in *c.* 460; and in the right contexts (e.g. the provinces of Beyond the River: below p. 122) native dignitaries need not have lacked for some enjoyment of a real sense of power.

Lack of imperial uniformity can be highlighted by considering some phenomena which are occasionally and misleadingly adduced to demonstrate its presence. Elsewhere in this volume Dr. Carradice describes a standardized royal coinage which was *not*, however, the coinage of the empire. A Babylonian weight system ('the stones of the King') was imported into Egypt (and has been presumed in Palestine), but it was only Babylonian *in name* (the shekel being 8.76 g not 8.4 g), and it coexisted with a separate, native standard ('the stones of Ptah') which is the normal point of reference in demotic texts.[15] Moreover, certain formulae in Aramaic texts imply that the Babylonian *karš* (ten 8.4 g shekels) was a familiar unit in the same region.[16] At least *three* weight standards, therefore: no uniformity here. In Babylonia itself there is occasional reference to disbursement of commodities by 'royal measure' (Dar. 158, TCL 13.128, 159, VS 3.131–2, TuM 2/3 137) but temple measures are also encountered, and the commonest measure in debt-payments is that of the creditor (San Nicolò/Ungnad 1935:233). Then there is the question of law. Darius speaks of the peoples of the empire obeying *his* law;[17] Ezra was told to punish those who disregarded the King's Law (*Ezra* 7.25, *I Esdr.* 8.23); and royal *data* is mentioned in Babylonian documents after 519 BC in connection with slave-sales, tolls, and cash deposits (Dar. 53, VS 3.159, UET 4.101; cf. also VS 6.99, using the Akkadian word for 'law', and VS 6.128 mentioning a man 'set over the *data*'). But the legal codification ordered in Egypt by Darius was of Egyptian law as it stood in 525 (and the law of the demotic papyri is largely unchanged from Saite times),[18] Ezra was also told to enforce the 'law of your God', and the Elephantine Jews had their own legal code (with Babylonian and Egyptian elements),[19] as did Babylonians and Greeks within their cities. All Darius' boast need mean is that, if a

[15] Stones of the King: AP 5, 6, 8–10, 14–15, 20, 25, 28, 43, 46, BP 3–5, 5, 7–10, 12. Stones of Ptah: AP 11, P. Berlin 3078, 3110, P. Loeb 44, 45, 48, 49, 68, P. Louvre E 9292, P. Turin 228. Palestine: Stern 1982:215 f. (but there will have been local standards too, ibid.).

[16] Porten 1968:305–7; and ibid. 62–72 on the whole metrological topic.

[17] DB8, DNa 3, DSe 4, XPh 3 (and cf. Aesch. *Pers.* 594 f.).

[18] Diod. 1.94, P. Bibl. Nat. 215 verso c 6–16 (Spiegelberg 1915:30), Seidl 1956:70.

[19] Yaron 1961, Porten 1968:191, Bresciani 1958:159 f., 1969:344.

place was within the empire, there would be some matters in which Persian-imposed legal regulations might apply—and the king could in principle multiply these endlessly if he wished (which he often did not). Alternatively (or additionally) we may accept the argument of Frei 1984, that there was a procedure for royal authorization of the laws of local communities. Either way it would be misleading to speak of the empire being bound together by a uniform legal code.

Thirdly, 'it is notoriously difficult to separate military and court ranks in the Achaemenid empire and may indeed be a pointless exercise' (Smith & Kuhrt 1982:207). This is true, and one possible implication is that even persons who are attested in purely military capacities and without a title or other indication to 'place' them in the structure of permanent garrisons or civil functionaries may nonetheless deserve consideration in the present context. I have not, however, succumbed to this line of thought and attempted to catalogue such persons exhaustively in order to guess at their possible administrative significance: there are enough uncertainties as it is. Nor, indeed, shall I say as much about the garrison structure as the present subject would perhaps warrant: some amends may be made for this by the discussion in Tuplin n.d.(b).

I GEOGRAPHICAL DIVISIONS

I SATRAPIES AND THE PERSEPOLIS DISTRICT

Let us turn now to the constituent parts of the Achaemenid empire. In seeking to delineate these, we dispose of various sorts of systematic description or (more crudely) lists. Many Persian royal inscriptions provide lists of the lands/peoples (*dahyāva*) of the empire. Thirty-one different peoples appear at one time or another (counting various types of Ionian and Scythian as one, though more than one can appear at once), though no list has more than 26.[20] Although these lists are sometimes accompanied by formulae stressing the King's possession of the people in question, their fear of and obedience to him and his law, and their provision of tribute (DB 8, DPe 2, DNa 3, DSe 2, DSv, XPh 3), there is no explicit indication (nor any reason to infer) that they are administrative units. They simply express the empire's extent in terms of ethnic groupings (Cameron 1973). Similarly unhelpful are the *ethnē* in Herodotus' and other sources' extensive listings of the constituents of royal armies.[21] Of more use is Herodotus' list of 20 tribute-paying *nomoi* = *arkhai* = satrapies, mostly comprising several *ethnē* (3.89 ff.). Its status as 'document' is decidedly controversial (its geographical order certainly tells against an immediate Persian official origin) but it does bear some relation to parts of a third list, the one which we can compile for ourselves from the whole range of written evidence of the regions and places named in titles of attested imperial officials. This

[20] DB6, DPe 2, DNa 3, DN I–XXX, DSe 2, DSm 2, DSv, XPh 3, A?P, Suez canal *stelai* (Posener 1936: nos. 8–10), Susa statue base (Roaf 1974). The sources of materials for the Susa palace in DSf and DSz amount to a list of peoples, and in the shorter DSaa they are actually presented in that form (cf. Herrenschmidt 1983). In addition there are unlabelled representatives of imperial peoples on four royal tombs and at various points in the Persepolis palace (cf. Roaf 1974).

[21] Hdt. 7.61–99 (Xerxes); Arr. *An*. 3.8.3 f., 11.3, Curt. 4.12.6 f., Diod. 17.59 (Gaugamela); Curt. 3.2.1 f. (army review prior to Issus). The only other moderately extensive listing (of a non-royal army) is Nep. *Dat*. 8 (army of Autophradates).

is much the most voluminous evidence (though it suffers from variations of date and inconsistencies of terminology). Once it is compiled we can, as a first step, assemble a list of relatively large regions attested (with, admittedly, occasional changes of boundary and combination) as the responsibility of officials whom Greek sources regularly call satraps (a term also used e.g. in the OP text of DB). We can for convenience call these regions satrapies (the term is actually not specially common in ancient sources), and then recognize further satraps in individuals associated with the appropriate areas but given a large variety of other titles or periphrastic descriptions.[22] Satraps are not the highest level officers ever attested in provincial contexts. In the early years of Persian rule Babylonia was governed by Nabuahhebullit the *šakin mati* (governor of the land), an office already estabished in pre-Achaemenid times (and indeed held by Nabuahhebullit himself since at least 548/7) which was abolished in favour of an Iranian satrap of Babylonia and Beyond the River at the end of Cyrus' fourth year (San Nicolò 1941:61 f., Oppenheim 1985:544); and the circumstances of war with Greek powers over possession of western Anatolia led intermittently to the creation of superior officials of various sorts.[23] Nor do the satrapies exhaustively fill the imperial area: some largish regions which were under satraps in the fourth century were earlier ruled by local dynasts—Caria, Lycia and Cilicia are clear instances[24]—and no Achaemenid satrap is ever recorded for e.g. Cyprus or (for all their regular appearance in lists of peoples) Sogdiana, the Arabs, or the Scythians.[25] Moreover, there were always some peoples inside the empire who paid scarcely any attention at all to the King's rule[26] and

[22] An inexhaustive list of examples/references: hyparch (Hdt. 3.70, 126, 6.33, Arr. *An.* 1.12.8, Robert 1975), *praefectus* (Nep. *Dat.* 2.5, Curt. 4.6.2, Plin. N. H. 6.120), *praeesse* (Curt. 3.4.3, Nep. *Con.* 5.3), *praeponere* (Just. 1.6.16, 5.5.1), eparch (Joseph. *AJ* 11.89), ἄρχειν (Xen. *An.* 3.15.7, Theop. 115 F389, Hdt. 3.120.2), ἡγούμενος (Diod. 17.21), ἐπίτροπος/ἐπιτρέπειν (Hdt. 1.153, 7.7), ἐπισταθμός (Isoc. 4.162), combinations of ἄρχειν/ἔχειν, νομός or GN (Thuc. 1.115.4, Hdt. 1.192, 3.127 and—pace Cook 1983:178—5.102), *provinciam habens* (Nep. *Dat.* 1.1), κρατῶν (Polyaen. 7.28.2), 'to whom Egypt is entrusted' (P. Berlin 13539–40), *pḥt*, *pīhat* or LU.NAM (Camb. 344, Oelsner 1976:316, BE 10.101, 118), ʿl (Cooke 1903:149A6). The reasonably clear satrapies are: Lydia, Hellespontine Phrygia, Great Phrygia, Cappadocia (latterly divided in two), Caria (+ Lycia) (cf. n. 24), Armenia, Cilicia (cf. n. 24), Beyond the River ('Syria'), Egypt, Babylonia, Media, Susa, (?) Persis (cf. p. 115), Hyrcania/Parthia, Arachosia/Drangiana, Areia, Carmania, Bactria. But this list is probably incomplete (in particular there is the question of a possible Indian satrapy at some dates).

[23] Some are also satraps, e.g. Tissaphernes (Thuc. 8.5.4, Diod. 13.36.5, Xen. *Hell.* 3.2.13, 4.1.37; the import of ib. 3.1.3, Diod. 14.26.4 is arguable), Cyrus (Xen. *Hell.* 1.4.3, *An.* 1.1.2, 9.7, (?) Plut. *Artox.* 2, Diod. 14.12.5, 19.2), (?) Tiribazus (Xen. *Hell.* 4.8.12, Diod. 14.85.4), (?) Struthas (Xen. *Hell.* 4.8.17, Diod. 14.99). Others are not, e.g. Tithraustes (Diod. 14.80.7), (?) Ariaeus and Pasiphernes (Hell. Oxy. 19.4), Mentor (Diod. 16.50.8, 52.2), Memnon (Arr. *An.* 1.20.2 f., 2.1.1, Diod. 17.23.6, 29.1), Pharnabazus (Curt. 3.13.14). There are many uncertainties here, to which can be added individuals who are generals or 'rulers' or satraps of (coastal) Asia or the coast: Artabazus (*epist. Them.* 16), Orontes (Diod. 15.90), Harpagus (Diod. 9.35.1), Otanes (Hdt. 5.25), Artaphernes (id. 5.30.5), Hydarnes (id. 7.135.1).

[24] Caria: Hornblower 1982:1–34. Lycia: 'never subdued by Persia' (Isoc. 4.161); no satrap of Lycia attested until TL 44b 26 (precise import obscure) or thereafter until FX VI pp. 32 f. = SEG 27.942 (a satrap of Caria and Lycia). Coinage establishes the existence of many dynasts. Cilicia: local ruler called Syennesis (Hdt. 5.118, 7.98, Xen. *An.* 1.2.12 f., 4.4, Diod. 14.20.1). Non-satrapal according to Xen. *Cyr.* 7.4.2, 8.6.7, Iranian satraps appear in the last generation of the empire, with Cilicia sometimes combined with Beyond the River.

[25] Cyprus: non-satrapal in Xen. *Cyr.* 8.6.7. Literary/numismatic evidence reveals only city-kings/dynasts etc. (The case of Phoenicia for most of the imperial period is perhaps only different in that, not being an island wholly separate from the Levant, it is more easily assumed to be part of Beyond the River.). A satrap of Paphlagonia (anonymous) appears in Diod. 14.11.3, but the remainder of the evidence is consistent with Xenophon's view (*Cyr.* 8.6.7) that it was non-satrapal.

[26] e.g. mountainous hinterland of Mysia (Xen. *Hell.* 3.1.13, *An.* 3.2.23, *Mem.* 3.5.26, Hell. Oxy. 21; contrast Hdt. 3.90.1, 7.74.1 f., 9.32.1); Pisidia/Lycaonia (absent in Hdt. 3.90; and cf. Diod. 11.61, Ephor. 70 F91.94 f., Xen. *Mem.* loc. cit., *Hell.* loc.

others (notably the 'agro-pastoralists' of the Zagros) whose relation with him consisted rather in receiving regular 'gifts' than in paying tribute, though they did furnish manpower for royal armies (Briant 1982b:57–112). The former were certainly not effectively within satrapies and the latter probably scarcely more so, except insofar as they might be commanded by the appropriate satrap in the context of military service. But, despite these important qualifications, satrapies do constitute a basic large-scale administrative framework of the empire; and more detailed discussion of Achaemenid administration is generally concerned with the structures and procedures one might find within a satrapy.

There is, however, one voluminously important exception. The Persepolis Fortification tablets, though emanating from an imperial capital, do not relate to the whole empire. But neither do they relate to the satrapy of Persis. There may indeed have been no such satrapy at the time (the first attested satrap of Persis appears in 331/0 and even he is only so designated by one source (Arr. *An.* 3.18.2)), but in any case one of the four subregions covered by the archive is beyond the Persian Gates and arguably not in Persis (Hallock 1977) and some of the tablets relate to operations at Susa (PF 88–92, 136, 318, 337, 1752–3). We can see various administrative elements in this exceptional region (cf. studies cited in n. 4). There is a chief administrator, notably Pharnaces, the King's uncle, with an attendant chancellery. There is the Persepolis treasurer, presumably also the ultimate controller of other treasury sites (below pp. 130 f.). There are two types of person associated with the worker-groups whose sustenance is so prominent a subject in the archive: (i) those (not numerous) who 'assign' them—the three commonest are 'chiefs of workers', their seals help to define the subregions and Hinz 1971 regards them as the chiefs of the whole system of food-stores, itself divided into five commodity departments (grain, wine/beer, fruit, animals, and fowls); and (ii) those who 'apportion' them, i.e. produce lists of workers and indications of size of rations. Then there are the supply officers at particular locations (though sometimes responsible for several) who provide the commodities for workers' rations and in the other contexts which the archive covers. There are also a couple of tantalizingly uninformative references to what may be a *dahyupatiš* (Hinz 1975: 92), i.e. a man in charge of a *dahyu*, the word used for entities in royal lists of lands/peoples. On a different tack, Sumner has recently pursued the principles laid down by Hallock for analysing the geography of the area covered by the archive and, by charting the associations of individual places in the transfer of produce or issue of rations, has produced an analysis in which Hallock's subregions I and II (Persepolis/Shiraz/Narezzaš [seals 1, 32] and Kamfiruz [seals 3, 30] respectively: Hallock 1977:109) break down into 'a regional model centred on Persepolis... with three urban regions [viz. Matezziš, a place immediately adjacent to Persepolis, Kaupirriš, and Shiraz] and a dozen rural districts composed of large or smaller towns and associated villages' (Sumner 1986:18 f., esp. 21–22). The model is based on only a fraction of the possibly relevant material (for a more systematic treatment we are still awaiting the dissertation of A. M. Arfaee and, it seems, are likely to be doing so for some time to come). Moreover Sumner presents only his

cit., *An.* 1.2.19, 3.2.23, Nep. *Dat.* 4.4, 6.1, Polyaen. 7.27.1).

results, not the detailed working that led to them, so it is difficult to evaluate them without immense labour. But any even casual reader of the texts will be aware that the operation is in principle feasible (and desirable), and Sumner's preliminary report may represent the start of an analysis which will eventually reveal the medium-size administrative districts of Achaemenid Fars. If so, however, one will expect his very large Shiraz 'urban region' to dissolve into units closer in scale to the Matezziš and Kaupirriš ones; and the prerequisite of any precise results in this direction must remain proper analyses of the interlocking workings of attested 'officials'. From that goal we are still very distant, and the already evident fact that particular individuals can combine several functions is not going to make things easier. All the same, the *general* picture of individual supply points (which can include private estates), storehouses, granaries, treasuries, and various regions is clear enough, even if the precise interrelationships of the various stages are not. Also clear is the very great complexity. It is a major question whether we can assume quite this sort of complexity everywhere, especially in areas where there were not such huge numbers of quasi-servile workers (15,376 persons at 108 locations over the period 509–494 according to figures in Dandamayev 1975).[27] These *kurtaš*, who are overwhelmingly non-Iranian, clearly include deported prisoners of war, literary evidence about whom almost always involves deportation to the central and eastern parts of the empire.[28] If the Persepolis tablets are archives of the royal 'palace economy', their bearing on places far from royal palaces might be thought debatable. And yet the differences may be largely ones of scale. Moreoever, not all deportees ended up geographically close to the royal capitals and there were certainly equivalents of *kurtaš* not only in Babylonia but also in Egypt.[29] In fact the significance of the royal capitals should not be overstressed: after all, there was royal land and land in the hands of members of the royal family all over the empire.

Few officials, apart from the satrap, have titles suggesting an office applying to the whole of a satrapy. The 'treasurers of Beyond the River' in *Ezra* 7.21 would be an example, if the text refers to officials of a central satrapal treasury rather than

[27] As Lewis 1984:594 remarks these figures are not entirely accurate (the number of locations, for example, is actually 112), but must be of the right order.

[28] Mesopotamia: Diod. 17.110.4, 19.19.2 (Boeotians). Upper Tigris: Strabo 747 (Eretrians). Middle Tigris: Arr. *An.* 3.8.5, 11.5, Diod. 17.110, 19.12.1 (Carians). Babylon: Grayson 1975:no. 9 (Sidonians). Cissia: Hdt. 6.119 (Eretrians), Ctes. 688 F13 (10), (?) 14 (38 f.) (Egyptians). Tigris mouth: Hdt. 6.20 (Milesians). Persis: Curt. 5.5.5, Diod. 17.69, Just. 11.14 (Greeks), Diod. 17.68.5, Curt. 5.4.4, Plut. *Alex.* 37 (Lycians). 'Red Sea' islands: Hdt. 3.93.2, 7.80. Hyrcania: Euseb. 112, Jerome 113, Oros. 3.7, Syncell. 486.10, Joseph. *Ap.* 2.134 (Jews)—a disputed case, cf. Stern 1982:255. Bactria: Hdt. 4.204 (Barcaeans), id. 6.9.4 (Ionian girls: but cf. 6.32), Curt. 7.5.28 f., Strab. 517, 634 (Didyma priests). An exception is the Paeonian deportation to Phrygia (Hdt. 5.12 f., 98). The very mixed racial constituents of the population of Babylonia (Dandamayev 1984a:339) may be relevant here, though it is in some measure due to deportations by Assyrian and neo-Babylonian kings.

[29] Babylonia: (i) *gardu*: VS 3.138/9, FP 32, BE 9.15, 101, 10.95, 118, 127, PBS 2/1 2, 204, CBS 12985, with Cardascia 1951:79, Dandamayev 1963:148, 1984c:568 f., Stolper 1974:100 f. In Murašu texts the *gardu* are organized in fief-collectives (cf. p. 153), seem exclusively associated with royal possessions and include non-Babylonians. (ii) *šušanne*: common in Murašu texts, see also (earlier) VS 6.276, TCL 13.147, YOS 7.106, 111, 114, Cyr. 158. See Stolper 1974:120f., Dandamayev 1984c:626f. Egypt: AD 7, 9, 12 (*grd'*, who are branded, appropriated to estates, receive provisions and can have property; an estate-manager is expected to secure extra ones during local disturbances, presumably as prisoners), Saqqara 19.6 f. (*grd'* on whom tax is paid). Arsames' branded slaves (*ʿbd*) 'appointed in my domain' (AD 5) may be relevant. *Prmnkry'* in AP 26.4 f. could be foremen of *gardu* like the **framanakara* in PT 44, 78.

collectively to the officials of all the satrapy's treasuries, which is an open question. (A similar problem arises with the 'inspectors of the province Beyond the River' in ibid. 5.6, 6.6.) On the whole, officials operating within a satrapy are either not 'placed' at all (being on record without informative title or other indication of hierarchical position[30]) or are presented either as subordinates/associates of the satrap himself[31] or as officers of some area smaller than the complete satrapy. Xenophon's Elder Cyrus tells his satraps to create courts modelled on the royal one (*Cyr.* 8.6.10 f.). Without pursuing all the implications of this (*via* evidence about the royal court), one can (as an example with other satrapal and royal parallels) register the evidence about the younger Cyrus' *philoi, homotrapezoi* and *skēptoukhoi* (who, *inter alia*, were constituents of the 600 cavalry who fought alongside him at Cunaxa)[32] or the commanders of Pharnabazus' cavalry (Xen. *Hell.* 3.4.13, *An.* 6.4.24 f.) or, at a subsatrapal level, the 'kinsmen' and 'men under the governor' who appear in *Nehemiah*, a work which also speaks of the governor's table.[33] Cyrus' entourage included people actually related to one another,[34] and the notion of kinship recurs with the 40 *syngeneis* accompanying Spithridates at the Granicus (Diod. 17.20.2, 21.1). Their status is, however, debatable (they may simply be high-ranking persons who were members of the *royal syngeneia*), and we shall have to rely rather upon the *Nehemiah* passage just mentioned (referring strictly to a subsatrapal level) and upon speculation about the satrapal court cavalry of Xenophon *Cyropaedia* 8.6.10 if we wish to believe that a satrap's aping of the King actually included the maintenance of an order of Satrapal Relatives.[35] The absence of any corresponding evidence in connection with the younger Cyrus strikes me as a powerful reason for caution on this issue. (There seems, incidentally, to be no evidence for a satrapal order of Benefactors to match the royal one.[36])

When passing through Dana (i.e. Tyana) Cyrus had occasion to execute two

30 e.g. Hieramenes (Xen. *Hell.* 2.1.8, Thuc. 8.58, TL 44c.12), Mithravahišt (AP 70: addressed with a quasi-pharaonic formula), Bagamarazdiya (named on a seal from Upper Egypt: Aimé-Giron 1939:45), Armantidata, Spentadata (P. Aram. Berlin 23000 = Grelot 1972:no. 109), Šytrḥʾ or Mytrḥʾ, the army chief (Smith & Kuhrt 1982), Asaph, keeper of a royal *paradeisos* (*Neh.* 2.8). Such a list could easily be greatly extended.

31 e.g. *dassija* (? = OP *daši-/dašya, 'expert': Zadok 1976b:5 f.): BE 10.91, ROMCT 2.48; *mar sipri* ('agent'): Pohl 1.61, Michigan 89; *mašennu*: TuM 2/3 147, cf. p. 133; *viθfrasa: cf. n. 44; scribe: cf. n. 39; and (of course) 'servant/slave' (BE 10.84–5, VS 4.152).

32 *Philoi*: Xen. *An.* 1.9.31, *Oec.* 4.19 (Other satraps: e.g. Nep. *Dat.* 9.2, Polyaen. 7.23.1. The King: Diod. 15.10.3, 16.50.7, 17.35.2 f., Plut. *Them.* 29, *Mor.* 174B, Agath. 472 F6, Hdt. 7.39.1). *Homotrapezoi*: Xen. *An.* 1.8.25, 9.31. (Other satraps: Xen. *Cyr.* 8.6.11, 14. The King:Hdt. 3.132, Xen. *Cyr.* 8.1.39, 6.11, 14, *Oec.* 4.8, Ctes. 688 F14 (43), Heraclid. 689 F2). *Skeptoukhoi*: Xen. *An.* 1.6.11, 8.28. (The King: id. *Cyr.* 8.3.15). Cunaxa cavalry: Xen. *An.* 1.8.6, 21 f. This is the same group as οἱ περὶ αὐτόν in ibid. 1.5.7, 6.4 (they wear the same fine clothes as a *skeptoukhos* (1.8.28) and are addressed as *philoi*). On royal friends/benefactors cf. Wiesehöfer 1980.

33 *Neh.* 4.23, 5.10, 14–18. cf. also Sanballat's companions (ibid. 4.2.).

34 Cf. Xen. *An.* 1.6.10—assuming (cf. 6–8) that Orontes had been a *philos* like those, including his relatives, who tried and condemned him.

35 Diod. loc. cit. implies they included persons of high status from outside Spithridates' satrapy (e.g. Atizyes, satrap of Phrygia; Mithrobuzanes, hyparch of Cappadocia) and the royal *syngeneia* is a well-attested honorific order whose members are not permanently attendant upon the king (cf. Arr. *An.* 7.11.1, 6, Xen. *Cyr.* 1.4.27, 2.2.31, Diod. 16.50.7, 17.35,3, Heraclid. 689 F5, Curt. 3.3.21, 25, 6.2.7, *I Esdr.* 3.4 f., 442, Joseph. *AJ* 11.34 f.—some of these texts imply that the relatives are a separate, higher status group, from mere *philoi*). On the other hand an élite cavalry unit of 1000 *syngeneis* appears at Gaugamela (Arr. *An.* 3.11.5, Diod. 17.59.2—and cf. perhaps the two units of 1000 picked horse in Hdt. 7.40 f.), and one might think that the satrap's court cavalry, imitative of the King's (Xen. *Cyr.* 8.6.10), was a copy of these 'Relative Cavalry'.

36 Hdt. 8. 85, Thuc. 1.129.3, Arr. *An.* 3.27, 37, Strab. 724, Aelian *VH* 12.40 etc.

dignitaries, one of whom had the title 'royal *phoinikistēs*', i.e. scribe (Xen. *An.* 1.2.20, Lewis 1977:25 n. 134). This person was presumably a subordinate of Cyrus within the Cappadocian satrapy, and the title recalls Herodotus' statement that every hyparch (the context shows this means, or includes, satraps) had a royal *grammateus* (3.128.4). Spiegelberg's translation of a demotic letter of Pherendates includes a 'royal scribe' among its signatories (1928:605 f.), although a more recent rendering (Hughes ap. Porten 1968:56) expels the word 'royal'. In any event, this text, together with signature formulae in Aramaic satrapal letters[37] and in Elamite letters from Pharnaces at Persepolis,[38] seems to reveal high functionaries in what can be called a satrapal chancellery, viz. a chancellor, a scribe, and other persons who communicate between the two.[39] (It is important to note that these persons include many non-Iranians, and one of them is called Yauna, 'the Greek'.) Some have also seen the Chancellor in the mysterious personage at Memphis to whom one Petesis appealed for protection against enemies at El Hibeh.[40] He is clearly a high personage (though subordinate to the 'Master of Egypt'—satrap or king?), addressed in quasi-pharaonic terms, possessor of a priesthood once the preserve of the Saite governor of upper Egypt, and surrounded by his own entourage of 'notables' as well as Egyptian subordinates.[41] His demotic title is one used later of Hellenistic *dioikētai*, but it appears only once more in the Persian period, where it is held by an Egyptian.[42] Alternative identifications include the satrap himself (Bresciani 1969:343) or the satrap's *juridicus* (Seidl 1956:33). For the latter idea titular parallels could be adduced from Babylonia—the 'judge of the satrap Gobryas'[43] and the '*databara* of (the satrap) Artareme' (PBS 2/1 34, 185, Stolper 1974:134 n. 67), of whom the latter is a Babylonian, despite his Iranian title. (Of course, titular parallel is no guarantee at all of substantial similarity.) And an Egyptian Aramaic text in turn mentions a *ptyprsn*—commonly interpreted as OP **patifrasa*, i.e. inspector (cf. the cognate **frasaka* of Beyond the River (*Ezra* 5.6, 6.6) and of the *mašennu* household (below, p. 133))—who is active at Memphis and could also be relevant.[44]

[37] AP 26.22 f.: 'Anani the scribe (and) chancellor (*bʿl ṭʿm*). Nabuaqab wrote it' (judging from handwriting neither is the scribe of the *letter*). AD 4, 6–10: all have the formula 'X is cognizant of this order (*ydʿ ṭʿm znh*), Y is scribe' (again palaeographic arguments show Y is not the actual writer).
Note also in Babylonia a Mede with the title *bal te-e-mu* who appears in Michigan 89 (a 'palace account' text) in some connection with the satrap Gobryas.

[38] See Hallock 1969: 51 f., Hinz 1971:310 f., Lewis 1977:10, n. 38, Stolper 1984:305. Up to three persons are named, a scribe (often Iranian, even though the texts are Elamite—hence not the writer) and two others.

[39] A 'royal scribe' appears in YOS 7.114, but he is actually a temple official (see below p. 151). Note also a palace scribe (CT 22.242)—perhaps involved in inspecting royal workers—and the King's Son's scribe (Cyr. 177, 199, 364). For scribes associated with satraps or governors cf. BE 9.48 (Rušunpati, scribe of Artareme, and landowner), Camb. 344 (of the governor of Egypt), Pohl 1.61 (of Gobryas the elder), PBS 2/1 70, 72, 133, BE 10.101, 118, CBS 12985 (Gobryas the younger), Amherst 258 (Uštanu). These need not be very senior persons (cf. Zadok 1978:70) though the Iranian Rušunpati could have been.

[40] P. Rylands 9.1–5. The word is *pꜣ prʿḥ* (Parker 1961:181). For identification with the chancellor cf. Ray n.d.

[41] Master of Egypt: 2/16. Pharaonic address: 3/11 (and cf. 2/3, said to recall Egyptian idiom for the pharaoh's travelling court). Prophet of Amun, once a priesthood of the Saite Master of Shipping: 8/2. Notables: 3/4, 4/12 (so too the Master of Shipping: e.g. 7/1, 10/2). Powerful subordinate agents: 1/1, 2/5, 3/5 ff., 5/2 f.

[42] Unpubl. Saqqara papyrus, mentioned in Tait 1977:30 f., and dated no more exactly than 525–332 BC. The holder is one Udjahorresnet, but there is apparently no particular indication of connection with the famous homonym (cf. p. 4).

[43] PBS 2/1 105, 133, 224, BE 10.84, 97, 128, CBS 12961, 12966.

[44] AP 37.3, 12. Compare Lloyd 1983:334, Ray n.d. Note, however, that the supposed Akkadian version of the same OP word in BE 10.97 (where the person involved is also a 'judge of the satrap

The 'royal' scribe is not the only 'royal' official encountered in provincial contexts. A number of titles of this sort will be encountered in various contexts later in this paper, but this is the appropriate place to mention one with which readers of Herodotus and other Greek sources will be familiar, namely the 'royal judges'. These are persons appointed for life who 'try cases among the Persians and interpret ancestral customs' (Hdt. 3.31.2). They are often found in the entourage of the king himself,[45] but the status was consistent with holding high office far from the royal court,[46] in which case, however, it becomes effectively an honorific rank rather than an administrative position. Royal judges also appear in non-Greek sources. In Cyr. 312 a court variously called 'the king's nobles and the judges of Cyrus, king of Babylon, king of lands' or 'the nobles and judges in charge of the palace' deals with a marriage contracted in somewhat dubious circumstances. The setting of the affair is evidently exalted (one of the parties being a palace official who denied having acted as witness to the union), and the tribunal seems to be one within the palace and (witness the unusual use of the actual king's name) one standing in quite a close relationship with the monarch. We might therefore be dealing here with royal judges of the sort found in Greek sources. It is much less certain that this is the case in three other documents in which royal judges (YOS 7.159, 189) or 'the royal court-house' (YOS 7.31) are, a little surprisingly, concerned with thefts of temple property (San Nicolò 1932:338 suggested that we are dealing here with an appeal or with a case in which one party was not a temple-member); and the significance of the 'judge of the palace gate' and the 'man set over the *data*' who are encountered simply as witnesses of a determination of monthly rations (VS 6.128) is decidedly opaque.

Egyptian documents provide us with a single attestation of 'royal judges' at Elephantine (AP 1.3), a text in which they are responsible, together with the garrison commander, for reaching a decision about what may be colonial allotments (see below n. 150). It is hard to be sure whether they actually constitute a higher board than the 'provincial judges' of AP 16.7 and 27.9 or indeed than 'Damidata and his colleagues the judges' in AP 6.6.[47] (After all, 'royal' sometimes simply designates someone who is part of the Persian system—? i.e. on Persian rations—not merely of the native one,[48] and the 'Royal House' of Elephantine might as well be called a 'provincial' treasury [see below pp. 128].) The fact that in AP 16 the provincial judges appear to sit with the *prtky'* (assessors) of the garrison commander (Porten 1968:47, Grelot 1972:134), not with the latter himself, might seem to support a differentiation of the 'provincial' and 'royal' boards. However, a

Gobryas'), PBS 2/1 63, 73 should perhaps in view of a more recently published text, ROMCT 2.36, be read differently and derived from OP *viθfrasa ('court interrogator'?). Whatever the correct reading the document only mentions this official as a witness and therefore casts no light on his functions.

[45] Hdt. 3.14.5, 31.2, Plut. *Artox*. 29. Diod. 15.10, Ctes 688 F27 (70) presumably also refer to royal judges.

[46] Hdt. 5.25 (Otanes, 'general of the coast'), 7.194 (Sandoces, hyparch of Cyme).

[47] Other (plain) judges appear in AP 6, 8, 16, 42, 45 (cf. Porten 1968:153), Saqqara 16, 27, 30a, 79, 121. The only Iranian besides Damidata is Paisana (AP 42.2, cf. 37.9, 40.2), apparently at Memphis; he, too, could be a royal judge. *Databara* appear in Saqqara 13 (mentioning their 'chiefs'), 14 (where they issue an order, *ṭʿm*). In the Murašu texts judges before whom documents are drawn up are normally Babylonian, but at least one Iranian Judge of the Sin Canal appears, Urdatu = *Xvardata (Cardascia 1951:20 n. 1, Hinz 1975:100).

[48] e.g. Ashor 'the royal builder' (AP 15), Ashanyahu 'the royal servant' (Stern 1982:207), Abla 'the royal boatman' (Peek 19).

homonym of the garrison-commander is mentioned in the preceding line of this lacunose text as one of three 'judges', and the three may after all be the commander plus two 'provincial' judges. Moreover, the Jews' claim in AP 27 that the destruction of their temple should be investigated by provincial judges, *typty* and **gaušaka* seems a little odd if there was in fact a higher judicial authority whose area of activity included the Elephantine garrison (as did that of the royal judges of AP 16). Of course, it is not impossible that the royal judges were too grand to undertake investigation themselves or that the anonymous addressee of the appeal in AP 27 was actually one such royal judge.

In the case of the satrap's royal scribe, at least, it seems reasonable to suppose that he is appointed by the King, and he could therefore be construed as among other things a royal spy upon satrapal loyalty (cf. Xenophon's remarks, *Cyr.* 8.6.1 f., on the role of royally appointed garrison commanders). Xenophon also mentions annual inspections of satrapies by the king or his agents, who could include the 'King's Eye', a personage attested (in largely uninformative contexts) in other Greek texts.[49] Another passage of Xenophon (*Cyr.* 8.2.10 f.) is sometimes taken to deny that there was only one 'Kings's Eye' and to suggest a whole spy system of Kings' Eyes and Ears, an interpretation in connection with which one could adduce the Egyptian provincial official called **gaušaka* or 'listener' (AP 27.9), the *didakka* of BE 10.118 (chief of the *hadru* of 'army scribes') and the postulated **didiyaka* (Hinz 1975:98 f.) of the Persepolis documents (both these words have the sense 'one who sees'). But more careful reading of Xenophon suggests a different interpretation. His point is not that there were many officials called King's Eyes and Ears (for however many there were they would all be open to the criticism of their utility which Xenophon advances against *the* King's Eye, viz. that everyone knew who they were) but that, although there *was* a single, very senior King's Eye, the King's practice of rewarding information *from whatever source* means that people behave as though he has many eyes and ears and is always looking and listening, because they have no idea who might betray any seditious utterances. In Xenophon's view, therefore, surveillance is above all informal, exemplified by the sort of mutual criticism of officials to which he refers in *Oeconomicus* 4.9. Moreover, the whole run of Greek evidence requires us to postulate no more than a single King's Eye and no King's Ears at all. There need be no conflict between Greek and non-Greek sources on this point: after all neither the *gaušaka* nor the officials in Babylonia and Persis is actually attested as a spy.

2 PROVINCIAL SUBDIVISIONS OF SATRAPIES

Among officials associated personally with the satrap one particular group consists of their so-called hyparchs.[50] Occasionally such persons are also described as

[49] *Cyr.* 8.6.16, *Oec.* 4.6; perhaps some royal journeying in Persepolis texts or e.g. Ael. *VH* 1.31 f. belongs to inspection trips. King's Eye: Aesch. *Pers.* 980, Hdt. 1.114.2, Arist. *Acharn.* 92 f., Plut. *Artox.* 12.

[50] Tamos (Thuc. 8.87.1), Arsaces (ibid. 108.4), Stages (ibid. 16), all hyparchs of Tissaphernes; Ariaeus, hyparch of Cyrus (Xen. *An.* 1.8.5), Condalus, hyparch of Mausolus (Ps. Ar. *Oec.* 1348a18). Additionally, the evidence about Philiscus (Dem. 23.141 f., Xen. *Hell.* 7.1.27, Diod. 15.70.2) and Zenis and Mania (Xen. *Hell.* 3.1.10 f.) amounts to their designation as hyparchs of Ariobarzanes and Pharnabazus respectively, as well as making clear that they are examples of a whole class of similar satrapal hyparchs. (So too, perhaps, Xen. *An.* 1.2.20: Cyrus executes a royal scribe and ἑτερόν τινα τῶν ὑπάρχων δυνάστην).

hyparchs of particular regions, and this was probably true in other, though not necessarily all, cases.[51] This brings us, therefore, to the various geographical subdivisions of a satrapy. Attested titles in Greek sources draw our attention to such areas as Ionia (hyparch: Thuc. 8.31.2), Ionia, Aeolis and neighbouring areas (satrap *alias epimeletēs*: Diod. 14.19.6), Troadic Aeolis (satrap *alias* hyparch: Xen. *Hell.* 3.1.10 f.), Lemnos (hyparch: Hdt. 5.27), Lycia (*arkhontes*: FX VI pp. 32 f. = SEG 27.942), and Cataonia (*Aspis qui Cataoniam tenebat*: Nep. *Dat.* 4.1). There is also the case of Sogdiana, which seems to have hyparchs but no satrap, unless we assume that Sogdiana was a subordinate part of the Bactrian satrapy (not something clearly attested). The relevant sources give varying hints about the internal nature of such areas. In Lycia it is still the (Carian) satrap whose authorization is required for the Xanthian decree which incidentally informs us about the *arkhontes*. In Troadic Aeolis we have a region of small *poleis* held by the hyparch's garrisons, who may be her 'private' troops rather than mercenaries strictly in the pay of her superior Pharnabazus. (I believe this to be the most logical explanation of Pharnabazus' apparent and imprudent failure to pay these mercenaries after Mania's murder by her son-in-law: cf. Tuplin n.d.(b).) To Pharnabazus she owes tribute and military service (Xen. *Hell.* 3.1.12–13). The hyparch of Ionia is similarly found in a military context (cf. n. 51) as is another of Tissaphernes' hyparchs, Stages, who is twice active in the same area of central Ionia but never actually designated hyparch of a particular region (cf. n. 51). I think that he fairly clearly *has* such a region, but it will be smaller than the likes of 'Ionia' or 'Lycia'. Not all hyparchs are alike, and in the last analysis the title lays more stress upon their subordination to someone else than upon their control of a particular sort of 'hyparchy'. (Hence, of course, the word can as well be used of a satrap in his capacity as subordinate of the king: cf. n. 22). Another approach to subdivisions of western Anatolian satrapies has been made by Sekunda n.d.(a) and (b), who sees Hellespontine Phrygia and Lydia as consisting of a small number of what he calls 'dukedoms', each providing contributions to the satrapal cavalry *via* ties of personal loyalty between individual cavalrymen and the 'duke'. There may be something in this, but identification of actual 'dukes' is tricky. Spithridates is the paradigmatic case (Xen. *Hell.* 3.4.10, 4.1.21, *An.* 6.4.24, 5.7 f., Hell. Oxy. 21), but Itamenes, for example, is on Xenophon's evidence (*An* 7.8.15) too lowly a figure to be another instance (see Tuplin n.d.(b)).

At the other end of the empire Briant 1982a: 197 f. has interpreted the evidence about Sogdian hyparchs in the Alexander historians as revealing a series of dynastic realms centred upon *petrai*, defensible strongholds housing stores of tribute collected by the hyparch-dynasts from their subjects, but this seems to me to go beyond the actual evidence for Achaemenid conditions, which treats the *petrai* as places of refuge rather than standard local 'capitals'—though we may well believe in the hyparchs' right to mobilize the populace for military purposes.[52]

[51] Tamos (cf. n. 50) is hyparch of Ionia (Thuc. 8.31.2). Zenis and Mania control a specific, tribute-paying area (Xen. *Hell.* 3.1.10 f.). Note that Stages is twice associated with the Teos/Colophon area (Thuc. 8.16, Xen. *Hell.* 1.2.5), Arsaces with the Adramyttium/Antandros area (Thuc. 8.108).

[52] Briant 1982a: 197 f. Relevant sources are Arr. *An.* 4.18.4 f., Curt. 7.11.11 f., Polyaen. 4.3.19 (Rock of Ariomazes, Sogdian Rock), Arr. *An.* 4.21.1 f., Curt. 8.2.19 f., Plut. *Alex.* 58, Strabo 11.11.4 (Rock of Chorienes *or* Sisimithres). Sogdian hyparchs: Arr.

Turning to areas where the evidence is predominantly non-Greek we may note first the case of Babylonia. The relevant evidence comes in various, not easily interrelatable forms. (i) The Nabondius Chronicle (ANET 306) reports that Cyrus appointed governors (*paḫat*) in Babylonia immediately after the conquest; but the only more precise information in that text concerns Ugbaru, governor of Gutium, who represents a rather special case (cf. Zadok 1981/2:138 n. 65). (ii) A number of documents refer to 'administrative districts' (*piḫatu/paḫatu* = *NÁM*) named after prominent cities, viz. Babylon (common), Borsippa (VS 3.182, 5.48, 92, TEBR 80), Dilbat (VS 6.71, Dar. 265, 295), Kish (Dar. 194, 245), and Sippar (Cyr. 26). The terminology continues neo-Babylonian practice, so we can probably add Nippur, Uruk, and Der to the list, even though they are only attested before 539. The purely geographical nature of the references in the texts means that no officials clearly associated with these districts are mentioned. One would expect the man in charge to be a *bel piḫati*, but this is an excessively vague term, equally applicable at various levels of secular and temple administration, and one could only identify a particular *bel piḫati* as governor of an administrative district of the sort in question here if there were appropriately specific evidence in addition to the mere title—which seems never to be the case. In any event the areas in question appear to be of relatively limited extent (considering, for example, how close Babylon, Dilbat, Borsippa, and Kish are to one another—they would all fit within the presumed area of the single Palestinian 'province' of Dor [see below]), and the terminology seems to disappear in later Achaemenid texts; so we are possibly not dealing with anything of great significance in our present context. (iii) The term *piḫatu* is occasionally (e.g. PBS 2/1 43, 72) used of canal-managers and the very existence of such officials (under whatever title) and of 'judges of the Sin Canal' and the like (cf. n. 47) doubtless shows that canals constituted administrative units. They might even be regarded as royal administrative units, insofar as the managers were crown-agents (cf. p. 133). But they are also, of course, extremely specialized and extremely local units: to speak of canal 'provinces' (Zadok 1978:281, 309) is a misleading perpetuation of Akkadian terminological vagueness. (iv) More important here are the various 'governors' whose title and/or area of competence suggests a higher position in the hierarchy, e.g. the governor of the Sealand (the area of the Tigris/Euphrates mouths) whose deputy appears (in a private capacity) in YOS 7.106, or Siḫa 'the satrap' (PBS 2/1 2: the Persian word is used in Akkadian transcription), or Belšunu, governor (LU.NAM) or 'satrap' of Babylon in 421–414 under the Persian satrap Gobryas, who is on record both in business documents relating to his and other proprietors' land and as adjudicator of a dispute about missing temple property (Stolper n.d.(a), (b)), and who is clearly too grand a figure to be merely in charge of what the earlier documents call the *piḫatu* of Babylon.

Other relatively copious material concerns Beyond the River (of which, incidentally, Belšunu was later satrap) and Egypt. In the former biblical texts, confirmed by inscribed coins and seals and by papyri from Wadi Daliyeh (Samaria)

An. 4.1.5, 21.1 (class), 4.21.2, 9 (Chorienes: Curtius calls him, under the name Sisimithres, a *satrapes*—just as Xenophon will use *satrapeuein* of the hyparch Mania, *Hell.* 3.1.10).

and Elephantine, reveal 'provinces' (*phwh* or *m^edinah*) such as Judah and Samaria (and also, less fully attested, Gaza, Ashdod, Dor, and others), under the command of native governors (*pḥt* or *peḥah*)—in the case of Samaria a succession of members of the same family—and with other officials such as prefects (*sgn'*), treasurers, and scribes (all appear in the Samaria papyri) and judges, commissioners, overseers, and chief officers (*Ezra* 4.8 f.—if these indeed *are* provincial officials).[53] On conventional interpretations of *Nehemiah* 3 the province of Judah at any rate was further subdivided into districts (*pelekh*) and half-districts (*ḥasi pelekh*) under chiefs called *sar* (Stern 1982:237 f., identifying 6 *pelekh*), but it has recently been suggested that the text is actually talking about groups of workers doing conscript labour (on the rebuilding of Jerusalem) as a form of tributary obligation (Demsky 1983, adducing Akkadian *pilku*). Be that as it may, the provinces certainly continue Assyrian and neo-Babylonian divisions and are perhaps the type of thing the author of *Esther* had in mind when saying that the empire consisted of 127 provinces (1.1, 8.9, 9.30); the word used is the same and (granted that some satrapies may have been richer in subdivisions than others) the total is reasonably consistent with the number of provinces per satrapy to be presumed for Beyond the River and for the other terminologically parallel case, Egypt.

Here there seems no reason to doubt the continued existence of the traditional nomes of Upper and Lower Egypt, though the direct evidence in Egyptian texts is not copious.[54] Equally, it is clear that there were units called 'provinces', two being attested by name, Thebes and *Tštrs* (the south).[55] Although the latter is designated a *tš* in P. Berlin 3110, which is a standard word for nome, it is evident that the provinces were larger than nomes, since Aramaic evidence implies that *Tštrs*, which includes Elephantine (AP 27.9, P. Berlin 13582), is adjacent to Thebes (AP 24.33 f.) and pre-Persian period evidence for the term is against its application just to Elephantine or to an area larger than the Elephantine nome but smaller than the whole region down-river as far as Thebes.[56] These provinces may be an innovation as compared with the Saite period, when there is no evidence for *Tštrs* as an administrative unit with associated officials (contrast a XXII dynasty reference to the scribe of the royal account of the *tš* of *Tštrs*[57]). There is also no evidence for Persian subsatrapal units *larger* than the province, for the concept *Ptores* (also 'the south') variously used of an area starting in Middle Egypt (P. Ryl. 9 1/2 (Persian),

[53] Stern 1982:237 ff., 1984:78 ff. Stern believes the province of Judah was only created after 450 BC.

[54] Hdt. 2.164.2, asserts the apparently contemporary division of Egypt *kata nomous*; cf. 2.4, 42, 46, 71, 91, 152, 165–6, 169, 172, 177. For possible nomes in Egyptian sources cf. (*tš*) P. Cairo 50060, P. Vienna 10.150, P. Louvre E 9292, Edfu Donation Text (Meeks 1972:passim); (*qʿḥ*) P. Loeb 46, P. Strasburg 5; also Posener 1936:no. 1 A1, D31, 41. The Aramaic word *spytkn* in AP 26.9, 22 f. has been derived from an older Egyptian term for nome, viz. *spꜣt*, yielding the title 'chief of carpenters in charge of the nome' (Grelot 1972:288).

[55] Thebes: AP 24.18b, 36, 37.6, 68.11r.2 *Tštrs*: AP 27.9 (cf. 24.39, 42, P. Berlin 13582, where the term province is omitted, and P. Berlin 3110 where it is called *tš*). Anonymous: AP 16.7, 17.1, BP 11.11. The relevant word appears in fragmentary and unintelligible contexts in Saqqara 101.6, 103.2.

[56] Relevant Saite texts: P. Turin 246, 246B, 247, 248 (many occurrences in definitions of site of land: written variously *Tꜣ-štꜣrsj* ('south district') or *Tꜣštꜣ-rs-Njw·t* ('south district of Thebes', i.e. area south of Thebes); the region includes Hermonthis); P. Louvre 7845A (where it includes land 'west of Thebes', i.e. an area on the west bank of the Nile opposite Thebes, which can have been in a different area from Thebes itself: it was in the Pathyrite nome in hellenistic times), P. Louvre 7858.

[57] Louvre Stele C112 (cf. Griffith 1909:143 n. 2). It has been claimed that this *Tštrs* stretched at least to Asyut, though the only evidence is the geographical spread of the scribe's priesthoods.

7/13 (Saite)) and (apparently) of the whole area south of the delta (P. Bibl. Nat. 215 verso) *can* be a purely geographical concept in both cases. (*Ptores*, in the larger sense, is last attested as an administrative unit long before the end of the Saite era.[58]) On the other hand, the (different) hieroglyphic terms used in the titles of Atiyawahy 'governor (*rpᶜt*) of Coptos' (Posener 1936: nos. 26, 30) and anonymous 'governors (*hꜣtjᶜ*) of nomes and cities' (ibid. no. 6 II.6) might be evidence for city-governors, including ones in nome-capitals, as distinct from nomarchs, though the former at least is archaic and could be essentially honorific, like his other title *srs* of Persia (Posener 1936: 24–30, Schott 1967: 88 f.). (This possibility is a perennial problem of Egyptian titulature.) Granted a province, nome, and (perhaps) city hierarchy, some attested officials fit in easily, e.g. the scribes, judges, **tipati* and **gaušaka* of the province (AP 16.6, 17.1, 27.9),[59] the 'chief (...) of the nome' (P. Cairo 50060) and 'scribe of the nome' (P. Vienna 10.150),[60] the commander (*rab hayla*) of the Elephantine/Syene garrison establishment (a person seen as much in judicial roles as in strictly military ones),[61] the eponyms (? commanders) of the *degelin* within the garrison.[62] But there are also various problems.

1) The *azdakara* (an Iranian title) who appear once might be city, nome, or provincial officials,[63] and Mithridates 'the boatman' of AP 26 is of uncertain status. Is he the chief of a 'house of boats' of the sort attested at Saqqara (Aimé-Giron 1931: nos. 5.11, 11a.4) or merely a subordinate official within such an insitution; and does the institution, if we are right to postulate it at all, count as part of the provincial structure or stand in a more direct relation to the satrap, to whom the matter in issue in AP 26, repair of a boat, has been directly referred?

2) P. Berlin 13552 speaks of the *tš* of Osorwer, an Egyptian whose house at Elephantine is a possible grain-storage place in P. Loeb 1. (He is also named in P. Berlin 13562, 13571.) Porten 1968: 45 n. 26 identifies him as a *fratarak* (see below), and wonders whether he was actually a Persian who had taken an Egyptian name (for which practice cf. Posener 1936: no. 33). Might he not alternatively be a nomarch?

3) In BP 8.23, (6 Tishri (VII) Darius year 8) the *rab haila* Waidrang is given the additional title *hptḥpt'*. There is little doubt that this *means* 'guardian of the/a seventh' (OP **haftaxva-pātā-*: Henning 1968, Bogoliubov 1974, Hinz 1975: 46), but the proper interpretation of this is another matter. I have just two observations.

[58] In P. Rylands 9.5/14, 18, 6/1 f., 7/11 f., 10/1 ff. it is the area from the south watch tower of Memphis (some 60 km south of Memphis: Yoyotte 1972) to Elephantine and is ruled by the Master of Shipping. In 10/8 it is designated *tš*.

[59] On *gaušaka* cf. above p. 120. **Tipati* (Ar. *typty'*) has been variously explained (Porten 1968: 50 n. 83). Hinz 1975: 92 denies that it recurs in Elamite garb in PF 1250, 1902. Possible provincial *accountants*: AP 68.11r.2, 11v.1.

[60] The former pays temple tax; the income of the latter's office is 'given' to another party like the income of religious offices in many other documents. Both are probably not directly part of the *Persian* administration.

[61] Judicial: AP 1.3, 16.7, 20.4, 25.24, 38.3, BP 8.2 f. Other: AP 30.7 (leading Egyptian troops against the Jewish temple), BP 13.7 (fragmentary), Grelot 1972: no. 75 (dedicatory inscription).

[62] Cf. Porten 1968: 29f., who also notes 'centurions'; and add Saqqara 3.6, 15.2, 63.3, 113.2. The Persons named in the formula *lyr* PN (under control of PN) in Aimé-Giron 1931: 5.11f., 11a.1, 2, 28.2 may be other such military officers.

[63] AP 17.5.7. Grelot 1972: 282 restores the text to locate them in 'the fort Elephantine'. One could as well read 'fort Syene' or even 'the province'. They are associated with the scribes of the province. The same text mentions 'Bigdan and his colleagues' without surviving title.

(i) The suggestion (Kraeling ad BP loc. cit., Henning 1968:138) that *hptḫpt'* represents a step on the promotion-ladder between *rab haila* and *fratarak* (the latter an office Waidrang held by 410 BC) is somewhat insecure, since Waidrang is once again plain *rab hayla* in AP 25.24 (3 Kislev (IX) Darius year 8) and it might be the case that *hptḫpt'* was simply a regular ancillary title of the *rab haila*, normally ignored in Jewish Aramaic documents. (ii) The recurrence of *hptḫ* (i.e. 'seventh') in Saqqara 63.4 in a fragmentary context also naming *degel* members (i.e. soldiers) suggests that we may be dealing with command of military units not administrative ones. It is certainly not safe to assume that our picture of the satrapy or its provinces/nomes (cf. Hinz loc. cit., Porten 1968:44) has to accommodate their division into seven districts.

4) P. Berlin 13582 refers to one Prnw as being 'in charge of *Tštrs* and the (?) fortress of Syene' in 488/7. The view that Prnw is identical not only with a homonym at Elephantine in P. Loeb 1 (which he is) but also with Prntt = Pherendates, satrap of Egypt before and after the date of P. Berlin 13582 (P. Berlin 13539–40) is incorrect. The names are (*pace* Spiegelberg 1928, Zauzich 1978) different (see Hughes 1984)—the non-Egyptologist can only wonder bemusedly why anyone should ever have thought otherwise. We do not therefore have to explain why a satrap should temporarily have a title relating solely to southern Egypt. But there is still a problem in the combination of the hierarchical levels of province (*Tštrs*) and city ('the (?) fortress of Syene' probably does not distinguish between the town and some institution within it in view of the interchangeable use of 'Syene' and 'the fort Syene' in Aramaic texts). Do we conclude that a provincial governor was normally also city-prefect of the provincial capital? Or does the specific reference here rather imply that these would usually be separate offices?[64]

5) A number of Aramaic documents use the titles *fratarak* and *sgn'*, whose interpretation poses certain difficulties. The *fratarak* (always an Iranian) appears both at Saqqara (Saqqara 27.5—the text also mentions judges) and Elephantine (AP 20.4, 27.4, 30.7 = 31.6). AP 20.4 names him as co-member with the *rab hayla* of a Tribunal of Nefa', and it is clear from the order of names in that text and from the personal career of Waidrang that the office is superior to that of *rab hayla*. Although Waidrang *writes* to his son and successor as *rab hayla* to order the attack on the Jewish temple (AP 30.7 = 31.6), it need not follow that his normal residence was not Elephantine/Syene. Several possible interpretations of the *fratarak* suggest themselves. (a) Nomarch (Porten 1968:47, Grelot 1972:200)—but I think one might expect nomarchs to be Egyptian, though, of course, the border nome and the Memphite nome could be exceptional. (b) A provincial military commander-—the trouble with this is that it involves postulating an official for whose existence there is no independent evidence. (c) Provincial governor (Bresciani 1969:324 f., Ray n.d.). This is the best solution. AP 37.6 is not a serious objection, since the asumption that it designates the Thebes provincial governor as *pqyd* is unfounded;[65] and although Palestinian parallels (p. 123) might lead one to expect the term

[64] Two more apparent Persian officials on record at Elephantine in the same period are Artabanus (P. Loeb 1) and Ravaka (P. Berlin 23584).

[65] The word may actually be a verb, not a title, and even if not (so Porten 1968:54 n. 102) could designate an estate-manager (this being the title's association elsewhere in Egypt (AD passim) and Babylonia (cf. p. 134)).

pḥt, the only attestation of that title in Egyptian Aramaic is in reference to a plurality of evidently lower-rank officers (Bresciani 1960, Fitzmyer 1962) and we need not after all assume the Palestinian and Egyptian cases to be identical: the fact that the Egyptian provinces are a Persian innovation could account for a special (Iranian) title.

Sgn' differs from *fratarak* in two respects. Firstly, although it is not a specifically Iranian title, it is attested in two other parts of the empire. Samaria Papyrus 14 (cf. Cross 1974:18, 1986:7) is a document executed before 'Yeshua, son of Sanballat and Hanan the *sgn'*', the latter being therefore an associate/subordinate of the provincial governor (for other texts establish that Yeshua held that position). The word recurs in *Nehemiah* 5.17 of persons who ate at the governor's table in Judah, and Stern 1984:81 sees them as commanders of small military garrisons. Further east, one interpretation of the inscribed mortars, pestles, and plates found at Persepolis is that they refer to a hierarchy of officials in Arachosia, a treasurer responsible for three fortresses, each of which has a *sgn'* (? fortress commander) and sub-treasurer.[66] There is no proving that the officers in Palestine and Arachosia are substantially comparable with the Egyptian case (though they are at least all of lower stature than the provincial governor), but their existence makes it unsurprising that one should encounter *sgn'* in an Egyptian province. This, however, leads to the second difference between *fratarak* and *sgn'*. Whereas we do find references to actual, individual and named *frataraks*, the *sgn'* appears only in legal formulae which envisage or preclude legal proceedings 'before *sgn'* or judge' (AP 8.13, 10.13, 20) or 'before *sgn'* or lord' (AP 47.2, 7, BP 9.19, 10.13) or 'before *sgn'* or judge or lord' (BP 12.18). (We also once get 'before judge or lord' (BP 1.6).)[67] It is commonly supposed that 'lord' refers to the satrap or the *fratarak*, with *sgn'* therefore designating either the *fratarak* or the *rab hayla*. Of these the latter is preferable since it keeps the *sgn'* down to a level more consistent with that in non-Egyptian evidence. But it may be worth airing a different approach. The purpose of the formulae under discussion is evidently to preclude further legal activity 'in any court whatsoever'. But it is clear from particular cases that the legal problems of members of the Elephantine garrison could fall within the competence of various persons (the *fratarak*, the *rab hayla*, the latter's assessors, royal judges, provincial judges, plain unqualified judges), and if we essay precise identification of 'lord', *sgn'* and 'judge' we run the risk of rendering the formulae ineffective. Bearing in mind that all the terms are in themselves quite vague and capable of referring to a variety of specific officials,[68] it is possible that 'judge' covers any relevant official whose titular role is solely judicial and lord and/or *sgn'* covers other persons whose functions are wider than, though can include, the judicial. In

[66] Bowman 1970 publishes the texts, but they should be interpreted as by Levine 1972, Naveh/Sakhed 1973, Vogelsang 1985:85.

[67] For preclusion of suit without naming of possible judges cf. AP 5.8, 6.12, 8.14, 21, 9.15, 13.8 f., 14.7, 10, 15.25, 29, 20.10, 16, 25.10, 17, 28.12, 14, 43.8, BP 3.12, 4.12, 15, 22, 5.6, 15, 7.32, 8.5, 11.8, 12. Note also PBS 2/1 21, where suit is precluded before 'king, satrap or judge'.

[68] 'Lord' can be used of the satrap (AD 3.3, 4.2, 10.1, AP 16.8, 17.5, 27.2, perhaps 33.7, 13, 34.6) but also of lesser persons: estate holders (AD 7.4 f.), governor of Judah (AP 30.1 f.), anonymous addressee of AP 27, Mithravahist (AP 70), various Jews (AP 37.1, 38.1, 12, BP 13.1, 9). The word is not confined to Achaemenid Aramaic: cf. Dupont-Sommer 1948:43 f. (Saite). *Sgn'* can designate a 'chief' carpenter (AP 26.9, 22).

other words, the reference of lord and *sgn'* may differ depending on whether one or both are mentioned in the formula (thus helping to explain why the formula's variations do not apparently matter); and *sgn'* should be no more as the title of a particular official than is 'lord'. The argument would fall, of course, if anyone could demonstrate that the varied contents of the formula and the regular appearance of a title never attested in its own right in the Elephantine archives related to the particular and varied kinds of prospective legal action and point at issue. But to date there seems to be no reason to think that this is the case.

3 INDIVIDUAL PLACES AS ADMINISTRATIVE UNITS

After this prolonged consideration of material from Elephantine, we may turn to other evidence about cities or other individual places (as opposed to regions) which may count as administrative units. In fact, even villages could have their local authorities. The 10,000 had dealings with a *komarch* in northern Armenia,[69] while Saqqara 22 perhaps refers to a village elder (though in itself *qiryah* could mean 'town' as well as 'village'). One naturally assumes that these are native, and that they represent long established structures; Xenophon, though, does note that the Armenian *komarch* spoke Persian, as indeed did other inhabitants of a village in the same region (*An.* 4.5.10, 34). Iranian rule is pretty intrusive if a village-head can do to speak the conqueror's language. But at this level it is rather the intrusion of actual Iranians that is of particular interest, for the mere existence of manipulable local structures in any individual community, be they the magistrates of a *polis* or the officials of a Babylonian town,[70] is (as stressed at the outset) relatively banal. So far as cities are concerned, one could perhaps find this in the Iranian hyparchs of Sestos (Hdt. 7.33, 78, 9.115 f.) and Cyme (id. 7.194). Are they Persian city-governors imposed upon local administration? Should one assume that this was common, that it is reflected in Diodoran passages which report the issue of royal instructions 'to satraps and to cities' (14.80.7) or 'to satraps and the cities they ruled' (14.98.3)—the word satrap being used in both cases of a lowlier official than the satrapal viceroy—and that parallels can be found in the *praefectus* of Pasargadae (Curt. 5.6.10) or Damascus (id. 3.8.12, 13.2), Batis, the man in charge of Gaza in 333/2 (Arr. *An.* 2.25.4, Curt. 4.6.7, Joseph. 11.320), Rhathines the eparch of Gordium in 395 (Hell. Oxy. 21.6), the 'satraps' of Pura and Makkas in PF 679–681, or Atiyawahy the 'governor' of Coptos (p. 124)? The answer is probably no. The Sestos hyparch seems to be active in an area wider than just Sestos (he is therefore a type of regional hyparch), and the same was true at Cyme for all we know (or else the hyparch relates to the place's special role as fleet base). Indeed, it could be true

[69] Xen. *An.* 4.5.10, 24, 27–30, 32, 34–5, 6.1–3. There were several villlages in the vicinity (cf. 4.5.23 f., 30 f.) and at first sight two different komarchs are mentioned (4.5.10 and 4.5.24, with all subsequent references being to the latter), leaving open the possibility of a komarch for each village (cf. 24: 'the komarch of *this* village'). More probably however the komarch in 4.5.24–6.3 is in charge of all the villages (he has relatives in several (32) and it is he whom Cheirisophus and Xenophon later cross-examine), and when Cheirisophus and his contingent enter a village πρὸς τὸν κώμαρχην at 4.5.10 we should understand that they expected to find this one komarch but did not do so.

[70] e.g. *šakin temi* of Uruk (San Nicolò 1941:12 f.), Borsippa (VS 6.128) or Babylon (Camb. 276), *šangu* of Sippar (San Nicolò 1941:34), *šatammu* of Sippar (YOS 7.106), 'city-chief' (*ša muhhi* URU) of Sippar (Camb. 19) or Handidi (BE 8.80), NIN.KU of Babylon (Dar. 154, 206) or Kuta (BM 84.2–11.214), *šaknu* of Nippur (BE 9.23, 10.76, PBS 2/1 70—the city-quarters were under a *paqdu*: Zadok 1978:275).

in some of the non-Greek locations just mentioned, where one's greater uncertainty about the nature of *native* administrative institutions makes it dangerously easy to assume direct rule of a city (as opposed to a region centred upon a city) through an externally imposed official.[71]

Various other sorts of evidence confer special status upon individual places within a satrapy. The satrapal capital itself obviously comes into that category (when it can be identified), as do provincial capitals. But what about other locations? The evidence for satrapal palaces/residences beyond capitals is inadequate to lead to any particular conclusion.[72] That about treasuries is a little better. Major treasuries (places storing silver in sizeable quantities, as well as other valuables) were to be found in royal and satrapal capitals, and some of the vague references to 'the (royal) treasury' or the like may also relate to such installations.[73] Leaving aside Timaeus' claim that the Ephesian Artemision was rebuilt in the second half of the fourth century using Persian *parakatathekai* recovered from the temple, which may have little relevance to the ordinary system, even if it is credible at all,[74] several bodies of material do relate to treasury-sites of lower status. In Egypt there was a Royal House or Royal Treasury at Elephantine, which supplied payments in kind and in silver and is associable with 'officers', scribes, and treasury accountants.[75] The fact that the grain income in AP 24 is labelled as 'from *Tštrs*' or 'from Thebes' suggests that the treasury works at provincial level and we may assume that the presence of a treasury in a provincial capital was a standard phenomenon. The voluminous 'Philisto-Arabian', 'Philisto-Egyptian' and Yehud coinages will be a confirmation of this, if they were in fact minted at provincial treasuries (Stern 1982:221 f., 1984:111).

[71] In the case of Pura one should note that Karkiš 'satrap at Pura' and travelling thither in Year 21, month 7 (PF 681) may be the presumed satrap of Carmania, for whom cf. PF 1330 (same date).

[72] Possible examples: Hdt. 3.122 (Magnesia), *Neh.* 3.7 (Jerusalem), Diod. 16.41.5 (Sidon: cf. Clermont-Ganneau 1921, Contenau 1923), Xen. *An.* 1.4.10 (Belesys' palace in Syria), 3.4.24 (unattributed palace 8 days north of Nineveh), 4.4.2 (palace of satrap of Armenia), 4.4.7 (palace of hyparch of W. Armenia). Some *basileia* in E. Iran may be relevant (Arr. *An.* 3.25.1–6, 30.6, 4.5.3, Curt. 6.5.24, Strabo 723C). The *basileia* of Askalon (Ps. Scyl.78) is the seat of the governor of Ashdod, the Lachish residence that of the governor of Idumaea (Stern 1982:249). For residences/*paradeisoi* in satrapal capitals cf. Xen. *Hell.* 4.1.15 f. (Dascyleium), *Oec.* 4.20, Diod. 14.80.2 (Sardis), Xen. *An.* 1.2.7 (Celainai).

[73] Capitals: Susa: Hdt. 5.49, Polyclit. 128 F3, and cf. n. 109. Persepolis: Cameron 1948:9, Cahill 1985, Strabo 15.3.3, Curt. 5.5.2, (?) Nep. *Dat.* 5.3, Dinon 690 F23, and cf. n. 109. Pasargadae, Ecbatana: cf. n. 109. Babylon: Arr. *An.* 3.16.3, Curt. 5.1.20, *Ezra* 1.8 (?), 6.1 f., Strabo 731, and cf. text below. Memphis: (i) Temple of Ptah: cf. statue of Ptahhotep, 'treasury chief', found there (Cooney 1953) and references to 'stones of Ptah' (cf. n. 15); (ii) Royal House: Saqqara 17, 31, 83. (These need not be the same institution.) Sardis: Arr. *An.* 1.17.3, Diod. 17.21.7. Dascyleium: Hell. Oxy. 22.3 (?). Other items: Susa: *Esther* 3.9, 4.7. Egypt: Hdt. 2.149. Beyond the River: *Ezra* 6.4, 8, 7.20 f. (*I Esdr.* 6.25, 29). Tema: Donner-Röllig 1963:no. 228 (but I wonder if this royal treasury is really anything to do with Persia; the same doubt applies to the 'governor of Tema'—who is also son of the King of Lihyan—in Cross 1986b).

[74] Timae.556 F150b. Artemidorus dismissed the story, claiming that there were no *parakatathekai* and that if there had been they would have been burned.

[75] House: AP 2.12 f., 43.8, BP 11.6. Granary: AP 2.14, 11.6, (?)50.6, BP 3.9, 6.7, 10.4, 11.4. Overlap of terminology in AP 2, BP 11 guarantees their identity; and both are connected with payment of rations (BP 11.4, AP 2.5, 43.8) and salary (AP 2.16, 11.16). The *gwrn'* (granary) which appears as store-place for cereals not yet paid as rations (AP 24.41) and as the *royal* granary partly destroyed in the Elephantine riots (AP 27.5) is perhaps part of the same institution; AP 24 shows that it supplies both Syene and Elephantine. In P. Loeb 1 corn is to be 'assigned to the treasury' (translation doubtful)—perhaps at Elephantine. The 'bank' of the man in charge of *Tstrš* and Thebes (P. Berlin 13582) is obscure. AP 2.12 f. apparently names 'scribes of the treasury' (*'wṣr'*); and the treasury (*gnz'*) accountants of AP 26.4, 23 are evidently officials of the Royal House.

Babylonian texts refer to a considerable variety of storehouses, treasuries and the like. Many are of no particular relevance here, but at least seven categories of 'royal' or otherwise special storage places present themselves. A number of Murašu archive texts from Nippur disclose the existence of the *nakandu šarri*, 'royal storehouse' or 'treasury', which was in the control successively of Manuštanu (the king's nephew) and Artaḫsar (see below p. 135) and employed the labour of a category of dependent person (the *šušanne*). Unfortunately nothing much emerges about its functions as an institution (Stolper 1974:131 f.). A different set of Murašu texts repeatedly names the *bit šarri* (royal house) as recipient of *ilku* (or a part thereof) paid on bow fiefs (cf. pp. 153), and the same name recurs in an earlier text, VS 3.159, where a tax called *miksu* is paid to the royal house in accordance with royal law. (Ellis 1974 discusses the earlier history of *miksu* but is unhelpful on the Achaemenid period. In CT 22.5 it appears to denote a canal toll. The word appears in Aramaic guise in Egypt as a silver tax in Saqqara 19.) It is at least possible, however, that in this document *bit šarri* is simply an abbreviation for the 'royal *bit miksu*', an institution (at or near Gibi) mentioned in ROMCT 2.35 as the locus of a slave-sale. It is not unlikely that the (Egyptian) *rab miksu* named in a private capacity in VS 4.194 had some connection with this institution, and more or less certain that its personnel included a **hamarakara* (accountant), for one appears as a witness in ROMCT loc. cit. (There is also a royal *hamarakara* in BE 10.13, perhaps to be connected with a royal treasury of one sort or another; a *hamarakara* of Artaḫsar (PBS 2/1 84), one time controller of the *nakandu šarri* (above); and other less well-defined bearers of the title (BE 10.59, 80, 82, 97, Eilers 1940:56).) In the case of the *bit sutum šarri* (royal storehouse) attested at Sippar (Camb. 202, 256, 359, Cyr. 74) and Uruk (YOS 7.88) the only fiscal function for which evidence comes to hand is the supply of foodstuffs to what seem to be temple officials and workers, but the royal *bit kari* (evidently a storeplace despite the current translations 'quay' or 'harbour') is intimately associated with the crown and its agents in connection with rent due to the superintendant of royal dates (ROMCT 2.23, at Isin), payment of the 'King's Share' (BE 8.85; cf. p. 149) and disbursement of 'royal' barley for *uppaiata*, i.e. OP **upayata*, the word used in Elamite garb in the Persepolis documents for (royal) food supplies (Dar. 244, Stolper 1977:254 f.). Evidently this is the storeplace for the produce of specifically royal property. Finally there are two institutions not designated 'royal' but nonetheless evidently linked with the Persian organization of Babylonia. In BE 9.19 a debt is to be paid 'in the enclosure at the *hanbara* gate', where *hanbara* = OP **hampara*, Elam. *ambaraš*, the standard word for storehouse in the Persepolis texts. We can tell nothing of its functions, but the unique use of foreign terminology in a formula where numerous parallels lead us to expect an Akkadian term must disclose a special institution (Stolper 1977:254), though perhaps one at an administratively low level. Much more substantial is the *kaṣir* (treasury) whose chief was the Iranian Bagasaru, variously called *rab kasir* and *ganzabara* (Dar. 105, 296; the former title recurs much later as that of a witness in PBS2/1 68, but the 'scribes of the *bit kaṣiranu*' of Camb. 384 are not relevant, at least to Babylonia, if Zadok 1976a is correct in thinking that the document was written in Persis). We only hear of the *kaṣir* casually, in documents concerned with Bagasaru's private business transactions, but bearing in mind that the latter's landholdings were round Babylon we may well be dealing with the treasury of the capital itself. The same may, of course, be true of the 'royal house' and the *nakandu šarri* of Murašu texts (that is, these could be other examples of vague references to royal treasuries actually relating to installations in royal/satrapal capitals: cf. n. 73). But the other items just reviewed must fairly certainly be located at a more 'provincial' level.

At the centre of the empire the Persepolis archives reveal treasuries explicitly attested as such or as locations of 'treasury workers' at Persepolis (Cameron 1948:9, Cahill 1985), Pasargadae (PF 62–3), Shiraz (59–61, 128, 865, 877, 1944), Matezziš (70–1, 2017, PFa 30; also *Camb*, 384 with Zadok 1976:69 f.), Rakkan (PF 65–6, 866, 1947), Hiran (58), Hunar (406), Kaupirriš (405), Ankarrakkan (863), Kurpun (879, 1158), Narezzaš (878, 1825, 1852) and Urunduš (864).[76] To these Koch 1981 adds a further eight by identifying the officials Karkiš and Šuddayauda in ration documents bearing Seal 1[77] and in some entries in account texts as successive *Hofschatzwarte* in 508–503 and 502–497 BC (Hinz 1971:283 thought they were *Vize-Intendanten*) and then tracing their worker-groups on the assumption that the latter will in fact be 'treasury-workers'.[78] (If so, not all worker-groups at treasury-sites were treasury-workers, since we find such groups under other apportioners and assigners in 508–497 at many of the relevant places. But that is not particularly surprising. The facts that we do not find workers associated with Karkiš and Šuddayauda at all explicitly attested treasuries and that explicitly attested treasury-workers and treasury officials can be discovered who are connected with other higher authorities are a little more worrying, but might have special explanations.[79]) Assuming Koch is right, we have therefore at least 19 treasuries in the Persis/Elam administrative region outside Persepolis itself. Almost all are in Hallock's Persepolis-Shiraz-Narezzaš area—necessarily so in the case of Koch's additional items, since their identification depends on use of seal 1, which is characteristic of the area. (Where a further more precise localization can be made in terms of Sumner's division of the area into two 'urban regions' [cf. above p. 115] the treasuries are more often in the Shiraz district than the Matezziš one: this will

[76] Unnamed treasuries appear in PF 67–8 (prob. Rakkan, cf. 65–6), 73–6, 129–31, 1442, 1788–9, 1800. 73–5 and 76 name two sets of otherwise unknown officials and should concern two treasuries not among those named in the comparable texts, 58–66. The anonymous treasury-worker sites in 1013–5 and 1120 are associated with Shiraz (reason unclear) and Barniš (?cf. 1212) respectively by Koch 1982:235, 243. The Persian *gazophylakiai* in Strabo 15.3.6 may be only Persepolis and Pasargadae, but 15.3.3 is perhaps acceptable evidence for Achaemenid treasuries at Gabae and Taoce.

[77] But not similar documents with other seals, cf. Koch 1981: 235 (Karkiš), 240 f. (Šuddayauda): in the latter case Koch postulates a distinct homonym. Koch does, however, count PF 1105 (Šuddayauda, seal 312: workers in the fort) and 1109 (Karkiš, seal 252: workers of Irdabamma), although 1042–3 (Karkiš, seal 76: workers of Irdabamma) is discounted and we do not have to assume that treasury and fort are institutionally equivalent.

[78] The additional places are Mandumattiš, Parmizzan, Pittanan, Šala/Kuntarturrizzan, Tenukku, Tukraš, Uskannaš, Zikara. The summary tabulation at Koch 1981:244 f. suffers from certain omissions and inaccuracies.

[79] Karkiš and Šuddayauda do not appear at Hunar or Kaupirriš: an accident perhaps, but possibly worrying since these places are not badly represented in the archive and happen to be the only two treasuries *outside* the Persepolis/Shiraz/Narezzaš triangle. The treasury 'delivery man' at Rakkan gets rations under a sealed document of Zissawiš in 502–1 BC (PF 1947:31): perhaps individual functionaries were dealt with differently from worker-groups? Treasury-workers at Kurpun are assigned by Midadda (PF 1158). This has no date, so he *might* be a short-lived *Hofschatzwart* between Šuddayauda and Baratkama (attested from 495 BC).

be partly a function of the disparity in size between the two regions, though one notes a particular concentration in the western end of the Shiraz region, directly connected with Shiraz itself.) The only treasuries *outside* the Persepolis-Shiraz-Narezzaš triangle are Kaupirriš (chief city of the Kamfiruz area) and Hunar, which is evidently in the Fahliyun (cf. its association in PF 11, 2019, 1092 with places to be located there), but this is presumably to some extent an accident of evidence: one can surely assume, by analogy with the rest of the data, that the Kamfiruz and Fahliyun areas actually had more than one treasury apiece. So far as function is concerned, these treasuries clearly resemble (e.g.) the Elephantine Royal House in not being confined to the storage of silver, as is evident from the types of treasury-worker employed in them (PF 864–6) and from the delivery of hides to them (58–76), possibly for use in manufacture of leather goods (Hinz 1971:268, Koch 1981:232,–Cahill 1985:375, relying on an argument from silence, doubts whether the Persepolis treasury itself had manufacturing functions). But it is not entirely clear that the treasuries were storeplaces for grain or the like to be used as rations for 'treasury workers' or any other category of worker or (e.g.) garrison soldier. The surviving evidence gives us little in the way of titles for local treasury officials;[80] and the large number of places involved, including some (especially among Koch's additional items) which are only rarely mentioned in the archive in any capacity, suggests that the treasuries cannot *all* be 'provincial' ones of the sort suggested by the Egyptian evidence. (A similar problem of classification affects e.g. Arad, a garison-site where a (non-Iranian) **ganzabara* is on record (Stern 1982:45), and the three Arachosian fortresses mentioned above (p. 126), under the overall supervision of a treasurer and each having its own sub-treasurer, where we have to choose between satrapy/province and province/sub-province as the spheres of responsibility of the treasurer and sub-treasurer respectively.) We can, however, be reasonably sure that the Persis treasuries form a different, smaller and more important category of storage place by comparison with the 'granaries' and 'storehouses' found in the Persepolis archives both at treasury sites and elsewhere, not to mention the many other locations at which provisions or supplies are provided for workers or high officials or travellers but which are never explicitly designated 'storehouse' or anything else. It is perhaps with sites like this that one should compare e.g. the evidence in Xenophon's *Anabasis* for villages in Syria (1.4.9, 19), Babylonia (2.2.13 f., 3.4, 21 f.), north Mesopotamia (3.4.17 f., 31, 5.1, 12) and Armenia (4.4.2, 7, 5.24) as convenient sources of accumulated natural produce for hungry mercenaries[81] (though it is rare for attested Persepolis archive storehouses to be actually called 'villages'[82]) and some at least of the Palestinian sites where excavation has revealed storepits or granaries (Stern 1982:237).

A different sort of distinction between places within satrapies is suggested by a rare Greek attempt to describe systematically their internal workings, viz. that

[80] A treasurer (*kanzabara*, **ganzabara*) appears at Rakkan (1947.19) but the Elamite synonym *kapnuskira* normally refers to workers not officials. The delivery man (1947.10 f.) and scribes (866.7, 1947.17) are also *kurtaš*.

[81] For the importance of villages in the imperial landscape cf. Briant 1982:137 f.

[82] Muran: granary (1636), village (1857). Hidali: storehouse (200), village (2057). Tandari: royal food-supply (116, 124), village (1736). Some eight other villages are named, and anonymous references occur in 45, 694, 1573, 1967, 2033, 2057, the places often being sources of supplies.

conducted by Xenophon in two related but distinct passages, *Cyropaedia* 8.6.1 f. (a purported account of Cyrus' institution of satrapies) and *Oeconomicus* 4.5 f. (a commentary on the Persian King's great interest in agriculture and war). Prominent in both is the question of garrisoning, on which matter the following consistent picture seems to emerge (cf. Tuplin n.d.(b)). Every satrapy contains a complement of *phrouroi*, all receiving payment which comes (ultimately) from the satrap and is drawn, like tribute, from local resources, all engaged in protecting the province (a job which is the satrap's responsibility), and all under commanders who are subordinate to the satrap but (like him) appointed by the king, in an attempt to ensure that they are not *necessarily* incapable of resisting satrapal disaffection. The garrisons are not, however, uniform, since a distinction is drawn beween *akra* garrisons (guarding relatively few important urban citadels) and troops distributed widely and in small units through the *khōra*. This physical contrast corresponds to four further administrative distinctions. (a) Each *akra* garrison has a phrourarch, but the *khōra* troops are organized under chiliarchs, commanders of artifical units defined in principle by numbers, not by topographic settings (i.e. fortresses). (b) There are various hints that the *akra* garrisons are 'King's Men' in some unexplained fashion not true of the *khōra* garrisons (since all receive pay from the satrap, this is not a distinction connected with source of remuneration). (c) All *phrouroi* receive payment, but Xenophon occasionally reserves the word *mistho-phoroi* for *akra* garrisons, as though *their* maintenance depends more totally upon direct and literal payment. One might guess at a distinction between 'pure' mercenaries and e.g. maintained military communities. In short, the analysis appears to suggest a special category of places which are 'royal garrison' sites. Unfortunately systematic comparison with evidence in Greek and near eastern sources about actual garrisons does not triumphantly vindicate this analysis, and one has to abandon absolutely strict interpretation of Xenophon's descriptions to avoid significant inconcinnities. One may note among other things that Xeno-phon's use of 'chiliarch' in this context is otherwise unparallelled in Achaemenid period sources (though, as we will see, there is something relevant in a hellenistic source), that, although there are traces of 'royal' forts, they do not all appear in the sort of urban centres Xenophon leads one to envisage, and that the apparent distinctions between 'pure' and other mercenaries is hard to maintain, at least so long as it is allied to the distinction between royal and other garrison sites. (This is one of the apparent strict implications of Xenophon's picture which needs to be abandoned.) At the same time, another interpretation of garrison distribution, Briant's thesis that the empire's basic fiscal units were military circumscriptions centred upon fortress-treasuries (1982a: 191 f.), also proves hard to justify, at least from actual Achaemenid evidence. Among the known treasury sites which might be held to exemplify the scheme—Briant adduces those of Persis / Elam (whose role as garrison-sites is not strictly attested[83]) and the Elephantine Royal House, and might have added Arad and the Arachosian forts—Elephantine certainly corres-ponds to an administrative unit larger than those Briant has in mind: for he appeals

[83] Hinz 1971: 266 f. finds treasury guards in PF 864–5, but the text only *says* treasury-workers. Only Persepolis and Shiraz are on record in the archives as having both a fortress and a treasury.

in this context to Xenophon's chiliarchs, who are precisely *not* in places like Elephantine which must be a good candidate for a *royal* garrison-site on the Xenophontic scheme. And we have already noticed that the status of the other sites is at least hard to judge.

4 ESTATES

So far I have been pursuing 'public' administrative units. But in the general context of Persian methods of exploiting the empire, there are other sorts of unit of perhaps equal significance, namely parcels of land (including villages, even cities) placed in the hands of various beneficiaries of the ruling and exploiting power. 'Estates' of one type or another (sometimes spawning their own internal administration) matter for a rounded impression of what the empire was like quite as much as satrapies or provinces. First there is the real estate of the King and other members of the royal family. Babylonian documents refer to e.g. royal canals, reservoirs, *usbarra*-land (an Iranian term of uncertain import), fiefs of the royal table, throne fiefs, royal treasury land, royal land, not to mention stables, barley, poultry, cattle, and dates (the last three appearing in references to the officials in charge of these commodities).[84] Only a certain amount can be seen of the administration of such property. The man in charge of feeding the royal cattle receives payments listed in a text labelled 'palace account' by its editor (Michigan 89). The job of the superintendent of royal dates includes collecting rent from royal property (ROMCT 2.23–25). In Murašu documents the 'land of the royal treasury' is held by a fief-collective of *šušanne* of the royal treasury ultimately subordinate to very high-ranking persons (cf. above, p. 129, below, p. 153). Again, canal managers, who are mostly Babylonian, whose powers include conscription of labour from other landowners and whose subordinates include canal inspectors, are themselves subordinate to a class of *mašennu*-officials (sometimes Iranian, sometimes not, and at least once designated 'royal' [BE 9.59]) which appears to be concerned with all sorts of crown property (in one text the Murašu firm pays rents on 'all lands which are crown property' to the *mašennu*'s agents). They are in turn associated with **frasaka* (investigators), their household includes a fief-collective of canal-workers, and one of their servants is foreman of another collective of grooms. They are perhaps immediately subordinate to the satrap: one recorded canal rent goes to a servant of the satrap Gobryas (Stolper 1974:61 ff.). Outside Babylonia royal property appears in the form of villages near Priene (Tod 185.9 f.—assuming continuity from Achaemenid conditions) or herds of Median horses (Strabo 11.13.7) or royal *paradeisoi*[85] or indeterminate 'royal land' in Egypt[86]

[84] Canals: Dar. 41, VS 3.68, YOS 7.162, TCL 13.155, BIN 1.7, GCCI 2.390, TEBR 25, FP 53, 63, BE 9.7, 73, PBS 2/1 2, 58–9, 73, 158. Reservoirs: BE 9.7, PBS 2/1 158, TuM 2/3 147. *Usbara*: BE 9.28, 32a, 67, 73, 10.31–2, PBS 2/1 124, 150, TuM 2/3 147, CBS 5205. Fiefs...: VS 5.128, PBS 2/1 65, 186, Strassmaier *8th Congress* 31. Royal Treasury Land: BE 10.34 = PBS 2/1 41. Royal Land: land is designated as royal property with various formulae in YOS 7.156, TCL 13.203, VS 5.55, FP 1, ROMCT 2.9, 23–5, BIN 1.118, PBS 2/1 36 = BE 10.46, BM 116622. Leases could include a guarantee that land was not the King's (VS 6.171). Stables: TEBR 47, TuM 2/3 124, 183, PBS 2/1 114. Barley: Dar. 244. Poultry: BE 9.20, 10.128, PBS 2/1 63, 76, 133, 160. Cattle: Michigan 89, BIN 1.7, YOS 7.77, 146. Dates: ROMCT 2.23–5.

[85] *Nehem*. 2.8, Arr. *An*. 6.29.4, Strabo 730. For other *paradeisoi* cf. n. 130; they are not normally called specifically 'royal', but note Plut. *Artox*. 25 (at a royal *stathmos*), Diod. 16.41.5, Curt. 7.2.22 f. (for royal diversion).

[86] Meeks 1972: passim. Royal land is also mentioned in P. Lille 22, 23 under Nectanebo I, but is

or a 'royal estate' in Persis (PF 1987) or an irrigation system in Chorasmia (Hdt. 3.117: see below, p. 144).

As for the rest of the royal family, Greek sources knew of cities or villages or land (especially in Egypt and Syria) being allocated to provide the Queen with clothing.[87] They also knew of Queen Parysatis' villages/cities in western Media, while Babylonian texts provide evidence for her holdings in Babylonia, as also for an 'Estate of the Queen'.[88] Irtašduna, Darius' wife, has an estate in Persis (PF 1836–7), as does her son Arsames (Hallock 1978:113) and another royal lady, Irdabamma (PFa 27): there is also mention of a 'village of Irtašduna' (PF 718). Back in Babylonia we hear of a Crown Prince's Estate[89] and of landholdings of various other 'sons of the (royal) house',[90] and, apart from two references to accountants in Persepolis texts (PF 1837, PFa 27), it is again Babylonia, and especially the Murašu archive, which provides most evidence of the internal workings of such estates (Stolper 1974:89 ff.; but cf. n. 89 for the sixth century Crown Prince's Estate). They consist of various types of land (including royal *usbarra*-land and bow-fiefs) and they are administered by managers who can be slaves (e.g. BE 10.84–5) and who receive rations from the estate-produce and/or fief holdings of their own within it. Such managers are variously designated *paqdu* or *ustarbar* (the latter being a Persian term only attested in the later Achaemenid period and sometimes found with the additional qualification 'of the king'). Various other officers are also visible, e.g. judges of Parysatis' estate. All these people tend to be Babylonians, although *ustarbar*-officials with Iranian names appear in e.g. BE 10.9, 15, BM 54025 = Eilers 1940:107.

Beyond the confines of the royal family similar sorts of pattern emerge. Greek sources speak of the satrap Tissaphernes' Carian *oikos* (something substantial enough to merit full-scale military attack[91]) and generalized references to satrapal *idia* or royal gifts to successful officials may conceal (among other things) similar sources of wealth.[92] Governors of Judah often 'acquired land' while in office (*Nehemiah* 5.14 f.) and evidence has been claimed for tax-exempt satrapal estates in Moṣah and Gibeon (Stern 1982:209, Briant n.d.(a)). A text from Babylonian Šatir (TEBR 31) mentions governor's land in a boundary definition and Herodotus' account of the Babylonian satrap's personal perquisites (Hdt. 1.192)

generally not very evident in any Late Period sources (Lloyd 1983:327).

[87] Xen. *An.* 1.4.9 (Syria, Parysatis), Hdt. 2.98, Athen. 33F (Egypt), Plat. *Alcib. I* 123B, Cic. *Verr.* 3.33.

[88] Parysatis: Xen. *An.* 2.4.27 (corn, sheep, *khrēmata, andrapoda*), PBS 2/1 38, 50, 60, 75, 105, 119, 133, 146–7, BE 10.97, TuM 2/3 185. Estate of Queen: BE 9.28 = TuM 2/3 179. BE 9.50, Stolper 1974:92 ff. The estate of Lady Amisri (? Amestris) appears in BE 9.39, 10.45, CBS 5199.

[89] BE 10.5, 31, 45, 59, 101, PBS 2/1 51–2, 90, 133, 202, Stolper 1974:89 f. The Crown Prince's Estate appears also earlier in the Achaemenid period: VS 3.210 (where a debt of barley owed to it is collected by an agent of the man 'in charge of the tax-demands of the Crown Prince's Estate'), 5.60, 129 (which both mention the steward, *rab biti*, of the estate, a type of agent encountered in other Persian landholdings (see below)). Cyr. 177 records the loan of silver which is the Crown Prince's property, and there were Crown Prince's palaces (YOS 7.8 [Uruk], CT 57.36 [Sippar]).

[90] Stolper 1974:96 f. (at least nine individuals).

[91] Tissaphernes: Xen. *Hell.* 3.2.13, Nep. *Ages.* 3.1. (His 'property' realized 920 talents in 395/4: Hell. Oxy. 19.3)

[92] *Idia*: Thuc. 8.45.6, Xen. *Hell.* 1.5.3, Hell. Oxy. 19.2. (The *idioi phoroi* of Xen. *Hell.* 2.1.4, 3.8 are a special, controversial case: Lewis 1977: 119, Tuplin n.d.(a).) For satrapal treasure in the form of metal, clothing etc. cf. Polyaen. 7.23.1 (Mausolus). Idrieus was 'the richest man in Asia Minor' (Isoc. 5.103). Gifts: Xen. *Oec.* 4.7 f., *Cyr.* 8.1.39. Satraps were also, of course, on salary scales like the dignitaries of the Persepolis archive.

surely presupposes land-holding, as does the title 'steward of Gobryas' estate' in a document also referring to the 'canal of Gobryas' (PE 8.80; and cf. TEBR 89). The Elamite version of DB 47 even appears to describe the fort Aršada as the *irmatam* (estate) of the Arachosian satrap Vivana. Much more informatively, texts from Babylonia and Egypt illustrate the estates of the Egyptian satrap Arsames in some detail.[93]

Nor is it only satraps that come into question. On the one hand Artoxares (Artḫašar) an influential court figure in Ctesias (688 F 14–15), turns up as landowner in eleven Babylonian texts (Lewis 1977:21) and Xenophon envisages the elder Cyrus giving members of his personal court *oikoi*, *khōrai* and servants (? *kurtaš*-workers) in provincial areas which will provide them with *dasmos* and be available for direct use on the occasion of official visits to the relevant area (*Cyropaedia* 8.6.4–5). On the other hand Xenophon also says (ibid. 10) that members of the satrapal court were given land, and this proposition can be easily illustrated from Near Eastern sources. The Persepolis archives refer to a number of estate holders, including some known in official capacities in other texts.[94] An Iranian secretary of the Babylonian satrap turns up in BE 9.48 as owner of a field, and an *ustarbar* (cf. p. 134) who bears two names, one Babylonian and one Iranian, has a plot described as 'gift of the king' (*nidintu šarri*; Eilers 1940:107). Belšunu (cf. p. 122) possessed both crown-grant land (*nidintu šarri* again) and land not so designated, which may have been his prior to appointment (YBC 11586, Stolper 1986 and n.d.). Bagasaru the treasurer (cf. p. 129) owned and received income from land near Babylon (some of it held jointly with a member of the Egibi banking family) which he administered through a *rab biti* (Dar. 105, 296, 527, 534, 542). More generally there are plenty of Iranian landowners in Anatolia, Egypt, and Babylonia known to us only by name, some of whom will be officials of the satrapal entourage. Some texts speak of, for example, the farm of Bagadata (BE 9.65) or the 'estate of the Persian' (VS 4.87/8, BE 10.101) or the canal of Uštana (BE 9.65).[95] Another treats the town of Rabiia as virtually belonging to (a different) Bagadata (BE 10.9). In BE 9.48 Bagamiri, son of Mitradata, leases property (some of it acquired from his late uncle) and a dwelling-house to the Murašu firm for a 60-year period.[96] In UET 4.99 Bagiš lends a large quantity of barley through the agency of his *rab biti*; the latter's title indicates that Bagis has a considerable estate (cf. above) and in a similar fashion we can identify additional estate owners in the Murašu archive because documents associate them with 'managers' with the same

93 Babylonia: Stolper 1974:94f. Egypt: AD passim.

94 e.g. Šutezza (PF 150–5), Ištimanka (180, 1802), Irtuppiya (330, 1527, Fort. 1091), Dauriša (PF 331), Dayakka (581), Bakabada (1256), Bakankama (1857), Marriya (1898), Mišparma (2027), Miturna (2070), Uštana (2071). The estates appear to be close to place(s) of official activity in the cases of Šutezza (150–4 with 520–1, 637–8, 640–1) and Ištimanka (1802 with 405, 925–8). Other named estate holders appear in 444, 1855, 1857, 2025, 2075. Anonymous estates: 1368, 2079. On Persis estates see now Sumner 1986:26–7 (incorporating investigations by Stolper).

95 Note also certain Persian toponyms (one a palace site) discussed in Zadok 1976a:72. Elsewhere in the empire note the fortified manor-house of Asidates in Xen. *An.* 7.8.8 f.

96 Distinct from Bagamiri, son of Aspadaštu, a bow-fief holder (BE 9.106, 10.50, PBS 2/1 77, 192) but conceivably identical with a Baga... attested as estate manager in the Queen's Estate in the same year.

titles and functions as those known in royal estates.[97] For the sort of landholdings we are now considering seem in general to be characterized by the same type of internal administration. The most copious and interconnected evidence is that about the estates of Arsames and two otherwise unknown Persians, Warohi and Warfiš, in Egypt.[98] From this emerges a picture of the owner running his estates or domains through a manager (or managers) who are responsible e.g. for supervising the workers (*gardu*) and slaves within it and collecting 'tax' due from it (the term used, *mndt*, is one also applicable to royal tribute, and it comes in a form which can be carried to Babylon, i.e. silver).[99] In performing his duties he is sometimes associated with accountants and can call upon the services of a local military commander, though there is no proving that this is a private militia as has sometimes been claimed.[100] His rewards include a *dwšn* (AD 2), apparently a grant of either land within or some sort of revenue from the estate. (He is also a slave owner.) This recalls Babylonian evidence, as does another text (AD 8) which also casts light on the sources of Arsames' 'tax': this records Arsames' assignation to an Egyptian of a domain (*baga*) consisting of land which, if untenanted, would be directly incorporated into the estate. In return the assignee pays rent (*hlk*) to the estate, which we now see consists at least partly, like Babylonian counterparts, of smaller, dependent estate-units. (The use of the term *hlk* also particularly recalls the payment of *ilku* (etymologically cognate) by Babylonian bow-fief holders to the authorities of the larger estate of which the bow-fief was part (see pp. 153 f.). But it would perhaps be unwise to infer that the Egyptian case is in all respects parallel.) The situation in AD 8 must be distinguished from that of Warohi's domain: this too is given to him by Arsames, but appears to be quite separate from the latter's holdings, the gift being from Arsames *qua* satrap, not *qua* estate owner. I say this without prejudice to the imponderable question of whether Arsames has his Egyptian estates because and only so long as he is satrap. Either way he will doubtless have them thanks to royal grant.

It is this sort of background that we should have in mind when we read in a Greek source about the *khōra* of Memnon[101] or of Tithraustes[102] or of the King giving an *oikos* or land to such worthies as Miltiades' son Metiochus (Hdt. 6.41),

[97] e.g. Parrinus (PBS 2/1 70, 98, 102, BE 10.103), Ipraduparna (BE 10.114), Umartašpa (PBS 2/1 10), Unnatu (CBS 12981), Gibbu (PBS 2/1 43), Artaumanu (CBS 4998), Mitrata (BE 10.114), Pitibri (BE 10.29, TuM 2/3 148). In the Kasr archive there are many Iranian proprietors of real estate (Stolper n.d.).

[98] Arsames: AD 1, 2, 4, 6–8, Warohi: AD 10, Warfiš: AD 12. (I assume that *baga* (domain) and *byt'* (estate, house) in these documents are not distinct categories of holding). Arsames had estates in Lower *and Upper* Egypt, but this was perhaps rare, the lack of evidence for Iranian estate-holders in demotic texts being conveniently explained if most such estates were in the delta. *Baga* recurs in Saqqara 41, 46, 47 ii, in which last case the owners have semitic or Egyptian names. Saqqara 6, 48 speak of a type of estate called *ʿšk*.

[99] Manager: passim. They are variously Egyptian, Babylonian and, at least once, Iranian (Maspat, AD 12). Succession of father by son appears in AD 2. *Pqyd* recurs in Saqqara 64b, 85, AP 37 (cf. p. 125), Grelot 1972:no. 99. *Gardu*/slaves: AD 5, 7, 9, 12. Tax 10, 11.

[100] Accountants: AD 8–11. Porten 1968:46 thinks these are 'public' officials also active in private contexts, but cf. p. 133f. for estate officials elsewhere. Military help: AD 4.

[101] The sources relate to two different areas: (i) western Troad: Dem. 23.154, 157, Ps. Ar. *Oec.* 1351b1f, (ii) Aesepsus valley: Strabo 587, (?) Arr. *An.* 1.17.8. Polyaen. 4.3.15 might belong with either.

[102] FGH 105.4. Tithraustes might be one of the royal satraps of the same text, but it still would not follow that the *khora* was his satrapy. That Chares chose to attack it does not settle the question (cf. n. 91), and Tithraustes' 20,000 cavalry (Schol. Dem. 4.19) are a possibly suspect quantity, since the scholiast is commenting on complaints about 'paper' Athenian armies of ten or twenty thousand mercenaries.

Phylakos of Samos (id. 8.85), Democedes of Croton (id. 3.132) and even the deposed Babylonian King Nabonidus.[103] But we should beware of putting everything under the same head. The various texts relating to donations of cities,[104] though consistent in some cases with the recipient actually residing in and ruling the city in question (this was certainly the position of Themistocles at Magnesia and of the Gongylids and Demaratids in Aeolis), are perhaps strictly speaking gifts of portions of royal revenue not of estates which happen to coincide with whole political units.[105] Again, there are various land-grants distinguished from the above by being much smaller (no question of internal administration, though the recipient may lease it to another tenant) and more explicitly tied to the provision of service or other dues to the crown, e.g. Babylonian bow-fiefs, landholdings of Egyptian garrisons (cf. pp. 152 f.), the settlement of exiled Delians and of Egyptians in Aeolis (the former at least carrying military obligations),[106] the apparent concentrations of Iranian settlers, perhaps 'military colonists', in three distinct areas of Lydia and in Cappadocia,[107] and the land in Egypt occasionally described by a demotic term later associated with hellenistic *katoikoi*.[108] A final, and quite different, sort of 'settlement' is that of transplanted prisoners of war (cf. n. 28)—quite different because these are the tools and objects of exploitation, not its beneficiaries, creating wealth for the king and getting (as Persepolis texts show) no more than bare subsistence in return. It is time now to turn to that other, most obvious form of exploitation, viz. tribute.

II TRIBUTE

1 GENERAL CONSIDERATIONS

Tribute was fundamental to the empire. In Aeschylus (*Persae* 585) the fear that Persian power might collapse is the fear that subjects will no longer keep Persian

[103] Beross. 680 F9, a residence in Carmania. Abydenus 685 F6 speaks of *hegemonie* (cf. the claim that Astyages was made ruler of Hyrcania: Ctes. 688 F9a, Just. 1.6.6). It is tempting to suppose that Timagoras and Calligeitus (Thuc. 8.6, 39) and Nicogenes of Aegae (Plut. *Them.* 26) are also beneficiaries of royal or satrapal land grants.

[104] Themistocles: Thuc. 1.138.5, Diod. 11.57.7, Plut. *Them.* 29, Nep. *Them.* 10, Athen. 29F, Aristodem. 10.4, Schol. Ar. *Equ.* 84. Pytharcus: Agathocles 472 F6. Amyntas: Hdt. 8.134. Lycon: Ctesias 688 F15 (53). Gongylus: Xen. *Hell.* 3.1.6 f., *An.* 7.8.8 f. Demaratus: two gifts, one of 'land and cities' *c.* 490 (Hdt. 6.40), the other of Teuthranias/Halisarne after 479 (Xen. *Hell.* 3.1.6, *An.* 7.8.18). Alcibiades: Nep. *Alc.* 9.2. Croesus: Ctesias 699 F9, Justin. 1.7.7.

[105] In Pytharcus' case (n. 104) one wonders if the cities are more than villages—in which case estate-holding may be the appropriate category. Similar doubts are possible with Lycon, given that Ctesias calls Parysatis' villages 'cities' (n. 88, Ctes. 688 F16 (65)). For a gift of villages and the right to Persian dress by Alexander, presumably imitating Achaemenid practice, cf. Plut. *Alex.* 31.

[106] Delians: Thuc. 5.1, 32, 8.108.4. Egyptians: Xen. *Cyr.* 7.1.45, *Hell.* 3.1.7. Anderson 1970:168 questions the claim that this settlement went back to the sixth century. In the same general area we have Hyrcanian and Assyrian royal mercenaries at Comania (Xen. *An.* 7.8.13).

[107] Lydia: substantial evidence exists for the survival of Persian cults in the Sardis-Magnesia-Thyateira triangle, at Hypaipa and in the Katakaumene (evidence can be assembled from Keil 1923: 250 f., Robert 1963: nos. 225, 233, 1975:308, 326 f., 1978:283 f., 1982:372 f., TAM 5/1 267). The first area is that of Hyrcanis (Robert 1948:16 f., Strabo 629, the latter mentioning Persian *epoikoi*), Dariukome (Foucart 1885, 398, 1887:90 f., Robert 1982: 373) and perhaps Cyrupedion (Strabo loc. cit.—others put it in Katakaumene). Cappadocia: Strabo 733 (fire-worship, many Persian temples), and cf. 512. Other scattered evidence for cults in Anatolia: Diogen. 692 F1; Robert 1963:349, 1978:277. There is also, of course, much personal Iranian nomenclature.

[108] P. Loeb 45, P. Cairo 31046, P. Moscow 424; and cf. P. Rylands 9.17/2 (Saite). The term is ḳ-land (*nb ḳ* = *katoikos*): Malinine 1967:78.

laws, do *proskynesis*, or pay *dasmos*: compare the formulae of royal inscriptions mentioned earlier (p. 133) and note that tribute also appeared as a symbol of Persian power in the Suez Canal stelae (Posener 1936: no. 8.6). Herodotus' claim that Persis itself was non-tributary (3.97.1) accords with this symbolic character, but it is not straightforwardly true. The inclusion of Persis in a List of Peoples associated with the formula about tribute in DB 6–7 might be an oversight, but the Persepolis documents certainly establish that some tribute payments went on in Persia (Koch 1980). Perhaps the exemption applied only to the nobility (Briant 1982a: 342, 501)—but in that case why did Herodotus not have a figure, albeit a low one, for Persian tribute?—or only to silver tribute (Dandamayev 1972: 43).

Darius says that his subjects bore him tribute, and this is not merely a figure of speech. Throughout Herodotus' Tribute List (3.89–96) the size of an area's tribute is consistently expressed as 'such-and-such a sum went to Darius', the metal being presumably supplied in bullion form and certainly stored thus, perhaps after further refinement (cf. Oppenheim 1947), to be coined as and when required, and for other evidence we can turn to Polyclitus' remarks (128 F3) about the treasuries in Susa built to receive the tribute (both silver and other non-perishable natural produce), to the large silver accumulations captured by Alexander (see below),[109] to statements in Greek sources about satraps sending tribute (including horses) to the King[110] or about a rebellious regional governor stealing *quae regi portarentur* (Nep. *Dat.* 4.2), and to various Persepolis texts which refer to treasure or silver or tax being transported to Susa or Persepolis or from Susa to Matezziš.[111] But we should not necessarily assume that *all* the silver tribute quota of a particular region was carried off to Mesopotamia or Iran. Herodotus himself notes that a portion of the Cilician *phoros* (28 per cent) was retained in the satrapy to pay for garrison cavalry and arrangements of this sort may have been quite common: after all, Xenophon (*Cyropaedia* 8.6.3) makes it appear that the satrap's payment of garrison *misthos* and execution of other unidentified functions (ἄλλο τελοῦσιν ὅ τι ἂν δέῃ) was standardly a consequence of tribute-collection, and Herodotus (3.91.3) records tribute in kind (corn) levied in Egypt for Persians and *epikouroi* in the satrapy. This supposition may help with the problem some have perceived in the surprisingly small percentage (about seven per cent) of the theoretical total tribute income for 520–331 BC which Alexander actually found in Susa and Persepolis[112] and the surprising parsimony of the king in providing cash to pay for the military defence of his own interests e.g. in western Anatolia. Cawkwell 1968: 4 confronts

[109] Susa (Arr. *An.* 3.16.7, Diod. 17.66, Curt. 3.2.11, Plut. *Alex.* 36, Strab. 15.3.9), Persepolis (Plut. *Alex.* 37, Diod. 17.70, Curt. 5.6.3, Strab. loc. cit.), Pasargadae (Curt., Strab. 11.cc.), Ecbatana (Strab. loc. cit.).

[110] Cyrus: Xen. *An.* 1.1.8. Mausolus: Ps. Ar. *Oec.* 1348a4f. Idrieus: Isoc. 5.104. Armenian satrap: Strabo 530 (20,000 horses at the time of the Mithra festival: but surely a tribute payment).

[111] PF 57 (tax, Maturban-Susa), 1357 (treasure, Babylon-Susa: carried by Patiasa, elsewhere a tithe-collector), 1342 (silver, Susa-Matezziš: carried by a treasurer, elsewhere attested as *bazikara*, tax-handler), 1495 (tax, Barrikana-Susa), PFa 14 and (unpubl.) Q 809 (treasure, Kerman-Susa). Patiasa also appears thrice accompanying groups of horses (PF 1394, 1472, 1570), which might be tribute (so Koch 1980: 123).

[112] For sources cf. n. 109. I assume 120,000 talents at Persepolis (Diodorus, Curtius) and some 180,000 for Susa, Persepolis and Pasargadae, respectively *circa* 4.5% and 6.5% of the theoretical total (190 × 14,560 talents). There is no figure for Babylon, and all we know about Ecbatana is that Darius III removed seven or eight thousand talents thence (Arr. *An.* 3.19.5, Diod. 17.74.4, Strab. loc. cit.).

this difficulty by discarding Herodotus' clear statement that a silver tribute was levied from all areas of the empire in favour of Polyclitus' claim (128 F3) that it was confined to the *paralia*, with the remaining (inland) regions paying produce instead (dyes, drugs, hair, wool, animals). The Achaemenid kings certainly did receive tribute in kind (see below), but we have evidence for silver-tax payments in the Persepolis documents[113] and in Babylonia (below pp. 153 f.)—and this despite the fact that silver is not native to Babylonia—so Polyclitus' simple picture is certainly wrong (inspired, perhaps, by his awareness of the irrelevant fact that only the empire's fringes had *coinage* economies). The problem about the bullion in Susa and Persepolis is better solved by supposing that only a certain proportion of the silver-tribute income had ever been in the major treasuries at the empire's centre. A recent discussion of the Persepolis treasury would make that proportion very low indeed or even eliminate it altogether. Cahill 1985 argues that the Persepolis treasury was above all a place of storage for gifts symbolic of the king's power not a centre for receiving tribute income and redistributing it into the imperial economy. He is not entirely clear about how he regards the bullion element of the treasury's contents, but the implication of his overall argument appears to be either that the bullion was not tribute at all or that, if it was, its transfer to Persepolis was in any case of ceremonial significance and the proportion of tribute transferred in this fashion was never much more than the *circa* five per cent represented by what Alexander eventually found there (cf. n. 112). The first of these alternatives stands in flagrant contradiction to the literary and inscriptional evidence unless one assumes that Persepolis was so totally a 'ritual' city outside the ordinary administrative structures as to be irrelevant to statements, even royal ones, about tribute being 'brought to the king'—a view which I find a little difficult to square with the existence there of an archive like that from the Fortification (irrespective of whether that archive was originally stored in the treasury). The second alternative is therefore the better one. But the small surviving corpus of treasury tablets, almost entirely concerned with silver payments given to workers in partial or (rarely) total replacement of payment in kind and interpreted by Cahill as something quite exceptional, is surely an unreliable reflection of the whole range of the treasury's activities and Cahill must be overestimating the purely symbolic import of the bullion holdings. The fact that the treasury contained some things which were not easily redistributable does not prove that everything it contained was practically in that category, and on Cahill's own view Susa was 'presumably' a place where 'taxes and other revenues for imperial purposes [were] collected and stored' (1985:387)—this in contradistinction to Persepolis—and yet some 50,000 talents were discovered in the Elamite capital by the Macedonians. I should suppose, therefore, that the proportion of silver tribute income actually brought to the king and stored in the major treasuries of Mesopotamia and Iran was decidedly higher than five or seven per cent.

In 3.89 Herodotus attributes the establishment of a regular silver-tribute system

[113] Cf. n. 111. PT 85, an Akkadian text mentioning silver tribute, found at Persepolis, was probably written there or at least in Persis: cf. Zadok 1976a (who identifies a Babylonian presence at Matezziš in 526–21 BC, and would have PT 85 written there), Stolper 1984 (publishing another Akk. text definitely written at Persepolis in Darius' reign).

to Darius, his predecessors having merely received unregularized gifts. The same view is asserted by Polyclitus 128 F3, is certainly assumed in a story in Plutarch *Moralia* 172F and Polyaenus 7.11.3 about Darius' first tribute assessment, and is presumably implied by Plato's claim (*Laws* 695C) that Darius incorporated into the law 'the *dasmos* of Cyrus which he (i.e. Cyrus) had promised to the Persians'. Other texts, however, appear to deny Darius' primacy. Some are admittedly of doubtful weight. Xenophon's willingness to attribute tribute demands to the elder Cyrus (*Cyropaedia* 7.4.2, 8.1.9, 6.1 f. etc.) cannot be regarded as reliable evidence, nor can Arrian's statement that the Indians paid tribute according to the assessment of Cyrus (*Indica* 1.3), in view of uncertainty as to whether India was within the empire at the time (Indians are missing in the List of Peoples in DB 7, though appear regularly thereafter). Even Cyrus' own statement in the Akkadian Cylinder Text (ANET 316, Berger 1975:199) that the kings of all the world 'brought heavy tribute and kissed my feet in Babylon' must be treated cautiously: for since the text relates to Cyrus *qua* king of Babylon and belongs firmly and exclusively in the tradition of Mesopotamian royal building texts (Harmatta 1971, Kuhrt 1983), the expression of universal recognition of the new king's power by reference to tribute may be dictated by that tradition and the claim that tribute was actually paid may be valid only for the ex-Babylonian empire. (Wiseman's hint, 1967:504, that the fragmentary royal statements about tribute coming to Babylonia in BM 82684 + 82685 may be Cyrus' is far too speculative to help.) The other evidence at odds with Herodotus' statement in 3.89 is provided by Herodotus himself, when he says that Smerdis remitted tribute for three years (3.67.3) and speaks of Libyans and Cyreneans agreeing to pay tribute to Cambyses (3.13, 4.165). This does at least show that different views were current already in the fifth century (which will help to explain Xenophon's line in *Cyropaedia*), but still does not settle the truth of the matter; it was all too easy for classical Greeks to assume casually that the Achaemenid king had always received tribute as he did in their own time. On the whole, Herodotus' clear statement, when *not* addressing himself to the question casually, that Darius introduced a change seems to deserve precedence. The best view is perhaps this: the Achaemenid empire had come into existence by the Persian king's successive acquisition of large existing imperial entities (Media, Babylon, Lydia, Egypt), each with its own internal tradition of royal 'tribute'. These traditions were maintained separately for the benefit of the new Achaemenid ruler (and may in some cases have involved elements of relatively unregularized gift-giving). What Darius did was perhaps to create a somewhat greater degree of uniformity between the different areas of the empire (e.g. by laying down some uniform principles of assessment) and certainly to order a new actual assessment, which quite possibly increased the burden.

How great was that burden? One encounters some informal indications. Herodotus declares that Persian demands led the Babylonians to prostitute their daughters[114] and less frivolously *Nehemiah* 5.6 reports heavy borrowing in order to

[114] Hdt. 1.197. (A different connection between Persia and Babylonian prostitutes appears in Plut. *Mor.* 173C: maintenance of public prostitutes was a requirement imposed after a Babylonian revolt. This is evidently a reworking of what appears in Hdt. 1.156 about punishment of rebellious Lydia).

pay the king's tribute.[115] Cook 1961 saw the impoverishment of classical Ionia in terms of tribute, but this is a special case of an area (in his view) paying taxes to *two* imperial powers. At an earlier date Miletus, for example, was said to be at a height of prosperity after 40 years of Persian rule (Herodotus 5.28, Roebuck: 1959: 131—but contrast Tozzi 1978: chapter 5). Resentment of the tribute burden is, nonetheless, a possible explanation of the Ionian revolt, and it is more or less explicitly attested as a cause of rebellion in Egypt (Diod. 11.71.3, Curt. 4.7.1, Briant n.d.(b)). The recorded indications of royal tax rates in Babylonia are not obviously unduly harsh, though doubtless one can only really judge a particular obligation in the light of all a taxpayer's obligations to state, temple or whatever, and the payment of royal *ilku* could certainly lead to debt.[116] The only global figure on offer is that in Herodotus' tribute list (3.89–96), where each *nomos* is assigned a figure in Babylonian silver or Euboean gold talents and a final total is produced of 14,560 Euboean talents. But the manuscript figures do not add up, and the simplest emendation to make them do so involves postulating a conversion rate of 78 instead of 70 Euboean *minai* to the Babylonian talent.[117] The general order of magnitude is not perhaps much affected, though, and even some rather radical criticisms of Herodotus (e.g. the claim of Armayor 1978 that the individual *nomos* figures are Herodotean inventions) allows that the total may come from a reputable source. Cawkwell 1968: 4 notes that it is credible in the light of Antigonus' later annual tribute income of 11,000 talents (Diodorus 19.56.5). Compared with Athenian tribute income and allowing for the different scale of the two empires the figure is not disproportionately large.

On the other hand, tribute was not just a matter of silver payments. Several texts distinguish between obligations in silver and in kind, subsuming both under the heading of tribute. Herodotus' own list notes fish and corn in Egypt, horses in Cilicia, eunuchs in Babylonia.[118] The pseudo-Aristotelian *Oeconomica* (1345b28–1346a5) includes some produce taxes in the satrapal revenue, but τὰ κατὰ γῆν καὶ ἀγοραῖα τέλη could be cash dues. (For a full list cf. p. 146). The taxes of Beyond the River enabled its treasurers to provide both silver and commodities to the Jews,[119] and when Strabo (11.3.8) says that the Cappadocians sent the king 1500 horses, 2000 mules and 50,000 sheep in addition to *argurikon telos* and that the Medes 'paid' (ἐτέλουν) nearly twice this the animals are clearly tribute. At a more

[115] cf. *Nehem.* 9.36: 'today we are slaves and all the land's produce goes to the king whom Thou has set over us'. *Nehem.* 5.6 also mentions, though not specifically in connection with tax payment, pledging of children for a debt, a procedure rarely attested also in Babylonia (Dandamayev 1976: 438 f.). Voluntary temple serfdom appears in Late Period Egypt (Lloyd 1983: 315), as does abandonment of land due to tax burdens (P. Rylands 9.6/15 (Saite)).

[116] BE 9.94, 94a, 95–6, 10.51, 57, PBS 2/1 40, 89, CBS 5516, 12863, 12966, 13022, Cardascia 1951: 40, Stolper 1974: 159 f.

[117] The Indians pay 360 Euboean gold talents, i.e. 4680 silver talents. The other 19 *nomoi* should therefore produce 9880 Euboean silver talents. All MSS, save one, at 95.1 make the total 9540, and the exception (S) has the correct figure *in rasura* (i.e. as a correction). The actual total of individual figures for the 19 *nomoi* is 7600 Bab. talents. This equals 9880 Eub. talents if 1 Bab. talent = 70 Eub. minai. A complicated attempt by Descat n.d. to 'explain' the figure of 9540 also involves the wrong exchange rate.

[118] 3.91.2 (fish, sold for silver: 2.149); 90.3 (360 horses); 92.1 (500 eunuchs). Cilician and (cf. below) Median horses turn up in Egypt according to one reading of P. Aram. Florence 11913 (Milik 1960); contrast Bresciani 1959, Hoftijzer 1962, Swiggers 1980.

[119] *Ezra* 7.21 f. (*I Esdr.* 8.18 f.); cf. *Ezra* 6.8 (*I Esdr.* 6.29, Joseph. *AJ* 11.16).

local level, an army land-tax mentioned at Saqqara included silver and materials.[120] We also have individual references to tribute in kind. Horses recur at Aspendus and in Armenia,[121] sheep, goats, and cereals in Persis (PF 267–73). Several passages in Xenophon and biblical sources clearly connect tribute and agricultural produce.[122] It is tempting to think that the cereal stores destined for the Elephantine garrison in AP 2 and 24 (drawn in one case from the provinces of *Tštrs* and Thebes) represent tax payments and to suggest a similar explanation of the foodstuffs recorded in ostraca at Beer-Sheba (Stern 1982:45, Naveh 1973, 1979), Arad (Stern loc. cit., Naveh 1975), Yatta and Tell 'Ira (Naveh 1985).

Nor does so-called 'tribute' (whether in silver or kind) exhaust the range of offerings to the Achaemenid kings, there being (at least) two other areas worthy of note.

(i) A major element in the iconography of Persepolis is the extensive representation of the bringing of clothes, precious objects, animals, and the like to the King found in the so-called Tribute Bearer reliefs on the staircases of the Apadana, Palace H and the Palace of Darius (Walser 1966). Despite the modern label, these should not be regarded as an image of the tribute system: the delegates are presenting *gifts* and the composition symbolizes the empire's respect for the king not its mundane fiscal subjection to him (Root 1979:227 ff., Cahill 1985:387 f.). Nor is it *merely* a symbol if Cahill 1985 is correct to identify the constituents of such gifts in some of the contents of the Persepolis treasury. Gifts of this sort are normally additional to ordinary tribute, but Herodotus (3.97) notes that the Ethiopians, Colchians and south Caucasians, and Arabs had the privilege (cf. 3.91) of paying no tribute but merely offering regular gifts. Since Ethiopians and Arabs appear regularly in royal Lists of Peoples and therefore implicitly as payers of *baziš* we have a contradiction in the evidence. Either the two sources refer to different groups of Ethiopians and Arabs (and Herodotus failed to notice the ones who did pay tribute) or the King was disinclined to distinguish gift and tribute when glorifying his own power (but did not think the Colchians worth a mention). The suggestion of Eph'al 1982:206 f. that the frankincense given by the Arabs of Gaza/Ienysus was simply a tax upon the profits of supervising the incense trade on behalf of the King is an interesting variation of the second type of solution but one not obviously extensible to the other areas involved.

(ii) In an attempt to give some impression of the enormous wealth of Babylonia Herodotus reports (1.192) that the whole empire was divided up for the provisioning (*trophē*) of the King and his army and that under this system Babylonia was responsible for the provisions of four months out of every year. Herodotus says explicitly that this was additional to *phoros*, but leaves a crucial question unanswered: is this additional to *silver* tribute or to *all* species of tribute? Similar

[120] Saqqara 24.11. In another Saqqara text (Aimé-Giron 1921:56) the same tax apparently only involves silver. In Saqqara 31 something, (?) natural produce, goes from the 'fields of the army' to the Royal House.

[121] Arr. *An.* 1.26.3, Xen. *An.* 4.5.25, in both cases bred as '*dasmos* for the king'. Cf. also nn. 110, 122.

[122] Xen. *Oec.* 4.11, Xen. *An.* 3.4.31 (barley, wine, oats for horses 'collected for the satrap of the country'), *Nehem.* 13.10 f., *I Esdr.* 4.6 f., Joseph. *AJ* 11.46 f. And (?) cf. the storage jars of Judah (p. 147).

questions arise with certain texts about the King's Table,[123] with Xenophon's statement that satraps had to send the 'good things' of their satrapies to the king (*Cyropaedia* 8.6.6) or indeed with the building materials of the Susa Palace foundation texts (cf. n. 20), where the named sources amount to a list of peoples of the empire. Whatever the answer, the simple fact that such income existed is significant enough. The collection of natural produce and its redistribution as rations and salaries to agents of the ruling power is a central fact of the Persian system. Some evidence of this has always been there in the literary sources, alongside the perhaps more prominent references to apparently intermittent gift-giving on the part of the king or others. Heraclides 689 F2 knew that the king's *doryphoroi* and peltasts received food as *misthos*. The guardians of Cyrus' tomb got sheep, wine, and cereals (Arr. *An.* 6.29.7, Strabo 15.3.7), and the members of the royal harem received food allowances (*Esther* 2.9). The governor of Judah was entitled to claim 40 talents' worth of food per day for his table (*Nehemiah* 5.4 f.), the Babylonian satrap got horses as well as silver (Herodotus 1.192), and some said that Cyrus rebelled because of an inadequate salary (Plut. *Artox.* 4). It is also possible that stories in Aelian *Varia Historia* 1.31 f. about giving natural produce to the king during his travels are a dim reflection of documents about royal provisions in the Persepolis archives (PF category J). But documentary evidence has immeasurably enriched the picture with payments in kind to garrisons in Egypt[124] and (perhaps) Palestine (cf. p. 142) and Persis (PF 1857, with Sumner 1986:26 f.), rations for *gardu* in Egypt and Babylonia[125] and above all the whole bureaucratic system in Persis/Elam (p. 115) for distributing salary, rations, and provisions to the king and his court, high functionaries (some receiving prodigious amounts every day), *kurtaš*-workers, travellers of varied status, and even to animals—which brings us back to Greek evidence and the villages which had to feed the Babylonian satrap's dogs (Herodotus 1.192.4) or provide maintenance for a favourite royal camel (Plut. *Alex.* 31, Strabo 737). Silver is, of course, by no means absent from the overall picture: even in Persis the later series of Treasury Tablets shows the regular replacement of some portion of payments in kind with silver, though when grain is so replaced it is a sign of crisis (Hallock 1985:603, Hinz 1971:274 f.). But it cannot be too much stressed that to a very large degree the empire ran not only not on *coinage* but not even on precious metal.

The Achaemenids are notorious for an interest in gardens and in agriculture. Strabo reports a Persian song about 360 uses of the date-palm (742C) and makes agricultural skill (as well as the manufacture of the tools of war and hunting) play a role in Persian education (15.3.18). Cyrus astonished Lysander by his planning and

[123] Ctesias 688 F53 (dinner discussed in *On the Tribute of Asia*), Deinon 690 F12 (what is consumed is a quasi-*aparkhē* from the whole empire). Id. F23a implies that Ammoniac salt and Nile water were brought for the Dinner, 23b speaks of Nile and Danube water put in the *gaza* as a confirmation of the empire's extent. Strab. 735 (Assos wheat, Syrian wine, Eulaeus water).

[124] AP 2.5 (as restored in Grelot 1972), 24.39, 42, 43.8, BP 11.4. (Cowley's restoration of the relevant word, *ptp'*, in AP 37 is wrong.) It is possible that some/all of the otherwise unexplained lists of names in AP 12, 19, 23, 51, 53, Aimé-Giron 1931:no. 87 are connected with ration distribution. Saqqara 46 may also be relevant; and a different word for provisions appears in Saqqara 25. Soldiers did also receive salary (*prs*) in silver: AP 2.16, 11.6, (?) 16.4, Grelot 1972:nos. 22 & 25, Bresciani 1960:no. 1.

[125] Egypt: AD 9.1 (artist-*gardu*, including a sculptor and his womenfolk). Babylonia: VAS 3.178–9. Various texts name a 'ration-portioner' (*pitipabaga*) of the *gardu*: BE 9.15, 10.95, 127, PBS 2/1 202. For another ration-giver cf. Zadok 1976b:5.

planting of a *paradeisos* at Sardis (Xen. *Oec.* 4.20 f.), and this was just one aspect of the general requirement upon a satrap to ensure that this *khora* was well-populated and productive, provided with an abundance of trees and other agricultural produce (Xen. *Oec.* 4.8, 15, *Cyr.* 8.6.16). (Arsites' refusal to contemplate a 'scorched earth' strategy in 334—'not one house belonging to his subjects was to be burned' (Arr. *An.* 1.12.9–10)—has been thought a reflection of this, though it should be noted that Artaxerxes II, Darius III, and the Cilician satrap Arsames were less sensitive.[126]) We accordingly find evidence for the establishment of new crops in imperial areas, e.g. Gadatas' transplantation of crops from Beyond the River to Ionia (SIG^3 22), the planting of Chalybonian vines in Damascus (Posidon. 87 F68), or the introduction of pistacchios in Aleppo, sesame in Egypt and rice in Mesopotamia (Ghirshman 1954:182). It looks as though population and cultivation increased in Achaemenid Babylonia (Stolper 1974:199 f.) and there is talk of technical innovations in control of water-supply (Oppenheim 1985:578). The king certainly owned the canals, deriving direct profit from this on top of the profits raked off from the results of using canal water (Stolper 1974:61 f.). Royal interest of this sort is reflected in some Greek texts about Babylonia,[127] and elsewhere the Persians took good care of the Memphis dyke (Herodotus 2.99.3), encouraged the extension of *qanat* irrigation in Hyrcania[128] and exacted payment for water use in Chorasmia.[129] The numerous *paradeisoi* attested in literary sources,[130] Babylonian documents (Sippar: CT 22.198 i, Cyr. 222; Uruk: YOS 3.133; Nippur: CBS 13039) and the Persepolis archives, where at least 15 *partetaš* locations are named as playing a role in the bureaucratic system (PF index s.v., Hinz 1975:72), are actually only the tip of a phenomenon whose causes, it will be clear now, were thoroughly hard-headed; and Briant has even suggested, not entirely fancifully, that *paradeisoi* were actually meant *inter alia* to symbolize the whole empire's agricultural adornment—for profit as well as pleasure.[131] Certainly when Darius prays (DPd 3) for protection against enemies and The Lie (external and internal threats) and against Famine (a pairing which recalls Xenophon's stress in *Oeconomicus* 4.5 f. on

[126] Xen. *An.* 1.6.1 (401 BC), Curt. 3.4.3 (334/3), id. 4.9.7 f., 12 f., 10.12 f., Diod. 17.55.2 (332). Curtius does observe that Arsames *ought* to have been protecting his satrapy.

[127] Arr. *An.* 7.21.5, Strabo 16.1.9; Hdt. 1.189 (Cyrus' punishment of R. Gyndes is presumably a fanciful tale inspired by Achaemenid waterworks).

[128] Polyb. 10.28.3: those who brought water to previously uncultivated regions were entitled *καρπεῦσαι τὴν χώραν* for five generations, the privilege being presumably exemption from water-charges like those in Chorasmia (n. 131): cf. Briant 1982a:427 f. Archaeological evidence has been claimed for Achaemenid *qanats* in other areas, but in some cases the recent trend is to attribute the inception of such systems to other, sometimes substantially earlier, periods and stress lack of demonstrable Achaemenid intervention even later on (Oman: Salles n.d. Qatif: Potts 1984:109. Bactria: various views in Briant 1982a:424, 1984:47 ff., Gardin & Lyonnet 1978/9:136 f.) An Achaemenid date can still be maintained at e.g. El Khargeh (Egypt), al-ʿUla (Hejaz): Briant 1982a:424, Nasif 1980. For irrigation-works near Persepolis cf. Sumner 1986:13 f.

[129] Hdt. 3.117: here it is not a question of *extending* cultivation but of the king extracting revenue on top of *phoros*.

[130] General Xen. *Oec.* 4.13, *Cyr.* 8.6.12, Ael. *VH* 1.33 (where the King's reaction to a fine pear is 'Which *paradeisos* does it come from?'). Dascyleium: Xen. *Hell.* 4.1.15 f., 33. Celainai: id. *An.* 1.2.7 f. Sardis: id. *Oec.* 4.20, Diod. 14.80.2, (?) Plut. *Alc.* 24. Syria: Xen. *An.* 1.4.10. Sidon: Diod. 16.41.5, Clermont-Ganneau 1921. Palestine/Beyond the River: *Nehem.* 2.8. Babylonia: Xen. *An.* 2.4.24 f., Strab. 741. Susa: Ctes. 688 F34, *Esther* 1.5, 7.7. Pasargadae: Arr. *An.* 6.29.4, Strab. 15.3.7, Stronach 1978:107 f. Persepolis plain: Sumner 1986:27. Ecbatana: Curt. 7.2.22. Media/Cadusia: Plut. *Artox.* 25. Sogdiana: Arr. *An.* 4.6.1, Curt. 8.1.11 f. The regular features are trees, other produce, running water and animals (for hunting). For a hunting ground not called *paradeisos* cf. Strab. 589.

[131] Briant 1982a:451 f. On gardening, hunting and royal ideology cf. Fauth 1979.

the twin royal concerns for *georgika* and *polemika*), Famine is not just a natural disaster but a direct fiscal catastrophe. And the connection of *georgika* and *polemika* in the Xenophon passage just mentioned is simple: if military control is good, there will be peace and the land-workers will produce the maximum *dasmos*—to pay among other things for the military control.

2 SATRAPIES AND PROVINCES

So much, then, in general terms. What can be said in more detail about the ways in which tribute was collected? The largest visible tax unit is the satrapy. In Herodotus' Tribute List the 20 *nomoi* are satrapies, *Ezra* speaks of the tax of Beyond the River,[132] the satrapal economy in pseudo-Aristotle (1345b20f) is entirely a matter of collecting revenue to feed the royal economy, Alexander orders the Hellespontine Phrygian satrapy to provide 'the same tribute as under Darius' (Arr. *An.* 1.17.1), and in Xenophon's analysis of satrapal duties oversight of *dasmos* is stressed (*Cyr.* 8.6.3, 16, *Oec.* 4.5, 11). Accordingly we find satraps pressed for arrears by and dispatching due *dasmoi* to the king,[133] the revolt of satraps cuts off royal income (Diod. 15.90.4), and at a more local level it is to the satrap that the hyparchs Zenis and Mania give their *phoroi* (Xen. *Hell.* 3.1.12), while the food stores in north Assyrian villages 'collected for the satrap of the country' (Xen. *An.* 3.4.31) may represent tribute payments. When Curtius reports that the Mallians and Oxydracae once paid tribute 'to the Arachosians', the latter phrase presumably stands for the Arachosian satrap.[134]

The satraps' role could include assessment: they performed this task for Darius at the supposed institution of the system (Plut. *Mor.* 172F, Polyaen. 7.11.3) and Artaphernes made a new assessment of Ionia after the revolt (Hdt. 6.42.2). The complaints of Darius (SIG^3 22) about Gadatas' exaction of *phoroi* from Apollo's *phytourgoi* and his insistence upon their cultivating profane land (in order to increase the tribute-producing area) represents royal reaction to a bit of piecemeal satrapal assessment—assuming, as most historians do, that Gadatas was a satrap (rather than e.g. a *paradeisos*-keeper as suggested by Dandamayev 1984b:114). Mausolus certainly was and is represented as responding to demands for *phoroi* by instituting *eisphorai* (Ps. Ar. *Oec.* 1348a4f)—the satrap can evidently invent what imposts he likes to meet the King's global requirements.[135]

Artaphernes' assessment of the Ionian tribute was based solely upon measurement of the cities' land, but Herodotus does not explain how exactly this led to an assessment being fixed. Evidence has been produced for the existence in Babylonia of a detailed land register (*karamarri*), showing property boundaries, ownership, and tax obligations,[136] and traces of the same may be discerned in Persis,[137] while the Edfu donation text mentions information about land from the 'Office of

[132] *Ezra* 6.8 (*I Esdr.* 6.29 (Coile Syria and Palestine), Joseph. *AJ* 11.16 (Samaria)).

[133] Thuc. 8.5.5, Ar. *Oec.* 1348a4f, Xen. *An.* 1.1.8, Isoc. 5.104.

[134] Curt. 9.7.14. On Arachosian/Indian relations see Vogelsang 1985.

[135] It is also indirectly relevant that Mausolus can grant *ateleia* to a city outside the empire, Cnossos, ὁπόσης Μαύσσωλλος ἄρχει (Labraunda 40).

[136] Dar. 551, BE 9.55, CBS 12859, with Stolper 1974:47 f., 1977:259 f. Stolper would also connect the *didakka* and *hatru* of army-scribes (p. 120) with this register.

[137] cf. PF 779, 1245 recording a *karamaras* (person) who also (Fort. 3562) 'writes people down', a function further associated (1620, 1242–3, Fort. 3568) with 'making inquiries' or 'investigating'. (The word for this is cognate with *patifrasa* (n. 44)).

Writings'.[138] But the claim advanced by Stolper (n. 136) that Artaphernes was constructing a similar register of Ionian land is only questionably coherent with Herodotus' implication that Artaphernes assessed each *polis* rather than all individual land-holdings (cf. p. 148). The point of his measurements may have been simply to re-establish how much cultivable or otherwise useful land each *polis* had, from which an assessment might be calculated by some rule of thumb. (Descat n.d. suggests, on the basis of a hellenistic text from Sardis (cf. p. 147) and of reworking of Herodotus' Tribute List figures, that the rule involved a valuation for tax purposes of 60 darics for each area of one parasang perimeter. The argument is speculative, to say the least.)

That tribute requirements were generally calculated on land is obviously credible in view of everything already said. But there are traces of various other sorts of basis. The pseudo-Aristotelian *Oeconomica* claims (1352b27) that Alexander revived an obsolete, presumably Achaemenid, tax on imports into Babylonia. Various passages in *Ezra* (4.13, 20, 7.24) provide an apparently complete list of the three taxes applicable to inhabitants of Beyond the River which are under the control of the Treasurers of that satrapy, viz. *minda*, *b^{e}lo* and *halak*. *Minda* is a rather general word for tax, used elsewhere of 'the tax of Beyond the River' (*Ezra* 6.8), the 'King's Tribute' (*Nehem.* 5.3), tax paid on garrison colony land (cf. n. 150), a land owner's income from tenants (AD 10, 11), and even the wages earned by a slave hired out by his owner (Saqqara 21.1—Akkadian *mandattu* is used in a similar context: Dandamayev 1976:436, 440, 1984a:331). *Halak* recalls Babylonian *ilku*, a land tax (cf. pp. 153 f.), or the tax owed to Arsames' estate by a tenant in AD 8. The middle term, which recurs in Egypt (Saqqara V, XXIV, Delaporte 1912:73, 78–80, 95), is perhaps here a tax on something other than land: the NEB renders it poll-tax. An even fuller list of satrapal revenues is provided by pseudo-Aristotle (1345b28f), embracing taxes on agricultural produce, animals, commercial activity, a poll-tax (*epikephalaion*), and a worker-tax (*kheirōnaxion*)—for which last compare an impost in Saqqara 19, apparently charged in accordance with the number of *gardu*-workers in a particular tax unit.

Just as we can attempt to divide satrapies into constituent general administrative units, so we can attempt to discern smaller tax entities within them. The results are partially parallel. We have already noticed the hyparchs Zenis and Mania collecting *phoroi* for Pharnabazus (Xen. *Hell.* 3.1.12). Pseudo-Aristotle (1348a18f) records stories about Mausolus' hyparch, Condalus, gathering taxes to feed the satrapy's tribute quota. Condalus can apparently exercise some discretion in deciding upon what persons and materials to assess and exact dues, but the stories are sometimes disconcertingly far-fetched. For example, Condalus informs the Lycians that the King has ordered everyone to shave off his hair (in order to provide an eccentric tribute in kind) and then agrees to commute this to a cash payment—this being an example of levying *epikephalaion*. Excavations in Palestine have produced many storage-jar handles stamped with the name of the province of Judah (and sometimes also the title *pḥh*, 'governor'). Stern 1982:205 f., 237, 1984:108 argues that these are stamps of governors and lesser officials and that the practice is

138 Meeks 1972:20. For parallels cf. ibid 58, Wild 1954:181.

connected with tax-collecting, thus making the province a tax-unit in some sense. Certainly they must mark the jars' contents as *somehow* belonging to the provincial government or administration, just as do the earlier uninscribed imitation Achaemenid jar stamps (Stern 1982:209 f., 1984:109). The fact that Stern takes the *latter*, like the Moṣah stamps (from the name of a Jewish town), to be the trademarks of *produce* from royal estates (rather than of the tax income of the province) illustrates the uncertainty of any particular interpretation and may even damage the logic of his inference from the disappearance of the latter types and subsequent appearance of the Judah stamps that the province of Judah only came into existence after 450 BC. (Of course, the mere appearance of the Judah stamps and coins may in itself establish the truth of the proposition irrespective of earlier phenomena.) In any case, there can be no certainty about the precise relationship between stamped jars and the 'King's Tribute', and the same problem arises with two other items, Nehemiah's agricultural tithe to support Levites in the Temple (*Nehem.* 13.10 f.) and Bagoas' tax of 50 drachmai per lamb on temple sacrifices (Joseph. *AJ* 11.297). Both cases do, of course, illustrate a governor's right to invent new taxes. In Egypt Saite nomarchs are said to have played a role in tax-gathering (Lloyd 1983:334) but there is no such evidence for the Persian period; on the other hand, the corn of *Tštrs* and Thebes in AP 24 might, as already noted, be provincial tax dues. Xenophon's analysis of the garrison system (above pp. 131 f.) envisages chiliarchs in charge of garrison units in the *khōra*. Otherwise unattested in the Achaemenid period, they find a parallel in a hellenistic text from Sardis,[139] which describes an estate consisting of villages and *klēroi* and says that these entities owe particular sums of *phoros* to a named chiliarchy.[140] *If* this text is a guide to Achaemenid practice (Atkinson's downdating of the dispositions to which it refers to the late third century in contrast to the original editors' late-fourth century date makes this a real question) it emerges that one tax-collecting unit, much smaller than province or hyparchy, was the area controlled by a chiliarch (there is no telling whether the chiliarch has a role as assessor too). The fact that it is villages and *klēroi* that are encumbered, not just the estate they constitute, presumably shows that chiliarchies do not come into the matter because Mnesimachus, and his putative Achaemenid period predecessors, are some special sort of estate-holder: the implication is rather that all tax-liable parcels of land in a given region would owe *phoros* initially to the chiliarch.

3 TOWNS AND VILLAGES

Mention of villages brings one to place- rather than area-units. When Herodotus says (6.59) that newly-acceded Persian kings remit tribute arrears 'from all the cities' he is doubtless guilty of an unduly hellenic formulation, but various other texts confirm that the city is a possible tax-unit. Thus Aspendus breeds horses for tribute (Arr. *An.* 1.26.3), Cyrene and Barca submit to *phoros* (Hdt. 3.13, 4.165),

[139] Buckler & Robinson 1912 (republished as Sardis VII.1). See Atkinson 1972.

[140] col. 1.3 f. Later Mnesimachus' holdings are resumed as (i) 'villages, *klēroi*, attached *oikopeda*, *laoi* plus families and belongings, wine-jars (?), *phoros* in money and work, other income from the villages and much else' (col. 1.11 f.) and (ii) 'villages, *klēroi*, *khōria* and *oiketai*' (col. 2.5). Buckler & Robinson 54 assume that everything besides villages and *klēroi* is not subject to tribute in its own right.

Cyrus sends Artaxerxes due *dasmoi* from certain Ionian *poleis* (Xen. *An.* 1.1.8), the king of Cypriot Salamis is to pay tribute (Diod. 15.8.2), and after the conquest Alexander makes various dispositions about the *phoroi* previously paid by Ilium (Strabo 593), Ephesus, and Mallus (Arr. *An.* 1.17.10, 2.5.9). There is also Herodotus' account of the Ionian reassessment (6.42.2). After saying that Artaphernes summoned *angeloi* from the cities and compelled the Ionians to make mutual arbitration agreements, he continues 'He compelled them to do this and he measured their land and fixed *phoroi* for each of them (ἑκάστοισι)'. At first sight this might refer to assessment of all individual landowners in the relevant city territories. But the *synthekai* made by 'the Ionians' are, of course, beween cities, and the plural ἑκάστοισι, i.e. 'for each group', can, in the context of city-dwellers, only mean 'for each city'. Herodotus is therefore clear that the satrap carried out his assessment city by city, providing each *polis* with a tribute-quota. This does not prove that the cities were thereafter free to match it by whatever means they wished, but this is without doubt the simplest hypothesis.

After cities, three quasi-civic communities in Caria (two *koina*, one using *polis* terminology, and a *syngeneia*) which are on record granting tax exemptions to individuals, but excepting from these grants imposts variously described as *basilika telē*, *basilikoi phoroi*, and *apomoira* (a royal tax term in Ptolemaic times).[141] Three preliminary points. 1. When cities within the empire grant general tax exemptions there is never any reference to royal taxes.[142] Since the cities owed tribute *qua* cities, this phenomenon simply shows that the city could decide how to produce its quota, and on whom to make the burden fall, as it saw fit. 2. One of the Carian entities, Koarendeis, is also on record making an *ateleia* grant covering *geōrgia* and all other incumbent obligations with no further qualification.[143] Here, therefore, it is behaving like a city. 3. Another Carian entity, Plataseis, while insisting that the honorand pay *basilika telē*, does exempt him from 'whatever royal or civic *epigraphai* may fall upon it' (Labraunda 42). There are therefore *some* royal imposts which apply to Plataseis as a *koinon* and from contribution to which they can choose to exempt any individual—again behaviour just like that of a city. So long as we treat the three royal imposts as parallel there are three possible conclusions (Hornblower 1982:161 f. favours the first). (a) These imposts are actually obligations upon an individual (or upon an individual as member of some other entity than the ones in question here) and the texts are merely noting for safety's sake that these obligations are unaffected. Hence the Koarendeis can fail to mention the point without this actually mattering and the Plataseis can waive the apparently different *basilikai epigraphai*. (b) The imposts are obligations upon the entities (as tribute is one upon a city) and it merely happens that on some occasions these entities chose not to waive their right to collect contributions to such obligations, a choice which no city is ever recorded as making, and which the Koarendeis themselves once did not make. (c) The imposts are (again) obligations on the

[141] Labraunda 42 (Plataseis), SEG 26.1229 (Koarendeis), Sinuri 73 + Robert 1949:63 f. (*syngeneia* of Pelekos). *Apomoira*: OGIS 90, SEG 12.550. These texts and those in n. 143 appear in Hornblower 1982:364 f.

[142] Xanthus (FX VI p. 32 f. = SEG 27.942), Kios (Tod 149), Erythrai (Tod 155), Miletus (Tod 195, if this be pre-334). Cf. also Sinuri 75 A–B.

[143] SIG^3 311. Note also the Kildareis of Robert 1950:14.

entities, but the rules about tribute, imposed by the Persian authorities, were such that the entitites were not permitted to exempt persons who would normally be liable. This view requires us to assume that in those grants of *ateleia* which do not mention royal imposts it is simply taken for granted that bestowal of *ateleia* always refers to those *telē* which the authority in question is allowed to waive (i.e., in the hellenistic formula, those ὧν ἡ πόλις κυρία ἐστι). The disadvantage with solution (a) is that in at least two cases the text is certainly so formulated as to make all the imposts mentioned appear of comparable status vis-à-vis the exempting authority. The disadvantage of solutions (b) and (c) lies in the subjection of the Plataseis to *two* royal obligations. One could say that the *basilikai epigraphai* are extraordinary imposts, not covered by any hypothetical rules against waivers. But that creates the paradox that the city's own *epigraphai* (the only civic impost mentioned) also turn out to be intermittent and extraordinary. These disadvantages can be mitigated by *not* treating the three royal imposts as parallel. Let us assume, instead, that in the Plataseis text *basilikai epigraphai* refer to the community's regular obligation to pay royal tribute, whereas *basilika telē* are an individual's obligation, mentioned superfluously but perhaps understandably given that *basilikai epigraphai* have (also superfluously) been explicitly mentioned and waived. In the other texts *basilikoi phoroi* and *apomoira* are community obligations (equivalent to *basilikai epigraphai*) which the communities chose not to waive.

The villages of the Mnesimachus estate (p. 147) owe *phoros* to the appropriate chiliarchy, which seems to make them tax units in their own right. Comparably specific evidence from actual Achaemenid period sources is not all that plentiful. There is little to be gained from Saqqara 22 which Segal optimistically links with village taxation (no word for taxation appears, and the word translated 'collected' or 'exacted (taxes)' appears elsewhere only in texts which Segal prudently classifies merely as 'commercial'). Alexander's letter to Priene (Tod 185) shows him levying *phoroi* from local villages, apparently *qua* royal property. This may continue Achaemenid practice, but we are getting very close here to direct landlord/tenant relations, at the furthest remove from tribute as we normally understand it. One may compare the King's Share (PBS 2/1 32, 59, BE 8.85, 9.73) and King's Harvest (CBS 12922) attested in Babylonia in connection with crown property, as well as the **upayata* (cf. p. 129) of the 'town' Iqiša-ili (VS 6.160). Also in Babylonia, Herodotus reports (1.192.4) that four villages were *ateleis* on condition of providing sustenance for the satrap's dogs. It appears, therefore, that villages would normally be liable to *telē*. Or does Herodotus just mean that individual villagers were let off individual taxes in return for special food production (put another way, that the village only came to constitute a tax unit for the (effective) dog-tax)? Similar uncertainty affects the 17 horses for royal *dasmos* found in an Armenian village by the 10,000 (Xen. *An.* 4.5.24). It is tempting to regard the persophone *komarch* as the local official through whom higher authority channels its demand for tribute and to identify the village, therefore, as the unit of assessment (Briant 1982a:152). But even granted the premise, the conclusion need not follow.

4 TEMPLES

Given the importance of temples in landholding, especially in Egypt and

Babylonia, one looks with particular interest at their role in the tax system. On the western fringe of the empire Gadatas' injudicious attempt to extract *phoroi* from Apollo's *phytourgoi* (p. 144) presumably reflects the assumption that as a general rule sacred land is as liable to taxation as any other sort (assuming that he was not simply claiming tribute on the secular land he was trying to get them to cultivate). But for more copious evidence about the inter-relation of temples and the Persian administration one must look to Babylonia.

Achaemenid kings can be found making offerings *to* the Babylonian temples, e.g. wine from Beyond the River (Weisberg 1967:10) or 'provisions before the statue of Bel' (Joannès 1980:156(13)—though the execution of this is actually the duty of a temple prebend), and we have already noticed payments from the royal storehouse to temple personnel (p. 129). But other texts referring to workers apparently within the temple economy who are 'on royal provisions' (YOS 7.16, Camb. 333, Dar. 72) or to the king's fixing of norms for temple-slaves' rations (YOS 3.45, 81, 106, Dandamayev 1984c:501) possibly (in the first case) and certainly (in the second) concern payments actually made by the temple, evidently in connection with work done for the king (in YOS 3.45 a royal agent oversees the slaves' activities). Moreover, the Achaemenid kings departed from late neo-Babylonian precedent in exempting themselves, their families and entourage from regular tithes to the temples of the sort generally incumbent upon the satrapy's population (Dandamayev 1969b). In short, it is the king's receipt of obligations *from* the temples and his interference in their administration that is most prominent.

Various hints of such interference come in texts which say that failure to carry out some task will be a sin against (or will earn the punishment of) the king or the satrap. Sometimes the task is explicitly an obligation of temple to royal administration of the types noted below, but elsewhere we can only assume a direct or indirect royal interest in e.g. an artisans' oath of temple-service (YNER 1.1), the production of sacrificial animals (YOS 7.160, TCL 13.162) or fish (VS 20.87) for the temple, the supply of shepherds or a weaver (YOS 7.25, BIN 2.114), arrangements for guarding the Eanna sanctuary (BIN 1.169, GCCI 2.103; and cf. YOS 7.154), payment of quit-rent by bird-handlers (TCL 13.168), theft of temple property (YOS 7.192, TCL 13.142; cf. p. 119) and so on.

More specific and explicit evidence comes in a variety of forms. A temple fief owes royal *telitu*-tax in YOS 7.38 (cf. Joannès 1982:13). The income of a temple prebend can be royal property (YOS 7.79). Weisberg 1967:10 may refer to undefined dues to be transported from Eanna (Uruk) to Babylon, and two fourth-century documents (UET 4.48–9) apparently concern delivery of 'taxes of temple slaves' to the king (the details are disputed, witness the varied summaries in San Nicolò 1950:227, Oppenheim 1950:190, Dandamayev 1984c:125, 546. The word for tax is OP **barra*). But the major categories of evidence concern labour obligations and the supply of animals and natural produce, sometimes designated as the king's meal (*susbuti*) or 'provisions' and sometimes explicitly having its sources in the materials of temple sacrifices.[144] Connected with the latter is the so-called

[144] Labour obligations. King/Palace: CT 22.121, 244, YOS 3.133 (including establishment of *paradeisoi*: Dandamayev 1984b:: 114), YOS 7.77, 146, Michigan 89, BIN 1.7 (all connected with royal cattle), YOS 7.187. Satrap: TCL 13.150, 152, YOS

'royal basket' (*quppu*) which received those portions of temple income earmarked for the king (cf. San Nicolò 1941:31, Weisberg 1967:12, Dandamayev 1984c:56 f.). In BIN 1.7 we hear of soldiers guarding it during transport to Babylon, but most of our evidence for its existence comes from the title of the royal temple official at Uruk in charge of it (for a selection of references see San Nicolò 1941:20 f.). The designation 'royal' is sometimes dropped, so the person 'in charge of the basket of Ebabbara' may be the corresponding official at Sippar: one may certainly assume that there was one there and in all major temples. Nor were they the only royal officials introduced into temple administration, the senior echelons of which included a 'royal commissioner and overseer' at Uruk (San Nicolò 1941:18 f.) and Babylon (TCL 13.193), and a 'high officer and royal commissioner' at Nippur (Biggs 1978:132(26)). It is important to stress, however, that this intrusive royal supervision is in principle merely a continuation of late neo-Babylonian trends, though the royal commissioner at Sippar is not attested until Cambyses' reign and the 'royal commisssioner appointed in Eanna' and 'royal scribe appointed in Eanna' (YOS 7.107, 114, 118, 130, 131, 164, 198, TCL 13.170) are attested only in his reign, when they temporarily replace the long established *qipu*. It should also be noted that there were evidently royal commissioners *below* the very senior levels: in ROMCT 2.5 prosopographical considerations guarantee this, and some of the numerous individuals with the title who appear casually in documents, e.g. as witnesses, are probably in the same category (there is even one with an Iranian name in UET 4.1–2). The kings were clearly very concerned that the exaction of their dues should proceed with the maximum efficiency.

In Egypt the surviving picture is somewhat different. Initially Cambyses sought to impose restrictions on some temple income. The relevant text (P. Bibl. Nat. 215, *verso* d. 1–17 = Spiegelberg 1915:32) is obscure but seems to say that a whole range of commodities (ship timber, firewood, flax, livestock, fowls, silver, corn, (?) incense, papyrus) were no longer to be given to the temples, apart from three near Memphis (Yoyotte 1972). Instead the priests were wholly or partly to supply them for themselves, in some cases from specially designated areas. Figures are given which may express the silver value of some of the commodities, more than 1.5 times Herodotus' figure for the satrapy's silver tribute (cf. Bresciani 1969: 335, 1985:506). The implications of all this are somewhat unclear to me (and the information sits somewhat uneasily with Cambyses' alleged favour for the Neith temple at Sais: Posener 1936: no. 1). What sort of 'gifts' are outlawed, do they

7.137. (In TCL 13.150 a canal revenue agent orders provision of *urašu*-workers for canal maintenance, non-compliance to be punished by the satrap). Note also inspection of workers by temple officials plus a palace scribe (CT 22.242). Other references to worker-inspection (Cyr. 292, VS 6.249, 264) do not certainly involve the king. One naturally recalls (implied) supervision of workers in Xen. *Oec.* 4.9, *Cyr.* 8.1.9, though that will not be confined to temple-workers (royal *gardu*/*kurtaš* would be equally relevant). *Šuṣbuti*: YOS 7.86, 129; and cf. YOS 7.123, Pohl 1.67, GCCI 2.120 which do not use the term but the details of which connect them closely with the texts which do. Provisions: Cyr. 162, GCCI 2.126 (both mention the official in charge of provisions for the king), VS 6.179. Provisions from occasional sacrifices: VS 6.143, 162. Other reference to royal sacrifices: YOS 3.41, 7.8. In TCL 13.152 a royal commissioner and overseer of Eanna (cf. below) is exceptionally called 'royal - commissioner and in charge of regular royal sacrifices'. Other evidence: TCL 13.153 (sheep for the king, received by a palace steward), YOS 7.168 (superintendant of Ištar's dates provides dates for palace), Pohl 1.61 (inspection of Eanna animals by temple officials and satrapal scribe/agent).

come from temple tenants or outsiders, was the royal treasury planning to absorb the commodities which would otherwise have been given? In a sense the question is of passing importance, since Darius' codification of traditional Egyptian law (p. 112) ought to have swept the dispositions away. They do not constitute the only sign, however, of restraint upon temple wealth, even aside e.g. from claims about Xerxes' confiscation of huge amounts of land from the gods of Buto (Urkunden I.11 f.). For example, private donations to temples of the sort extensively attested under the Saites disappear from view, though royal donations continue, if the Edfu text is reliable (Meeks 1972:153, 1977:653). Since such donations provided costs for funerary cults, a function the need for which did not suddenly cease in 525 BC, the change must represent external interference in the temple's finances, and helps create the suspicion that there may have been other such interferences. All the same the temples certainly went on possessing land and receiving income from it. When such land was sold the temple continued to receive a tithe;[145] when it was leased provision still had to be made about payment of tax to the temple.[146] Several demotic papyri record temple tax receipts (P. Strassburg 5, P. Loeb 46, P. Cairo 50060), in the last case from an impost on beer and wine paid by a 'chief' (...) of the nome', soldiers, *pastophoroi* and other untitled persons. By contrast one can find no clear evidence for the state's levying of tax upon the temple, a problem which also exists in the Saite period, when just one possibly relevant text comes to hand.[147] Nor is it only a matter of silence, or a difficulty confined to temples. Herodotus says that members of the warrior class (*makhimoi*) possessed 12 *aroura* estates which were tax free, a privileged position only paralleled among priests,[148] and it is regularly assumed that this was true of the Persian period.[149] It begins to look as though the royal treasury's sources of income in Egypt were not distributed very evenly over the whole satrapy. Other evidence is meagre: we have already noticed possible income from tax in kind (p. 142), and Saqqara 19 records an (?) annual silver-tax of some sort (the payers are Egyptian). But paradoxically we can see as much evidence of revenue from the empire's own garrison troops as from native subjects. Members of garrisons at Elephantine and elsewhere apparently had some lands on colonial tenancy from the King;[150] four Saqqara papyri seem to concern tax from such land to the royal treasury (24, 31, 74a, Aimé-Giron 1921:56) and a somewhat obscure Elephantine text (AP 17) has been interpreted as referring to tax upon colonial allotments (*mnt*) received monthly by

[145] P. Louvre E 7128 = Malinine/Pirenne 1950/1: no. 18. For earlier practice cf. ibid. nos. 15–17 (P. Turin 246, 247, P. BM 10117).

[146] This is absent in P. Loeb 45, but see P. Aram. Bauer-Meissner = Grelot 1972:no. 1. (The relevant word for tax [*ms*] recurs in an ostracon [Segal 1969:173].) For earlier practice cf. P. Louvre E 7833A, B, 7836, 7839, 7845A (all in Hughes 1952).

[147] P. Rylands 9.21/16, cf. Meeks 1979:644.

[148] The text about Darius' legal codification (p. 112) gives special mention to three classes, priests, warriors and scribes, but there is no evidence about tax privileges for the last-named.

[149] cf. Lloyd 1983:309, Bresciani 1958:134 f. (Although Herodotus speaks of the existence of the *makhimoi* in the present tense (2.164 f.) and draws an implicit distinction between their numbers in the fifth century and earlier, he casts statements about their privileges in the past tense.)

[150] Holdings of *degel* or army: AP 16.2, (?) 80.5. Holdings of individuals: AP 7.2, 8.2, 33.6, BP 12.5. The crucial aramaic term is *mhḥsn*, also used of the 'possession' of a government boat by an Egyptian in AP 26.3. See Grelot 1970:30 f. Porten/Szubin 1982, 1985 take the term to denote hereditary property holders, but do not deny that it could designate 'military colonists'. The word *mnt* (portion) in AP 1.3, 17.2 has also been thought to refer to *klēroi* (Porten 1968:52, Grelot 1972:76).

three groups of officials, including provincial scribes, and accounted for by them to the satrap (Porten 1968:52). (It is fair to add that the same text has also been read as referring to payments *by* the said officials *to* the troops (Grelot 1972:280 f.).)

5 BABYLONIAN LAND-TAXES

Turning back to Babylonia a good deal of evidence comes to hand of taxes and other obligations incumbent upon various sorts of non-temple land. Imposts upon specifically crown property have already been mentioned (cf. pp. 133). What we are concerned with now is 'military' fief-land and land (or individual tax payers) whose status is undefined in the sources.

One of the best attested elements of landholding in Babylonia consisted of (theoretically) inalienable but heritable family-held fiefs, known as bow-fiefs or (more rarely) horse- or chariot-fiefs.[151] These are attested only from the start of the Achaemenid period (Dandamayev 1967, 1983) and the bulk of the information comes from the Murašu archive at Nippur in the reigns of Artaxerxes I and Darius II. But the phenomenon was certainly general in Babylonia, the terminology being attested at Babylon, Borsippa, Šahrinu, Šatir, Sippar, Ur, and Uruk (Joannès 1982:9); and the use of the term 'bow(-fief)' in the Akkadian version of DB 14 (Voigtlander 1978:17, 55) for that which Gaumata took away from the 'army' or 'people' suggests that something comparable existed elsewhere in the empire, perhaps specifically in Persis.

The evidence for taxes and other obligations upon such fiefs runs as follows. (i) In the Murašu archive the normal impost upon fiefs, although there is the odd exception (e.g. the payment called PA.U *šarri* in BE 10.15), is an annual silver tax designated as *ilku*, running at between 10 shekels and 17 minai, with a constant rate over time for any given fief (Cardascia 1951:100 f., Stolper 1974:206 n. 30). This tax was collected by the foremen (*šaknu*) of the collectivities (*hadru*), chiefly ethnic or occupational in title, into which the fiefs were grouped. (Such *šaknu*, it should be noted, represent a quite substantial layer of officialdom within the satrapy, one drawn largely from the Bablyonian population and imposed upon the *hadru* to represent it in relation to a higher authority (Stolper 1974:121 f.). They also seem, as collectors of a quasi-military tax—see below—to bear a distant similarity to holders of the same title in seventh century Assyria (Postgate 1980:75).) The further progress upwards of the proceeds of *ilku*-taxation is rarely visible, but there is in principle at least one further stage before the royal treasury is reached, that of the large estate-holders within whose estates the fiefs are often located (Cardascia 1951:104 f., Stolper 1974:121 ff.). The significance of *ilku* will be further discussed below.

(ii) Non-Murašu documents of earlier (the majority), contemporary and later date

[151] See in general Cardascia 1951, 1958, 1977, Stolper 1974:14 f., 111–47, Joannès 1982:8–45. Inalienability is deduced from Lutz 1928:269 f. = Cardascia 1951:179 f. = Ebeling 1952, where adoption is used to alienate a fief (another example of adoption appears in VS 6.188). But contrast TEBR 31, apparently a sale of a bow-fief. In BE 9.99 a bow-fief is actually called *nidintu šarri*, 'gift from the king', but even in default of such description one must assume that bow-fiefs are normally in origin royal grants. However UET 4.41/42 and Walker 1973:127 (17) describe fiefs as property of gods, suggesting that they had been granted by a temple (cf. Ries 1976:40). The reverse phenomenon occurs in VS 5.55 where a *bit ritti*, characteristically a temple fief is 'property of the king'. ROMCT 2.9 mentions land which is both a *bit ritti* and a *bit azanu* (? quiver-fief, i.e. bow-fief).

also refer to silver payments incumbent upon bow-fiefs. In many cases such payments are given no descriptive title (Dar. 199, 307, VS 4.77, 96, 125, 6.194, 277, TEBR 1), but elsewhere we find the terms *ilku* (VS 4.127, Michigan 43, TEBR 2), 'front of the bow' (VS 6.60, ROMCT 2.9, TuM 2/3 220–1) and *telitu* (Camb. 13). The documents rarely illuminate the official agencies by which these payments are received; but TEBR 2 does mention 'receivers of the *hadru*' collecting *ilku*, and in Michigan 43 it is paid to the *šaknu* of a collective just as in the Murašu texts. (Both these texts are contemporary with the Murašu archive.)

(iii) There is also evidence both in the Murašu archive and elsewhere for (labour) service obligations falling upon fiefs. In VS 6.302 eighteen bow-fief holders have to help move a boat and in VS 6.160 payment for work connected with the royal quay and delivery of *upayata* (cf. p. 129) comes (probably) from a fief-holder. VS 6.155 refers to a payment of silver for (i.e. in lieu of) royal work charged against the chariot fief of a temple official; and three Murašu texts speak of *pirqu*, apparently a *corvée* duty (BE 10.43, PBS 2/1 28, 107). Also noteworthy is TCL 13.203 which stipulates more generally that persons sharing a bow-fief shall 'serve the king' in proportion to their share. The Akkadian term used here recalls (a) VS 6.188, where share in a fief carries the obligation to 'perform *ilku*-service for the king' and (b) BE 10.15, CBS 12794, where *palah* LUGAL, 'service of the king', is an obligation incumbent on some land, though one fulfilled by a silver payment. It is possible that all these texts are actually referring to *ilku*-service (or its monetary equivalent) and relate more to military than labour service. (The fief in BE 10.15 belongs to a group whose 'professional' designation appears to be military: Ries 1976:40.)

This range of evidence about obligations is matched if one turns to documents not explicitly concerned with bow-fiefs and their holders. There are many references to *ilku*-payments (Michigan 15, 24, 26, Cyr. 89, Dar. 323, BE 8.100, TCL 13.197, 198, VS 4.109, 121 + 122, 123, 132, UET 4.60), including one where it appears to be in flour not silver (Berens 105). Other texts mention *telitu* (CT 22.5, 57.17–25), *miksu* (CT 22.5; cf. above p. 129), various 'gifts' to the king or palace (ROMCT 2.23, Pohl 2.10, YNER 1.2, TCL 13.153) and 'money for military outfitting' (see below p. 129). One of the royal 'gifts' is received by a palace steward and passed by him to a minor city administrator (TCL loc. cit.) but otherwise, as before, the official agencies involved are not evident. Labour or service obligations also recur: requisitioned *urašu*-labour (cf. n. 144) is found in Cyr. 8, 224, TCL 13.173, VS 6.119, 150, the obligations being fulfilled by fixed payment or by actually hiring a substitute. UET 4.48–9 apparently records one Kusurea's hire of persons to perform a task connected with taxes (cf. p. 150), while in UET 4.1–2 adoptive children are required to 'do the service for the Gods and the King' charged against (the land of) their parents. And just as VS 6.188 spoke of *ilku* as a service performed, not just a tax paid, so Strassmaier *8th Congress* 31 and TuM 2/3 172 require someone to perform (literally 'go') the royal *ilku* incumbent on some land.

This brings us to the further consideration of the significance of *ilku* promised above. In Murašu texts, by contrast with all other evidence, there is a regular formula which itemizes the constituent parts of *ilku* as 'soldier of the king, flour, *barra*, and the other dues of the royal house' (Cardascia 1951:98 f. For *barra* cf. above p. 150. *Ilku* and 'other dues' recurs in UET 4.60, and we have noted a case of *ilku* paid in flour, but these are at best very partial parallels for the formula from outside the Murašu archive.) The first item shows that *ilku*, which essentially means 'service', is specifically connected with *military* service—not surprisingly since we are here (as in some non-Murašu texts: above) dealing with fiefs named after a species of armament. Evidently *ilku* contains at least an element corresponding to the obligation to provide a royal soldier. We have already seen examples of the principle of money in lieu of service (including some which may refer to *ilku* under a different name). In specifically military contexts the principle can be illustrated by various other phenomena. A large number of texts from the reigns of Cyrus, Cambyses, and Darius refer to (money) for the outfitting of a soldier, often appearing as an annual payment. What is happening is that land-owners are providing money to pay a substitute to undertake their technical obligation to do military service—and not only money but provisions as well.[152] A century later we find the same thing in UET 4.109 (397/6) where Kusurea supplies pay, provisions, and armament for another person to undertake his royal *andesu*-service (apparently a Persian term signifying military levy). None of these texts relates explicitly to bow-fiefs. But a similar situation is in fact attested apropos of such a fief in 530 BC, when a pair of fief-holders provide a royal soldier, one Nabubelšunu, plus travel provisions and money (Camb. 13; cf. Joannès 1982:19, Dandamayev 1983:57), and such a substitution also appears to occur in Dar. 430 (bow fief) and (perhaps) Dar. 154 (chariot fief). These texts can in turn be compared with a set relating to bow-fiefs from a period of nine days in 422 BC. Five of these (BE 10.61–2, PBS 2/1 54, 167, 194, CBS 4992) are mortgages to cover debts for dress, equipment, provisions, and (perhaps) money in connection with a military expedition to Uruk. Nothing is said about an actual soldier, but in the sixth text we encounter an agreement between two joint-fief holders according to which one of them will actually go as a cavalryman to Uruk, while the other will provide equipment and one mina of silver for provisions (Lutz 1928, Cardascia 1951:179, 1958:5 f., Ebeling 1952). Clearly each fief was expected to provide an actual soldier and appropriate equipment and provisions. (Nothing establishes whether the soldier could be an outsider as was apparently the case 108 years earlier.) The first year of Darius II's reign saw a huge number of mortgage agreements between fief holders and the Murašu; normally the nature of the debt lying behind the agreements is unstated, but occasionally it is connected with payment of *ilku*, and it has been suggested that this was actually true in the majority of cases (Stolper 1974:162 f.). But if this is so the sums involved show that what is here being called *ilku* cannot be the regular annual tax from which we began (Joannès 1982:23). This situation has been hypothetically connected with large-scale mobilization in Babylonia in the context of struggles for the throne after Artaxerxes I's death (Stolper loc. cit.) and in this case *ilku* will be describing the sort of actual costs attendant upon mobilization seen in the texts from 422 BC.

[152] Cyr. 331, Camb. 17, 276, 291, 322, Dar. 46, 112, 141, 156, 164, 167, 220, 234, 253, 308, 481, VS 4.139. See Oppenheim 1945:239 f., 1985:573.

We have therefore to distinguish between (i) an annual monetary levy symbolizing the obligation of the fief holder to provide soldiers and provisions and (ii) the right of the king to call for additional actual supply of soldiers, equipment and provisions.[153] Since the copious Murašu archive only yields clear signs of this right being exercised in two years, it may have happened only rarely and in times of relative crisis by the later fifth century (for a further example see UET 4.109, above); and the Babylonian evidence as a whole could reflect the King's increasing reliance upon mercenary service paid for by taxation.

6 INDIVIDUAL TAX-PAYERS

Finally, after the tribute of satrapies, smaller regions, cities, villages, temples, and estates, some cases where tax payment cannot for the most part be clearly associated with any entity larger than the individual. Appropriately, perhaps, this brings us back to Persis. (On all of what follows see Koch 1980.) Eight Persepolis texts (267–273) refer to large or very large groups of sheep and goats received as tax (*baziš*—the word for tribute in royal inscriptions) and variously entrusted to individual officers (in one case for use in payment of food rations) or 'withdrawn' (again, once, for provisions) or used in what are apparently attempted trading transactions. Among the persons named in the texts is one Appitranka, known elsewhere (PF 1942.29) as a tax-handler. A further document, PF 2008, provides an account of sheep received as tax and entrusted to Makama for Harrena to apportion. These names provide connections both with the first set of texts (where two different persons named Makama appear in PF 268–9) and with another pair of tablets which offer some further details. In PF 2025 Raubasa and his colleagues, 'payers of the land' (Hallock) or 'Bergzahler' (Koch), take a total of 574 sheep and goats for the King's Tax and entrust them in two unequal groups to Makama the cattle chief at Uranduš (a treasury site, incidentally) and Umizza the herdsman at Hiran. The first group 'pertains to the *dalalaki* persons' in Hallock's rendering, though Koch says that *dalalaki* means *Steuerabgaben*, the second were 'at the sheepfolds'. In both cases the apportioner is (once again) Harrena. The tablet emanates from Pharnaces' chancellery, and in PF 2070 we have a letter from Raubasa and his colleagues to Pharnaces giving some more information about the animals entrusted to Umizza. (i) Raubasa had got them from six persons at Hiran: four (one a woman) have no title but are just said to be 'at the estate of Miturna, the *ansara* official and slaughterer', while the other two are a royal *rara* worker and a treasurer. (The only indication of origin in PF 267–273 is the mention of Marduka people in 273.) (ii) Umizza has now taken the animals to Pharnaces. Raubasa and his colleagues also say that they sent the tax-handlers to Pharnaces, and it may be

[153] With such exceptional cases Joannès 1982:22 associates VS 4.96 (519 BC, 'supplementary silver on the bow-fief' and 'first receipts of silver on bow-fiefs') and VS 4.126, Michigan 26 (both 513 BC, both connected with a year's service in Elam). But Michigan 26 at least explicitly refers to *urašu*-service, not therefore on the face of it military. I assume that texts such as TuM 2/3 183 and PBS 2/1 114 which relate just to payments for 'wages and provisions' for two or three 'soldiers of the king' do not have to be taken as referring to actual soldiers on campaign. If so, the 'soldier of the king' element of *ilku* may theoretically correspond to wages/provisions (rather than e.g. equipment) for a soldier (Cardascia 1951:99). But the facts that (i) wages and/or provisions are valued at 1 mina in PBS 2/1 114 and in the levy text of Lutz 1928 etc. (n. 151) and (ii) 1 mina is quite a common *ilku*-rate do not (*pace* Cardascia 1951:181 f., 1958:76 f.) constitute a significant coincidence.

that Umizza is to be construed as one such. At any rate we do have here more of a picture than usual of the journey of tribute from the individual payer up to highest administrative echelons—though one would still like a clearer statement of what Pharnaces was going to do with the animals.

Another series of documents concern, in Hallock's translation, 'deposits' of various commodities 'to the account of' named persons (generally otherwise unknown and sometimes female),[154] and it has been subsequently suggested, on the basis of the historical associations of the relevant Elamite verb, that they are really tax payments by private Persian landowners (Hinz 1971:189, Koch 1980:106 f.): it is to such people that other documents refer in which corn is described as 'from the people' (PF 113, 200, 454, 1973–7, 1985). The payments include cattle, corn, fruit, dates, figs, nuts etc. and may be tithes, since the seal of Patiasa the tithe-receiver (1942) sometimes appears on the tablets. Another associated person is the *rušdabaziya*, land-tax official (PF 1968). Koch does not raise the question of the relation beween the tax involved here and that in the first set of texts discussed above. Certainly distinct from both of them is what is found in yet another category of documents to which attention is drawn by occasional appearances of a *bazikara* (tax-handler).[155] These, it is argued, relate to a leasing practice by which the administration supplies seed and then claims a ten or thirtyfold return (depending on type of crop). The land involved can be either crown or private property, and the proceeds mostly go to provide provisions (i.e. worker rations), though a proportion is withdrawn and disappears from sight. The distinction between this lease income and the tax discussed above is underlined by a further circumstance. In some accounting texts a further deduction of a tenth or thirtieth is made from the former, something which also happens with the income of direct working of crown land by *kurtaš* but not with the tax received from private tax payers. Koch 1980:136 suggests that these extra deductions went to the personal provisioning of the king.

The material assembled in the preceding pages is easy to summarize in the literal sense of condensation, but difficult in any more interesting sense. I have shown that general analysis of imperial officials leads one's attention to such entities as satrapies, subregions (e.g. provinces, hyparchies of varying size, nomes, (perhaps) garrison chiliarchies), cities, individual fortresses, treasury sites and smaller storeplaces, villages, estates and their constituent estates, fiefs, etc. There are also plenty of attested officials whom it is hard to 'place', and perhaps types of region for which no pertinent official title survives. Again, evidence about tribute collection relates it to many of the entities just mentioned, as well as to temples or individuals. The problem lies in the interconnection of the highlighted details. Is 'hierarchy', with its implications of continuum of authority from top to bottom the appropriate term to use of the various agents of the ruling power within a satrapy? How should we envisage the inter-reaction of phenomena that look bureaucratic and ones that look

[154] PF 138–232, 1829, 1849–51, 1955.11 f., 1968–70, 1982–8, 2018–24, PFa 1.

[155] Account texts with headings 'set aside', 'provided for provisions', 'withdrawn' (e.g. PF 1955–65, 2075–6, PFa 32); all texts in Hallock 1969: categories F ('setting aside . . . '), G ('providing for provisions'). Tax-handlers appear in 438, 443, 451, 512, 567, 1942.25 ff., 1943.37, 1965.4 f. (cf. 492–3, 566, 645),

feudal? Granted the various types of evidence about taxation, how do we picture the actual stages of the process by which a satrap ends up with so and so much silver to forward to the king? Put another way, at how many removes do the tax payments I have described stand from 'The King's Tribute'? When an Egyptian estate owner pays *halak* to Arsames' estate, was he thereby making an (indirect) contribution to the royal tribute, or was he also encumbered with other unattested direct payments to that end? What *is* the relation between this Egyptian's situation and the Babylonian fief-holder paying *ilku* to a foreman put in position by the superordinate estate-holder? How far should we go in assuming that bow-fief procedures were to be found all over the empire (is a single attested *kleros hippikos* in hellenistic Magnesia ad Sipylum (SdA 492) good ground for postulating an extension even to western Anatolia)? What was, after all, the relation between *phoros* and the King's *trophe?*

One may, perhaps, still look for further assistance from the Persepolis archives. Despite the oddities of the area they cover, exhaustive analysis of the inter-relations of places, persons and seals can in principle reveal *possible* structures; and there are also, of course, many texts both from Persepolis and from Achaemenid Babylonia still awaiting mere publication, let alone analysis and combination. The proposition that 'there was no uniform infrastructure of Achaemenid rule in the satrapies, and no general system for the collection of tribute can be discerned' (Cook 1983:173) may be destined to stand (it may even be the simple truth), but we can at least hope to acquire better information about and understanding of the manifold varieties and of such 'system' as there may have been in particular satrapies.

Abbreviations

AD	G. R. Driver, *Aramaic Documents* (Oxford 1957).
Amherst	A. Ungnad, Neubabylonische Privaturkunden... Amherst, *AfO* 19 (1959/60), 74–82.
ANET	J. B. Pritchard, *Ancient Near Eastern Texts in Translation* (Princeton 1969).
AP	A. E. Cowley, *Aramaic Papyri* (Oxford 1923).
BE 8	A. T. Clay, *Legal and Commercial Transactions from Nippur* (Philadelphia 1908)
BE 9	H. Hilprecht/A. T. Clay, *Business Documents of the Murashu* (Philadelphia 1898).
BE 10	A. T. Clay, *Business Documents of the Murashu* (Philadelphia 1904).
Berens	T. G. Pinches, *Babylonian Tablets of the Berens Collection* (London 1915).
BIN 1	C. E. Keiser, *Letters and Contracts from Erech* (New Haven 1917).
BRM 1	A. T. Clay, *Babylonian Business Transactions...* (New York 1912).
Camb.	J. N. Strassmaier, *Inschriften von Cambyses* (Leipzig 1890).
CBS	Unpublished University of Pennsylvania tablets (cf. Stolper 1974).
CT	Cuneiform Texts... in the British Museum. (CT 22.1–248 translated in E. Ebeling, *Neubabylonische Briefe* (Munich 1949).)
Cyr.	J. N. Strassmaier, *Inschriften von Cyrus* (Leipzig 1890).
Dar.	J. N. Strassmaier, *Inschriften von Darius* (Leipzig 1892)
DB etc.	texts in R. G. Kent, *Old Persian*[3] (New Haven 1953).
FP	K. R. Nemet-Nejat, *Late Babylonian Field Plans* (Rome 1982).
FX VI	H. Metzger *et al.*, *Fouilles de Xanthos* VI (Paris 1979).
GCCI 2	R. Dougherty, *Archives from Erech...* (New Haven 1933).
Labraunda	J. Crampa, *Labraunda III* (Stockholm 1969, 1972).
Michigan	E. W. Moore, *Neo-Babylonian Documents in the University of Michigan Collection* (Ann Arbor 1939).
OGIS	W. Dittenberger, *Orientis Graeci Inscriptiones Selectae* (Leipzig 1903).
PBS 2/1	A. T. Clay, *Business Documents of the Murashu* (Philadelphia 1912).
Peek	T. G. Pinches, *Inscribed Babylonian Tablets in possession of Sir Henry Peek* (London 1888).
PF, PFa	Texts in Hallock 1969 and 1978 respectively.
Pohl 1, 2	A. Pohl, *Neubabylonische Rechtsurkunden...*, An.Or. 8 (1933), 9 (1934).
PT	Texts in Cameron 1948.
ROMCT 2	G. J. P. McEwan, *Late Babylonian Tablets in the Royal Ontario Museum* (1982).
Saqqara	J. B. Segal, *Aramaic Papyri from North Saqqara* (London 1983).
SdA	H. Bengtson, *Staatsverträge des Altertums* (Munich 1962).
SEG	Supplementum Epigraphicum Graecum.
SIG[3]	W. Dittenberger, *Sylloge Inscriptionum Graecarum* (Leipzig 1915–24).
Sinuri	L. Robert, *Le Sanctuaire de Sinuri* (Paris 1945).
Strassmaier *8th Congr.*	*Actes du 8e Congrès International des Orientalistes*, IIe partie, Ib (Leiden 1893), 281 f.
TAM 5	J. Keil, P. Herrmann, *Tituli Asiae Minoris* V (Vienna 1981).
TCL 13	G. Contenau, *Contrats Neo-babyloniens* II (Paris 1929) (translated in E. W. Moore, *Neo-Babylonian Documents* (Ann Arbor 1935)).

TEBR	Texts in Joannès 1982.
TL	E. Kalinka, *Tituli Asiae Minoris* I (Vienna 1901).
TuM 2/3	O. Krückmann, *Neubabylonische Rechts- und Verwaltungsurkunden* (Leipzig 1933).
UET	H. Figulla, *Business Documents of the Neo-Babylonian Period* (London 1949).
Urkunden II	K. Sethe, *Hieroglyphische Urkunden der griechisch-römischen Zeit* (Leipzig 1904).
VS 3–6	A. Ungnad, *Vorderasiatische Schriftdenkmäler* (Berlin 1907–8) (translated in San Nicolò/Ungnad 1935).
XPa etc.	see DB etc.
YBC	unpublished Yale University Library tablets.
YNER 1	D. Weisberg, *Guild Structure and Political Allegiance*... (Yale 1967).
YOS 3	A. T. Clay, *Neo-babylonian Letters from Erech* (New Haven 1919).
YOS 7	A. Tremayne, *Records from Erech*... (New Haven 1925).

Aramaic and Egyptian demotic texts are normally published with translations. Where the place of publication of demotic texts is not stated it can usually be located in E. Lüddeckens, 'Papyri, Demotische', *Lexikon der Ägyptologie* IV 750–899. Akkadian texts, on the other hand, are often initially published only in hand-copies of the cuneiform tablets. The whereabouts of such translations as exist can be sought in R. Borger, *Handbuch der Keilschriftliteratur I–III* (Berlin 1967–75).

Bibliography

Ackroyd, P. n.d., 'The written evidence for Palestine', *Proceedings Achaemenid Workshop*.

Aimé-Giron, N. 1921, 'Fragment de papyrus araméen provenant de Memphis', *JA* 18, 56–64.

——1931, *Textes araméens d'Egypte* (Cairo).

——1939, 'Adversaria Semitica', *BIFAO* 38, 1–63.

Anderson, J. K. 1970, *Military Theory and Practice in the Age of Xenophon* (Berkeley, Los Angeles).

Armayor, O. K. 1978, 'Herodotus' Catalogues of the Persian Empire', *TAPA* 108, 1–10.

Atkinson, K. M. 1972, 'A hellenistic land conveyance: the estate of Mnesimachus in the plain of Sardis', *Historia* 21, 45–75.

Balkan, K. 1959, 'Inscribed bullae from Daskyleion-Ergili', *Anadolu* 4, 123–8.

Ball, C. J. 1892, 'A Babylonian Deed of Sale', *PBSA* 14, 166–9.

Berger, P.-R. 1975, 'Der Kyroszylinder mit dem Zusatzfragment BIN 2.32 . . .', *ZA* 64, 192–234.

Biggs, R. D. 1978, 'Cuneiform Inscriptions', in D. McCown *et al.*, *Nippur* II (Chicago).

Boardman, J. 1970, 'Pyramidal stamp seals in the Persian Empire', *Iran* 8, 19–46.

Bogoliubov, M. 1974, 'Titre honorifique d'un chef militaire achémenide . . .', *Acta Iranica*, 1e série (Commemoration Cyrus), Hommage Universel II (Teheran–Liège), 109–14.

Bowman, R. 1970, *Aramaic Ritual Texts from Persepolis* (Chicago).

Bresciani, E. 1958, 'La satrapia d'Egitto', *SCO* 7, 132–88.

——1959, 'Un papiro aramaico da El Hibeh . . .', *Aegypt.* 39, 3–8.

——1960, 'Papiri aramaici egiziani di epoca persiana . . .', *RSO* 35, 11–24.

——1969, 'Egypt in the Persian Empire' in H. Bengtson, *The Greeks and the Persians* (London), 333–53.

——1985, 'The Persian occupation of Egypt', *Camb. History of Iran* ii, 502–28.

Briant, P. 1982a, *Rois, tributs et paysans* (Paris).

——1982b, *État et pasteurs* (Paris, Cambridge).

——1984, *Asie Centrale et les royaumes proche-orientaux du premier millénaire* (Paris).

——n.d.(a), 'Dons de terres et de villes: l'Asie mineure dans le contexte achémenide', *Proceedings of Bordeaux conference on Anatolia (April 1986)* (forthcoming).

——n.d.(b), 'Ethno-classe dominante perse et populations soumises dans l'empire perse: le cas d'Égypte', in A. Kuhrt & H. Sancisi-Weerdenburg, *Achaemenid History III: Methodology and Theory* (Leiden, forthcoming).

Bryce, T. 1983, 'Political unity in Lycia during the dynastic period', *JNES* 42, 31–42.

Buckler, W. & Robinson, D. M. 1912, 'Greek Inscriptions from Sardis', *AJA* 16, 11–82.

Cahill, N. 1985, 'The treasury at Persepolis . . .', *AJA* 89, 373–89.

Cameron, G. 1941, 'Darius and Xerxes in Babylon', *AJSL* 58, 314–25.

——1948, *Persepolis Treasury Tablets* (Chicago).

——1958, 'Persepolis treasury tablets old and new', *JNES* 17, 161–75.

——1965, 'New texts from the Persepolis treasury', *JNES* 24, 167–92.

——1973, 'The Persian satrapies and related matters', *JNES* 32, 47–56.

Cardascia, G. 1951, *Les archives de Murašu* (Paris).

——1958, 'Le fief dans la Babylonie Achémenide', *Rec. Soc. Bodin* 1² (Brussels), 55–88.

——1977, 'Armée et fiscalité dans la Babylonie achémenide', in *Armée et fiscalité dans le monde antique* (CNRS, Paris), 1–10.

Cawkwell, G. 1968, 'The power of Persia', *Arepo*, 1–5.

Clermont-Ganneau, C. 1921, 'Le paradeisos royale achémenide de Sidon', *BevBev. Bibl.* 30, 106–9.

Contenau, G. 1923, 'Sculpture provenant de la ville', *Syria* 4, 276–8.

Cook, J. M. 1961, 'The problems of classical Ionia', *PCPS* 138, 9–17.

——1983, *The Persian Empire* (London).

Cooke, G. A. 1903, *Textbook of North Semitic Inscriptions* (Oxford).

Cooney, J. D. 1954, 'The portrait of an Egyptian collaborator', *Bull. Brooklyn Museum* 15, 1–16.

Cross, F. M. 1974, 'The papyri and their historical implications', in P. W. & N. L. Lapp, *Discoveries in the Wadi Daliyeh* (Cambridge Mass.).

——1986a, 'Samaria Papyrus 1 . . . ', *Eretz Israel* 18, 7*–17*.

——1986b, 'A new Aramaic stele from Tayma', *Festschrift J. Fitzmyer*.

Dandamayev, M. 1963, 'Foreign slaves on estates of Achaemenid kings and nobles', *Proc. XXV Int. Cong. of Orientalists* (Moscow), II, 147–54.

——1967, 'Die Lehnsbeziehungen in Babylonien unter den ersten Achameniden', *Festschrift Eilers* (Wiesbaden), 37–42.

——1969a, 'Achaemenid Babylonia', in I. Diakonoff, *Ancient Mesopotamia* (Moscow), 269–311.

——1969b, 'Der Tempelzehnte in Babylonien . . . ', *Festschrift Altheim* (Berlin), 82–90.

——1972, 'Politische und wirtschaftliche Geschichte', in G. Walser, *Beiträge zur Achämenidengeschichte* (Wiesbaden), 15–58.

——1975, 'Forced labour in the Persian Empire', *Altorient. Forschungen* 2, 71–8.

——1976, 'Social stratification in Babylonia . . . ', in J. Harmatta & G. Komoročzy, *Wirtschaft und Gesellschaft im alten Vorderasien* (Budapest), 433–44.

——1977, 'State and Temple in Babylonia . . . ', in E. Lipinski, *State and Temple Economy in the Ancient Near East* (Leuven), 589–96.

——1982, 'Neo-babylonian Elders', in *Societies and Languages of the Ancient Near East* [Festschrift Diakonoff] (Warminster), 38–41.

——1983, 'On the fief in Babylonia in the early Achaemenid Period', in H. Koch & D. N. Mackenzie, *Kunst, Kultur und Geschichte der Achämenidenzeit . . .* (Berlin), 57–9.

——1984a, 'Babylonia in the Persian Age', *Camb. Hist. Judaism* 1, 326–42.

——1984b, 'Royal *paradeisoi* in Babylonia', *Acta Iranica*, 2e série (Hommages et opera minora), vol. ix (= Festschrift Duchesne-Guillemin) (Liège), 113–18.

——1984c, *Slavery in Babylonia* (Northern Illinois UP).

Delaporte, L. 1912, *Épigraphes araméens* (Paris).

Demsky, A. 1983, '*Pelekh* in Nehemiah 3', *IEJ* 33, 242–4.

Descat, R. n.d., 'L'inscription de Mnesimache et le système tributaire achémenide', *Proceedings Bordeaux conference on Anatolia (April 1986)*.

Donner, H. & Röllig, W. 1963, *Kanaanaische und aramäische Inschriften II* (Wiesbaden).

Dupont-Sommer, A. 1948, 'Un papyrus araméen d'époque saite . . . ', *Semit.* 1, 43–68.

Ebeling, E. 1952, 'Die Rüstung eines babylonischen Panzerreiters . . . ', *ZA* 50, 203–13.

Eilers, W. 1940, *Iranische Beamtennamen in der keilschriftlichen Überlieferung* (Leipzig).

Ellis, M. 1974, 'Taxation in ancient Mesopotamia . . . ', *JCS* 26, 211–50.

Eph'al, I. 1978, 'The western minorities in Babylonia . . . ', *Or.* n.s. 47, 74–90.

——1982, *The Ancient Arabs: nomads on the borders of the fertile crescent* (Leiden).

Fauth, W. 1979, 'Der königliche Gärtner und Jäger im Paradeisos . . . ', *Persica* 8, 1–54.

Fitzmyer, J. 1962, 'The Padua aramaic papyrus letters', *JNES* 21, 15–24.

Foucart, P. 1885, 'Inscriptions d'Asie Mineure', *BCH* 9, 387–403.
——1887, 'L'exploration de la plaine de l'Hermus', *BCH* 11, 79–107.

Frei, P. 1984, 'Zentralgewalt und Lokalautonomie im Achämenidenreich', in P. Frei & D. Koch, *Reichtsidee und Reichsorganization im Perserreich* (Freiburg / Göttingen).
Gardin, J. C. & Lyonnet, B. 1978/9, 'Prospection de la Bactriane orientale', *Mesopot.* 13/14, 99–154.
Ghirshman, R. 1954, *Iran* (Harmondsworth).
Grayson, A. K. (1975), *Assyrian and Babylonian Chronicles* (New York).
Greenfield, J. & Porten, B. 1982, *Bisutun Inscription of Darius I: Aramaic version* (London).
Grelot, P. 1970, 'Essai de restauration du papyrus AP 26', *Semit.* 20, 22–32.
——1972, *Documents araméens d'Egypte* (Paris).
Griffith, F. Ll. 1909, *Catalogue of Demotic Papyri in the John Rylands Library III* (Manchester).

Hallock, R. T. 1960, 'A new look at the Persepolis treasury tablets', *JNES* 19, 90–100.
——1969, *Persepolis Fortification Tablets* (Chicago).
——1973, 'The Persepolis fortification archive', *Or.* n.s. 42, 320–3.
——1977, 'The use of seals on the Persepolis fortification tablets', in M. Gibson & R. D. Biggs, *Seals and Sealings in the Ancient Near East* (Malibu), 127–33.
——1978, 'Selected Fortification Texts', *CDAFI* 8, 109–36.
——1985, 'The evidence of the Persepolis tablets', *Camb. Hist. Iran* 2, 588–609.
Harmatta, J. 1971, 'The literary pattern of the Babylonian edict of Cyrus', *AAAS Hung.* 19, 220 ff.
Henning, W. B. 1968, 'Ein persischer Titel im Altaramäischen', in *In Memoriam P. Kahle* (Berlin), 138–45.
Herrenschmidt, C. 1983, 'Sur la charte de fondation DSaa', *Rev. Assyr.* 77, 177–9.
Hinz, W. 1971, 'Achämenidische Hofverwaltung', *ZA* 61, 260–311.
——1975, *Neue Wege im Altpersischen* (Wiesbaden).
Hoftijzer, J. 1962, 'Ein Papyrusfragment aus El Hibeh', *VT* 12, 342–4.
Hornblower, S. 1982, *Mausolus* (Oxford).
Hughes, G. 1952, *Saite Demotic Land Leases* (Chicago).
——1984, 'The so-called Pherendates Correspondence', *Festschrift Lüddeckens* (Würzburg), 75–86.

Jelínková-Reymond, E. 1955, 'Paiement du président de la Nécropole (P. Caire 50060)', *BIFAO* 55, 33–55.
Joannès, F. 1980, 'Textes néo-babyloniens de Strasbourg', *RA* 74, 145–69.
——1982, *Textes économiques de la Babylonie récente* (Paris).

Keil, J. 1923, 'Die Kulte Lydiens', in W. Buckler & W. Calder, *Anatolian Studies* (Manchester), 239–66.
Kleiss, W. 1981, 'Ein Abschnitt der achämenidischen Königsstrasse ...', *AMI* n.f. 14, 45–54.
Koch, H. 1980, 'Steuern in der achämenidischen Persis?' *ZA* 70, 105–37.
——1981, 'Hofschatzwarte und Schatzhaüser in der Persis', *ZA* 71, 232–47.
——1983, 'Zu den Lohnverhältnissen der Dareioszeit in Persien', in H. Koch & D. Mackenzie, *Kunst, Kultur und Geschichte der Achämenidenzeit* (Berlin), 19–50.
Kuhrt, A. 1983, 'The Cyrus Cylinder and Achaemenid imperial policy', *JSOT* 25, 83–97.
——n.d., 'Babylonia from Cyrus II to Xerxes', *Camb. Ancient History* IV².
Kuhrt, A. & Sherwin-White, S. forthcoming, 'Xerxes' destruction of Babylonian temples', in H. Sancisi-Weerdenburg & A. Kuhrt, *Achaemenid History II: the Greek*

sources (Leiden).

Levine, B. 1972, 'Aramaic texts from Persepolis', *JAOS* 92, 70–9.
Lewis, D. M. 1977, *Sparta and Persia* (Leiden).
——1984, 'Postscript', in A. R. Burn, *Persia and the Greeks*² (London), 587–609.
Lloyd, A. B. 1982, 'The inscription of Udjahorresnet . . . ', *JEA* 68, 166–80.
——1983, 'The Late Period, 664–323 B.C.', in B. Trigger *et al.*, *Ancient Egypt: a social history* (Cambridge), 279–348.
Lutz, H. 1928, 'An agreement between a feudal lord and his retainer . . . ', *UCPSP* 9, 269–77.

Malinine, M. 1967, 'Partage testamentaire d'un proprieté familiale', *Rev. Egypt.* 19, 65–85.
Malinine, M. & Pirenne, H. 1950/1, 'Documents juridiques égyptiens', *AHDO* 5, 11–91.
McEwan, G. 1983, 'Late Babylonian Kish', *Iraq* 45, 117–23.
Meeks, D. 1972, *Le Grand Texte des Donations au Temple d'Edfu* (Cairo).
——1977, 'Les donations aux temples dans l'Égypte . . . ', in E. Lipiński, *State and Temple Economy in the Ancient Near East* (Leuven), 605–88.
Meuleau, M. 1969, 'Mesopotamia under Persian Rule', in H. Bengtson, *The Greeks and the Persians* (London), 354–85.
Milik, J. T. 1960, 'Lettre araméene d'El Hibeh', *Aegypt.* 40, 79–81.
Moore, E. 1939, *Neobabylonian Documents in the University of Michigan* (Ann Arbor).

Nasif, A. 1980, 'Qanats at al-'Ula', *PSAS* 10, 75–80.
Naveh, J. 1973, 'The aramaic ostraca', in Y. Aharoni, *Beer-Sheba* I (Tel Aviv, 1973), 79–82
——1975, 'The aramaic ostraca from Tel Arad', in Y. Aharoni, *Arad Inscriptions* (Jerusalem).
——1979, 'The aramaic ostraca from Tel Beer-Sheba (1971–1976)', *Tel Aviv* 6, 182–95.
——1985, 'Published and unpublished aramaic ostraca', *ʿAtiqot* (E.S.) 17, 114–21.
Naveh, J. & Shaked, S. 1973, 'Ritual texts or treasury documents?', *Or.* n.s. 42, 445–57.

Oelsner, J. 1976, 'Zwischen Xerxes und Alexander . . . ' *WO* 8, 310-18
Oppenheim, A.L. 1945, 'Studies in Akkadian Lexicography', *Or.* n.s. 14, 235–41.
——1947, 'A fiscal practice of the ancient Near East', *JNES* 6, 116–20.
——1950, 'M. Figulla: Business Documents . . . ', *JCS* 4, 188–95.
——1985, 'The Babylonian evidence of Achaemenid rule in Mesopotamia', *Camb. History of Iran* 2, 529–87.

Parker, R. A. 1961, 'The durative tenses in P. Rylands IX', *JNES* 20, 180–7.
Petrie, W. F. 1910, *Meydum and Memphis* (London).
Porten, B. 1968, *Archives from Elephantine* (Berkeley, Los Angeles).
Porten, B. & Szubin, H. 1982, 'Ancestral estates in Aramaic contracts', *JRAS*, 1–9.
——1985, 'Hereditary leases in Aramaic letters', *BO* 42, 283–8.
Posener, G. 1936, *La première domination perse en Egypte* (Cairo).
Potts, D. 1984, 'North-eastern Arabia in the late pre-Islamic era', in R. Boucharlat & J.-F. Salles, *Arabie orientale, Mésopotamie et Iran méridional dans l'âge du fer au début de la période islamique* (Paris), 85–114.

Ray, J. D. n.d., 'Egypt (525–404 B.C.)', *Camb. Ancient History IV*².
Ries, G. 1976, *Die Neubabylonischen Bodenpachtformulare* (Berlin).
Roaf, M. 1974, 'The subject peoples on the bases of the statue of Darius', *CDAFI*, 73–160.
Robert, L. 1948, 'Hyrcanis', *Hellenica* 6, 6–16.
——1949, 'Décret d'une syngénie carienne', *Hellenica* 7, 63–8.
——1950, 'Inscriptions cariennes', *Hellenica* 8, 5–21.

——1963a, 'Bulletin épigraphique', *BCH* 76, 121–92.
——1963b, *Noms indigènes dans l'Asie Mineure* (Paris).
——1975, 'Une nouvelle inscription grecque de Sardes', *CRAI*, 306–30.
——1978, 'Malédictions funéraires grecques', *CRAI*, 241–89.
——1982, 'Documents d'Asie Mineure', *BCH* 106, 308–78.
Roebuck, C. D. 1959, *Ionian Trade and Colonisation* (New York).
Root, M. C. *King and Kingship in Achaemenid Art* (Liège).

Salles, J.-F. n.d., 'Le golfe arabo-persique du 6e au 4e siècles', *Proceedings Achaemenid Workshop.*
San Nicolò, M. 1932, 'Parerga Babyloniaca VI–VIII', *Ar. Or.* 4, 325–48.
——1941, 'Beiträge zu einer Prosopographie neubabylonischen Beamten . . .', *SB Bay. Ak. Wiss.* (II.2).
——1950, 'Neubabylonische Urkunden aus Ur', *Or.* n.s. 19, 217–32.
San Nicolò, M. Ungnad, A. 1935, *Neubabylonische Rechts- und Verwaltungsurkunden* (Berlin).
Schott, E. 1967, 'Ein datierte Apisbronze', *Rev. Egypt.* 19, 88–98.
Seidl, E. 1956, *Ägyptische Rechtsgeschichte der Saiten- und Perserzeit* (Glückstadt).
Segal, J. B. 1969, 'Miscellaneous fragments in Aramaic', *Iraq* 31, 170–4.
Sekunda, N. n.d.(a), 'Patterns of Persian aristocratic settlement in the Dascyleion satrapy', in A. Kuhrt & H. Sancisi-Weerdenburg, *Achaemenid History III: Methodology and Theory* (Leiden, forthcoming).
——n.d.(b), 'Achaemenid colonization in Lydia', *Proceedings of Bordeaux conference on Anatolia (April 1986).*
Sherwin-White, S. 1982, 'Median Artemis in an early hellenistic funerary inscription', *ZPE* 49, 30.
Smith, H. S. & Kuhrt, A. 1982, 'A letter to a foreign general', *JEA* 68, 199–209.
Spiegelberg, W. 1915, *Die sogenannte Demotische Chronik* (Leipzig).
——1928, 'Drei demotische Schreiben aus der Korrespondenz des Pherendates . . .', *Sitz. Preuss. Akad. Wiss.* Hist.-Phil. Kl., 604–22.
Stern, E. 1982, *Material Culture of the Land of the Bible in the Persian Period* (Warminster).
——1984, 'The Persian conquest and the political and social history of Palestine in the Persian period; the archaeology of Persian Palestine', in *Camb. Hist. Judaism* 1, 70–114.
Stolper, M. W. 1974, *Management and Politics in Achaemenid Babylonia* (Diss. Michigan).
——1977, 'Three Iranian loan-words in late Babylonian texts', in L. Levine (ed.), *Mountains and Lowlands* (Malibu), 251–66.
——1984, 'The Neo-Babylonian text from the Persepolis fortification', *JNES* 43, 299–310.
——1986, 'Belšunu the satrap', *Festschrift Reiner* (New Haven).
——n.d., 'The Kasr Archive', *Proceedings Achaemenid Workshop.*

Stronach, D. 1978, *Pasargadae* (Oxford).
Sumner, W. 1986, 'Achaemenid settlement in the Persepolis plain', *AJA* 90, 33-31.
Swiggers, P. 1980, 'Note sur un papyrus araméen d'El Hibeh', *Aegypt.* 60, 93–5.

Tait, W. J. 1977, *Papyri from Tebtunis in Egyptian and in Greek* (London).
Tozzi, P. 1978, *La Rivolta Ionica* (Pisa).
Tresson, P. 1931, 'La stèle de Naples', *BIFAO* 30, 369–91.
Tuplin, C. J. n.d.(a), 'The treaty of Boiotios', in H. Sancisi-Weerdenburg & A. Kuhrt, *Achaemenid History II: the Greek sources* (Leiden, forthcoming).
——n.d.(b), 'Persian garrisons in Xenophon and other Greek and non-Greek sources',

AMI (forthcoming).

Vogelsang, W. 1985, 'Early Historical Arachosia . . . ', *IA* 20, 55–100.
Voigtlander, E. N. von 1978, *The Bisutun Inscription of Darius I: Babylonian version* (London).

Walker, C. B. F. 1973, 'Cuneiform Tablets in . . . Truro', *AfO* 24, 122–7.
Walser, G. 1966, *Die Völkerschaften auf den Reliefs von Persepolis* (Berlin).
Weisberg, D. 1967, 'A Neobabylonian temple report', *JAOS* 87, 8–12.
Wiesehöfer, J. 1980, 'Die "Freunde" und "Wohltäter" des Grosskönigs', *SI* 9, 7–21.
Wild, H. 1954, 'Statue de Hor-Nefer', *BIFAO* 54, 173–219.
Winlock, H. 1941, *The Temple of Hibis in El Khargeh Oasis: Part I Excavation* (New York).
Wiseman, D. J. 1967, 'A late Babylonian tribute list?', *BSOAS* 30, 495–504.

Yaron, Y. 1961, *The Law of the Aramaic Papyri* (Oxford).
Yoyotte, J. 1972, 'La localisation de Ouenkhem', *BIFAO* 71, 1–10.

Zadok, R. 1976a, 'Connections between Iran and Babylonia in the sixth century', *Iran* 14, 61–78.
——1976b, 'Three Iranian loan words in late Babylonian documents', *BO* 33, 5–6.
——1978, 'The Nippur region during the Late Assyrian, Chaldaean and Achaemenian periods . . . ', *IOS* 8, 266–332.
——1979, *The Jews in Babylonia* (Haifa).
——1981/2, 'Iranian and Babylonian Notes', *AfO* 28, 135–9.
Zauzich, K.-Th. 1978, *Papyri aus der Insel von Elephantine* (Berlin).

ACHAEMENID ADMINISTRATION

ADDENDA

p. 120: on the King's Eye see Cassio, *CQ* n.s.35 (1985), 41–2.
p. 126: on *sgn'* see now J. Greenfield, *Or.Suec.* 33/5 (1984/6), 153.
p. 136: on *dwšn* in AD 2 see now H. Szubin & B. Porten, *JNES* 46 (1987), 39–48.

THE SYMPOSIASTS

M. ACTON, Esq., Oxford.
Mrs. F. ACTON, Oxford.
Dr. KATHERINE ADSHEAD, University of Canterbury, New Zealand.
Professor A. ANDREWES, New College, Oxford.
Dr. R. ASHTON, London.
Dr. A. BURNETT, British Museum, London.
Professor T. V. BUTTREY, Cambridge.
Mrs. J. CARGILL THOMPSON, London.
Dr. IAN CARRADICE, British Museum, London.
G. L. CAWKWELL, Esq., University College, Oxford.
Dr. J. J. COULTON, Merton College, Oxford.
N. M. DE COURCY, Esq., Cambridge.
Professor J. K. DAVIES, University of Liverpool.
Dr. S. FRIED, New York.
N. M. HARDWICK, Esq., Oxford.
M. R. HAY, Esq., London.
G. K. JENKINS, Esq., London.
Dr. ALAN JOHNSTON, London.
JONATHAN H. KAGAN, Esq., New York.
Dr. PHILIP KINNS, Newbury.
Mrs. A. T. L. KUHRT, University College, London.
Professor D. M. LEWIS, Christ Church, Oxford.
Professor HAROLD B. MATTINGLY, University of Leeds.
Dr. DAPHNE NASH, Oxford.
Mme H. NICOLET, Bibliothèque Nationale, Paris.
Dr. M. JESSOP PRICE, British Museum, London.
Professor M. COOL ROOT, Oxford.
Dr. N. K. RUTTER, University of Edinburgh.
Dr. T. T. B. RYDER, University of Hull.
J. SPIER, Esq., Oxford.
Professor R. A. TOMLINSON, University of Birmingham.
Dr. C. J. TUPLIN, University of Liverpool.
MICHAEL VICKERS, Esq., Ashmolean Museum, Oxford.
Miss UTE WARTENBERG, Heidelberg.
Dr. D. J. R. WILLIAMS, British Museum, London.
R. T. WILLIAMS, Esq., St Davids.

www.ingramcontent.com/pod-product-compliance
Lightning Source LLC
LaVergne TN
LVHW071213210926
848482LV00015B/795

* 9 7 8 0 8 6 0 5 4 4 4 2 5 *